Counterinsurgency in Pakistan

Seth G. Jones, C. Christine Fair

RAND NATIONAL SECURITY RESEARCH DIVISION

Project supported by a RAND Investment in People and Ideas

This monograph results from the RAND Corporation's Investment in People and Ideas program. Support for this program is provided, in part, by donors and by the independent research and development provisions of RAND's contracts for the operation of its U.S. Department of Defense federally funded research and development centers.

Library of Congress Cataloging-in-Publication Data

Jones, Seth G., 1972–
Counterinsurgency in Pakistan / Seth G. Jones, C. Christine Fair.
p. cm.
Includes bibliographical references.
ISBN 978-0-8330-4976-6 (pbk. : alk. paper)
1. Pakistan—Politics and government—1988- 2. Counterinsurgency—Pakistan.
I. Fair, C. Christine. II. Title.

DS389.J66 2010
954.9105'3—dc22

2010015059

Published 2010 by the RAND Corporation
1776 Main Street, P.O. Box 2138, Santa Monica, CA 90407-2138
1200 South Hayes Street, Arlington, VA 22202-5050
4570 Fifth Avenue, Suite 600, Pittsburgh, PA 15213-2665
RAND URL: http://www.rand.org/
To order RAND documents or to obtain additional information, contact
Distribution Services: Telephone: (310) 451-7002;
Fax: (310) 451-6915; Email: order@rand.org

Preface

This document examines the evolution of militancy in Pakistan, assesses Pakistan's efforts to counter militants, and offers a range of policy recommendations. It is based on detailed research in Pakistan and an examination of the quantitative and qualitative literatures on counterinsurgency and counterterrorism.

This document results from the RAND Corporation's Investment in People and Ideas program. Support for this program is provided, in part, by donors and by the independent research and development provisions of RAND's contracts for the operation of its U.S. Department of Defense federally funded research and development centers. This research was conducted within the RAND National Security Research Division (NSRD) of the RAND Corporation. NSRD conducts research and analysis for the Office of the Secretary of Defense, the Joint Staff, the Unified Commands, the defense agencies, the Navy, the U.S. Intelligence Community, allied foreign governments, and foundations. For more information on the RAND National Security Research Division, contact the Director of Operations, Nurith Berstein. She can be reached by email at Nurith_Berstein@rand.org; by phone at 703-413-1100, extension 5469; or by mail at RAND, 1200 South Hayes Street, Arlington VA 22202-5050. More information about the RAND Corporation is available at www.rand.org.

Contents

Figures

Tables

Executive Summary

Beginning in 2001, Pakistan conducted a range of operations against militant groups in the Federally Administered Tribal Areas (FATA) and other parts of Pakistan. Because of Pakistan's nuclear status and the presence of international terrorist organizations, such as al Qa'ida, Pakistan's counterinsurgency campaign significantly affects the security of countries across North America, Europe, Asia, Africa, and the Middle East—including the United States.

U.S. President Barack Obama argued that Pakistan's border region is "the most dangerous place in the world" for the United States. The head of U.S. Central Command, General David Petraeus, noted that "it is the headquarters of the al Qa'ida senior leadership," which is planning attacks in the West.[1] U.S. intelligence agencies have linked several terrorist plots in the United States to networks in Pakistan, including Faisal Shahzad's May 2010 attempt to bomb Times Square in New York. Another notable threat was the al Qa'ida plot to detonate a bomb in the New York City subway that involved Najibullah Zazi. According to U.S. government documents, Zazi's travels to Pakistan and his contacts with individuals there were pivotal in helping him build an improvised explosive device using triacetone triperoxide, the same explosive used effectively in the 2005 London subway bombings.[2] Similarly, British Prime Minister Gordon Brown warned that "three

---

1 Yochi J. Dreazen, "Al Qaeda's Global Base Is Pakistan, Says Petraeus," *Wall Street Journal*, May 11, 2009.

2 United States District Court, Eastern District of New York, United States of America Against Najibullah Zazi, 09 CR 663(S-1), February 22, 2010; United States District Court,

quarters of the most serious plots investigated by the British authorities have links to al Qa'ida in Pakistan."[3]

This document examines counterinsurgency efforts in Pakistan and asks several questions: What are the roots of the militant challenge in Pakistan? What have Pakistan's primary operations against militants been? How effective have these operations been in achieving their goals? And what are the policy implications? To answer these questions, the document combines field research in Pakistan with a review of the literature on counterinsurgency and other relevant areas. While there have been numerous policy reports on Pakistan and its militant challenges, there has been little effort to systematically analyze the effectiveness of Pakistan's operations and to apply relevant theoretical lessons.

A Mixed Record

The study argues that despite some successes since 2001, militant groups continue to present a *significant threat* to Pakistan, the United States, and several other countries. As Figure S.1 illustrates, numerous militant networks—including al Qa'ida and other foreign fighters—exist in the FATA and North West Frontier Province. Other groups, including Lashkar-e-Taiba and Jaish-e-Mohammad, remain entrenched in other areas of Pakistan outside FATA. Some of these groups pose a grave threat to the Pakistani state, as the growing number of terrorist attacks in Pakistani cities demonstrates. Some also present a threat to the United States, which has at least two major interests in Pakistan. One is defeating al Qa'ida and other militant groups that threaten the U.S. homeland and its interests overseas. The second is preventing militant groups from acquiring weapons of mass destruction, especially nuclear weapons.

Eastern District of New York, United States of America Against Najibullah Zazi, 09-CR-663, September 24, 2009.

3 Sam Coates and Jeremy Page, "Pakistan 'Linked to 75% of All UK Terror Plots,' Warns Gordon Brown," *The Times* (London), December 15, 2008.

Figure S.1
Example of Militant Networks in FATA and the North West Frontier Province

RAND *MG982-S.1*

The militant threat persists for several reasons. One is Pakistan's challenge in developing an effective population-centric counterinsurgency strategy, which is necessary to counter militants and secure its population over the long run. Counterinsurgency is extraordinarily challenging; governments have won only 31 percent of counterinsurgencies since 1945. Insurgents have won 28 percent; 22 percent ended in a draw; and 18 percent are ongoing.[4] This study concludes that Pakistan will not be able to deal with the militant threat over the long

4 David C. Gompert and John Gordon IV, *Building Complete and Balanced Capabilities for Counterinsurgency*, Santa Monica, Calif.: RAND Corporation, 2008, p. 377.

run unless it does a more effective job of addressing the root causes of the crisis and makes security of the civilian population, rather than destroying the enemy, its top priority.

In addition, Pakistan's decision to support some militant groups has been counterproductive. Its use of militancy as a tool of foreign policy is not new and, in fact, dates back to the early weeks of statehood. Pakistan's acquisition of nuclear weapons appears to have emboldened its support of militant groups by dampening its concerns about Indian retaliation. The policy of supporting militants began to backfire after September 11, 2001, when such groups as the Tehreek-e-Taliban Pakistan conducted terrorist attacks in Pakistan from bases in FATA. By 2010, following the capture of senior Taliban leaders, such as inner shura member Mullah Abdul Ghani Baradar, some changes appeared to be taking place in Pakistan's policy. But Pakistan has not yet made a systematic break with militant groups.

Finally, Pakistan's army and Frontier Corps have demonstrated an uneven ability to clear and hold territory. Their performance during Operation Al Mizan—especially in South Waziristan in 2004—suggested serious deficiencies in conducting cordon-and-search operations and holding territory. Pakistani operations had improved somewhat by Operation Sher Dil in 2008 (Bajaur), Operation Rah-e-Rast in 2009 (Swat), and Operation Rah-e-Nijat in 2009 and 2010 (South Waziristan). Frontier Corps and army forces were better able to clear territory and integrate operations with local tribes. U.S. mentoring and training assistance, including that of U.S. Special Operations Forces, was helpful in building the capacity of some Pakistani forces, such as the Frontier Corps and Special Services Group. But the Pakistan Army has been reluctant to establish such a close relationship.

Pakistan's lack of an official counterinsurgency doctrine remains a lingering challenge. The government's focus on a war with India has ill-equipped it to contend with a growing domestic threat, although Pakistan's capabilities have improved. The Pakistan Army has long contended that it is the sole institution that can protect the country, yet Pakistan's police institutions have languished. The extensive literature on counterinsurgency and counterterrorism suggests that police-led—not army-led—approaches are usually more effective over the long run.

Pakistan's federal and provincial bureaucracies have also failed to provide systematic development and other aid to conflict-afflicted areas, offer adequate assistance to internally displaced persons, or engage in other efforts to secure the support of locals. The government's inability to provide immediate relief has exacerbated the army's reliance on scorched-earth policies in such places as South Waziristan, Bajaur, and Swat, which have alienated some locals.

A Population-Centric Strategy

Pakistan has demonstrated varying will and capacity to counter the militant groups operating on its territory. Four components are critical to adopting a more effective strategy.

First, Pakistan needs to establish a population-centric approach that aligns better with effective counterinsurgency efforts. As the counterinsurgency practitioner John Nagl argued, "Population security is the first requirement of success in counterinsurgency."[5] U.S. Special Operations Forces can be especially helpful, since they have both a history of involvement in insurgencies and counterinsurgencies, and good relations with Pakistan's security institutions. Of particular importance are the Pakistani police, which need to serve as a key "hold" force over the long run. Pakistan's police forces are poorly paid and poorly equipped, and there are too few of them. There is an urgent need to increase the number and capabilities of police forces. In addition, Pakistan's domestic intelligence agencies, including the police Special Branch, are underdeveloped and overshadowed by Pakistan's Directorate for Inter-Services Intelligence (ISI).[6] The United States is partly responsible for Pakistan's overreliance on military, rather than civilian, power because it has provided so much assistance to the Ministry of Defense.

---

[5] John Nagl, "Foreword to the University of Chicago Press Edition," in *U.S. Army and U.S. Marine Corps, Counterinsurgency Field Manual*, Chicago: University of Chicago Press, 2007, p. xix.

[6] C. Christine Fair and Peter Chalk, *Fortifying Pakistan: The Role of U.S. Internal Security Assistance*, Washington, D.C.: United States Institute of Peace, 2006.

FATA's outdated and idiosyncratic legal structure is also a challenge. Under the Frontier Crimes Regulation, there are no regular police in FATA; justice is draconian; and corruption appears to be rampant. The Frontier Crimes Regulation is also a barrier to the free movement of people between FATA and the rest of Pakistan. The High Court in Peshawar declared the Frontier Crimes Regulation unconstitutional. Despite the importance of this region, the Pakistani government has not developed a consensus on how it should move forward with the legal and constitutional issues surrounding FATA. Current plans contend with only development and defer important issues of legal status and governance.

Second, Pakistan needs to abandon militancy as a tool of its foreign and domestic policy. A key objective of U.S. policy must be to alter Pakistan's strategic calculus and end its support to militant groups. The United States should continue to make this position clear, as it began to do in 2010. Other states and international organizations, such as China and NATO, should issue similar statements. Indeed, the United States should enlist as many partners in this effort as possible. Pakistan's key allies, such as China, have become increasingly concerned about militant groups, including Uighur groups, that have used Pakistani soil for training and sanctuary. Anti-Americanism in Pakistan would likely make a coordinated message more effective in persuading Pakistan to alter its policy.

Third, the United States needs to reduce it reliance on Pakistan where feasible. In some areas, the United States will remain dependent on Pakistani cooperation, such as in targeting al Qa'ida and other militants based in Pakistan that threaten the U.S. homeland and its interests overseas. The ISI's Counter Terrorism Wing has been a particularly cooperative partner with U.S. government agencies in targeting terrorist groups. In other areas, however, the United States can seek alternatives if necessary. For instance, Pakistan provides an important and affordable land bridge to move lethal and nonlethal supplies to NATO troops in Afghanistan. The U.S. reliance on Pakistan indicates a notable vulnerability. The United States should continue seeking alternative routes for resupply, including through Iran and Central Asia.

Fourth, the United States should reexamine "carrots" and "sticks" in a comprehensive strategy. The United States should continue U.S. Special Operations Forces training programs and ensure that goods and services given to Pakistan are appropriate for counterinsurgency purposes. But it should withhold some aid until Pakistan makes discernible progress. Washington has had mixed success in persuading Pakistan to change course, partly because U.S. strategy has focused too much on carrots and too little on sticks.

The carrots offered include money and conventional weapons, which do not offer the strategic carrots Pakistan most values.Successful persuasion requires a mixture of carrots and sticks. The United States secured President Musharraf's cooperation in 2001 precisely because its strategy included carrots and sticks, which President Musharraf took seriously. In 2010, U.S.-Pakistani cooperation began to improve following a renewed diplomatic push that included both carrots *and* sticks. In a letter to Pakistani President Asif Ali Zardari, for instance, U.S. President Barack Obama bluntly warned that Pakistan's use of militant groups to pursue its policy goals would no longer be tolerated. President Obama also offered additional military and economic assistance, as well as help in easing tensions with India.

To accomplish these objectives, the United States needs to respect Pakistan's sovereignty and recognize that there is still considerable anti-Americanism among some Pakistanis. However, there is a tremendous amount at stake for the United States and Pakistan to deal more effectively with militant groups that threaten both countries' security. Some observers have focused on the periods of friction between the United States and Pakistan, including during the 1990s. But there is a rich history of cooperation. In a May 1950 meeting with U.S. President Harry Truman, Pakistani Prime Minister Liaquat Ali Khan remarked that

> the American people are not strangers to us. We have known them as educators and as men and women engaged on missions of peace. We have known them as soldiers who fought on our plains,

> our hills, and our jungles. And again since the birth of Pakistan we have known them as messengers of your goodwill.[7]

Cooperation today is just as important—if not more important—than it was during the Cold War. The United States and Pakistan need to come together to develop a more-systematic strategy to deal with the challenges that threaten both countries.

---

[7] Quoted in Shuja Nawaz, *Crossed Swords: Pakistan, Its Army, and the Wars Within*, New York: Oxford University Press, 2008, p. 95.

Acknowledgments

This manuscript would not have been possible without the help of numerous individuals. Stephen Cohen, Michael Semple, Samina Ahmed, and Arturo Muñoz provided useful help and information. James Dobbins provided a range of valuable comments, which significantly improved the quality of the manuscript. John H. Gill, Peter Chalk, and Ahmed Rashid reviewed the manuscript and offered frank, insightful critiques. Joya Laha and Sean Halpin provided helpful research assistance and helped shepherd the manuscript through production. We owe a special debt of gratitude to the government officials from Pakistan (including the Frontier Corps and army), the United States (including Special Operations Command Forward, U.S. Agency for International Development, and the Department of State), and the United Kingdom who took time out of their busy schedules to provide critical information about the state of the insurgency and Pakistan's efforts to counter it. Most did not want to be identified because of the sensitivity of the information they provided, so we have not thanked any of them by name.

Abbreviations

CIA	Central Intelligence Agency
DIA	Defense Intelligence Agency
FATA	Federally Administered Tribal Areas
FCR	Frontier Crimes Regulation
FIA	Federal Investigative Agency
HQ	headquarters
IRI	International Republican Institute
ISI	Directorate for Inter-Services Intelligence
JUI	Jamiat-e-Ulema Islami
LOC	line of communication
NATO	North Atlantic Treaty Organization
NWFP	North West Frontier Province
PIPA	Program on International Policy Attitudes
SOF	Special Operations Forces
TNSM	Tehreek-e-Nafaz-e-Shariat-e-Mohammadi
TTP	Tehreek-e-Taliban-e-Pakistan
UAV	unmanned aerial vehicle
USIP	U.S. Institute of Peace

CHAPTER ONE

Introduction

Since 2001, Pakistan has faced an increasingly serious threat from militant groups operating on its soil, as Figure 1.1 illustrates. In 2009, there was a 48 percent increase in terrorist attacks from 2008 levels, which killed 3,021 people and injured 7,334. The highest number of attacks occurred in the conflict zones of the Federally Administered Tribal Areas (FATA), North West Frontier Province (NWFP), and Baluchistan Province. But other areas of Pakistan, including Punjab,

Figure 1.1
Terrorist Attacks in Pakistan, 2006–2009

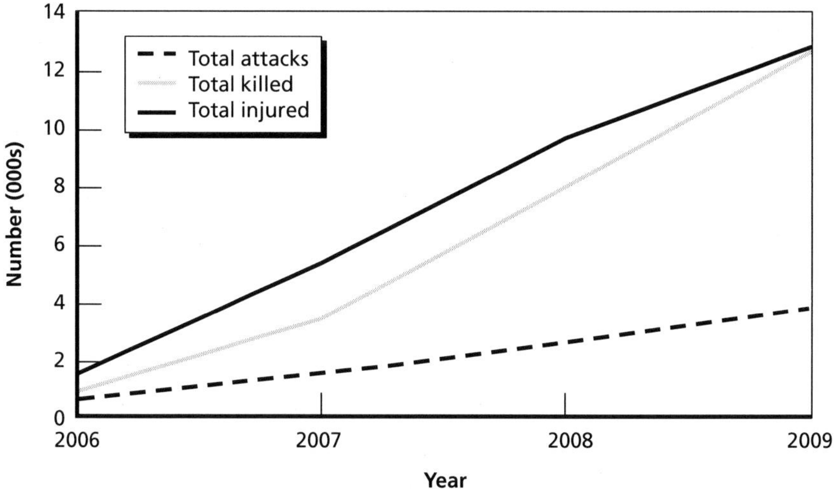

SOURCE: Pakistan Institute for Peace Studies, *Pakistan Security Report 2009.*
RAND *MG982-1.1*

were also targeted by a lethal campaign of bombings. Militant groups increasingly resorted to suicide attacks, which killed or wounded a growing number of civilians. There was a 32 percent increase in suicide attacks in 2009 from 2008 levels, which killed 1,299 people and injured 3,633.[1] These attacks targeted Pakistanis and foreigners—including U.S. government facilities. In April 2010, for example, militants mounted a multipronged assault against the U.S. consulate in Peshawar using a truck bomb, machine guns, and rocket launchers.

In addition, there were several serious international terrorist plots with links to Pakistan. In May 2010, Faisal Shahzad attempted to set off a car bomb in New York, but it malfunctioned. In December 2009, five Americans from Alexandria, Virginia—Ahmed Abdullah Minni, Umar Farooq, Aman Hassan Yemer, Waqar Hussain Khan, and Ramy Zamzam—were arrested in Pakistan and charged with plotting terrorist attacks. There were other plots to attack U.S. targets with links to Pakistan, including those involving Najibullah Zazi (who was arrested in 2009) and the British residents who planned to detonate liquid explosives on at least 10 airplanes traveling from the United Kingdom to the United States and Canada (who were arrested in 2006). In February 2010, Zazi pleaded guilty in U.S. District Court to "conspiracy to use weapons of mass destruction" and "providing material support for a foreign terrorist organization" based in Pakistan.[2] There were also a range of other plots and attacks in Germany, Spain, Netherlands, France, and India with links to militant groups in Pakistan.

In response to the growing violence and terrorist threats on Pakistani soil, Pakistani security forces conducted a number of operations against militant groups in FATA and other parts of the country. Yet there has been little effort to systematically analyze the effectiveness of Pakistan's operations and apply relevant theoretical lessons from the counterinsurgency and counterterrorism literatures. Consequently, this manuscript asks several questions:

---

1 Pakistan Institute for Peace Studies, *Pakistan Security Report 2009*, Islamabad, 2010.

2 U.S. District Court, Eastern District of New York, United States of America Against Najibullah Zazi, 09 CR 663(S-1), February 22, 2010.

- What are the roots of Pakistan's militant challenge?
- What have been Pakistan's primary operations against militants?
- How effective have these operations been in achieving their goals?
- What are the policy implications?

To answer these questions, we adopted several methodological approaches. One was a comparative case study to assess Pakistan's operations against militants. Case studies offer a useful approach to help understand the motivations of Pakistani leaders and the results of their operations.[3] As Alexander George and Timothy McKeown argue, case studies are useful in uncovering "what stimuli the actors attend to; the decision process that makes use of these stimuli to arrive at decisions; the actual behavior that then occurs; the effect of various institutional arrangements on attention, processing, and behavior; and the effect of other variables of interest on attention, processing, and behavior."[4]

A second was to review the literature on counterinsurgency and counterterrorism, since Pakistan's operations against militants have been affected by the *capabilities* and *political will* of its national security agencies. The army and Frontier Corps have at times struggled to clear and hold territory, as well as secure local support in FATA and NWFP. In addition, Pakistan has been willing to target some militant groups, but not others. These realities have enormous implications for the United States and its interests in Pakistan. Some U.S. policymakers

---

[3] On comparative case studies, see David Collier, "The Comparative Method: Two Decades of Change," in Dankwart A. Rustow and Kenneth Paul Erickson, eds., *Comparative Political Dynamics: Global Research Perspectives*, New York: HarperCollins, 1991, pp. 7–31; Charles C. Ragin, "Comparative Sociology and the Comparative Method," *International Journal of Comparative Sociology*, Vol. 22, Nos. 1–2, March–June 1981, pp. 102–120; Charles Tilly, "Means and Ends of Comparison in Macrosociology," in Lars Mjoset et al., *Comparative Social Research: Methodological Issues in Comparative Social Science, Vol. 16*, Greenwich, Conn.: JAI Press, 1997, pp. 43–53; Theda Skocpol and Margaret Somers, "The Uses of Comparative History in Macrosocial Inquiry," *Comparative Studies in Society and History*, Vol. 22, No. 2, 1980, pp. 174–197; Stephen Van Evera, *Guide to Methods for Students of Political Science,* Ithaca, N.Y.: Cornell University Press, 1997, pp. 49–88.

[4] Alexander L. George and Timothy J. McKeown, "Case Studies and Theories of Organizational Decision Making," in Robert F. Coulam and Richard A. Smith, eds., *Advances in Information Processing in Organizations: A Research Annual, Vol. 2*, Greenwich, Conn.: JAI Press, 1985, p. 35.

have expressed frustration that they cannot persuade Pakistan to do more despite giving the Pakistani government billions of dollars in assistance since September 2001.

The rest of the study is divided into several chapters. First, it assesses the roots of the militant challenge in Pakistan. Second, it explores Pakistan's military operations since 2001 and examines Pakistan's political will and capability to contend with its security threats. Third, it analyzes the counterinsurgency and counterterrorism literatures to identify key factors that have contributed to effective counterinsurgency operations. Fourth, the study concludes by outlining policies to alter Pakistan's political will to reject militancy as a foreign policy tool and bolster Pakistan's counterinsurgency capabilities.

CHAPTER TWO

The Militant Challenge

This chapter examines Pakistan's historical practice of supporting militant groups to achieve its foreign and domestic policy objectives.[1] Pakistan's first use of militant groups occurred in 1947, shortly after independence. Since then, Pakistan has relied on irregular fighters and *razakars* (volunteers), as well as regular fighters drawn from the military, paramilitary, and intelligence agencies. These regular fighters have sometimes been dressed "in mufti" and disguised as irregular fighters, perhaps to convince domestic and international audiences that the operations were conducted by nonstate actors, rather than instruments of the state.

The chapter argues that, while beginning to use asymmetric warfare in 1947, Pakistan significantly increased its support to militant groups after it acquired a covert nuclear capability by 1990 and an overt nuclear capability by 1998. Before then, several instances in which Pakistan used substate actors led to conventional conflicts with

[1] Pakistan has long tolerated anti-Shia groups and even Shia pogroms at different parts of its history. This is due in part to Gen Muhammad Zia ul-Haq's efforts to promote Sunni Islam and to contend with a militarized Shia response sponsored by Iran. While Pakistan has episodically cracked down on these groups, because they have overlapping membership with key Deobandi religious institutions and with groups fighting in India/Kashmir and Afghanistan, Pakistan has been reluctant to put them down decisively. See inter alia Vali R. Nasr, "International Politics, Domestic Imperatives, and Identity Mobilization: Sectarianism in Pakistan, 1979–1998," *Comparative Politics*, Vol. 32, No. 2, January 2000, pp. 170–191; International Crisis Group, *The State of Sectarianism in Pakistan*, Islamabad/Brussels, Asia Report 95, April 18, 2005, pp. 12, 19–20; A. H. Sorbo, "Paradise Lost," *The Herald* (Karachi), June 1988, p. 31; Muhammad Qasim Zaman, "Sectarianism in Pakistan: The Radicalization of Shi'a and Sunni Identities," *Modern Asian Studies*, Vol. 32, 1998, pp. 689–716.

India. Nuclearization permitted Pakistan to expand the scope, scale, and geographical boundaries of asymmetric conflict with limited fear of retaliation.[2] Such support began to backfire after 2001, when a growing number of decentralized militant networks expanded their power and influence across a larger swath of territory. Some also targeted the Pakistani state and orchestrated suicide attacks in major cities.

The remainder of this chapter is divided into four sections, followed by our conclusions. The first examines Pakistan's historical use of militant groups. The second section explains the ways in which nuclearization enabled Pakistan to expand the jihad deeper into India and other countries, including Afghanistan. The third section argues that any U.S. policy that aims to curb Pakistan's use of militant groups will likely contend with the nuclear umbrella. The fourth describes the militant landscape in Pakistan and the connections that exist among different groups.

Pakistan's Use of Proxy Warfare

Most accounts assume that Pakistan first engaged in using militants as a foreign policy tool during the anti-Soviet jihad in Afghanistan. Pakistan, the United States, Saudi Arabia, and others supported seven major mujahideen groups operating in Afghanistan. "The Mujahedeen could achieve nothing without financial support," acknowledged Brigadier Mohammad Yousaf, who headed the Directorate for Inter-Services Intelligence's (ISI's) Afghan bureau from 1983 to 1987, and was responsible for the supply, training, and operation planning of the mujahideen. "Almost half of this money originated from the U.S. taxpayer, with the remainder coming from the Saudi Arabian government

[2] This argument is developed in C. Christine Fair, "Leader-Led Jihad in Pakistan: The Case of Lashkar-e-Taiba," in Bruce Hoffman and Fernando Reinares, eds., *Leader-Led Jihad,* New York: Columbia University Press, forthcoming. See also Ashley J. Tellis, C. Christine Fair, and Jamison Jo Medby, *Limited Conflicts Under the Nuclear Umbrella: Indian and Pakistani Lessons from the Kargil Crisis*, MG-1450-USCA, Santa Monica, Calif.: RAND Corporation, 2001.

or rich Arab individuals."[3] In many standard accounts, Pakistan redeployed these battle-hardened operatives to Kashmir in 1990 when the Soviets formally withdrew from Afghanistan.

In fact, Pakistan has relied on nonstate actors to prosecute its foreign policy objectives in Kashmir since its independence in 1947. In that year, the state mobilized *lashkars* (tribal forces) to seize Kashmir while the Maharaja of Jammu and Kashmir, Hari Singh, debated whether to join India or Pakistan. The Pakistan Army supported the lashkars. Worried about being defeated by the lashkars, the maharaja asked New Delhi for military support. Delhi's price was accession to India, and the maharaja agreed. By October 1947, Pakistan's first foray into asymmetric warfare had precipitated the first Indo-Pakistani conventional military crisis (the 1947–1948 war). That war ended on January 1, 1949, with the establishment of a ceasefire line sponsored by the United Nations, which demarcated which areas were under Pakistani and which were under Indian control. The ceasefire line was converted to a line of control during the Simla Accords, which concluded the end of the Indo-Pakistani 1971 war.[4]

Following the failed effort to seize Kashmir in 1947, Pakistan supported numerous covert cells within Indian-administered Kashmir, sometimes using operatives based in the Pakistani embassy in New Delhi. In 1965, Pakistan assessed that a wider indigenous insurgency could be fomented in Indian-administered Kashmir.[5] Pakistan's interest in using proxy war may have increased during the 1950s, when the United States provided insurgency-specific training during the

---

[3] Mohammad Yousaf and Mark Adkin, *Afghanistan the Bear Trap: The Defeat of a Superpower*, Havertown, Pa.: Casemate, 2001, p. 77.

[4] For various accounts, see Shuja Nawaz, *Crossed Swords: Pakistan, Its Army, and the Wars Within*, New York: Oxford University Press, 2008; Shuja Nawaz, "The First Kashmir War Revisited," *India Review*, Vol. 7, No. 2, 2008, pp. 115–154; and Robert G. Wirsing, *India, Pakistan, and the Kashmir Dispute: On Regional Conflict and Its Resolution*, New York: St. Martin's Press, 1994.

[5] See also Sumit Ganguly, *The Crisis in Kashmir: Portents of War, Hopes of Peace*, Cambridge, U.K.: Cambridge University Press, 1999.

Cold War.[6] The United States was an important supplier of military equipment for several reasons, including to help balance against Soviet power in the region. Pakistan's military also undertook an important doctrinal shift under American influence and tutelage. As Stephen Cohen noted, Pakistan began intensively studying guerilla warfare during its engagement with the U.S. military. While the United States was interested in *suppressing* such wars, Pakistan was interested in learning how to *launch* such wars against India—or even to develop its own "people's army" as a second defense against India.[7]

With American assistance, Pakistan established the Special Services Group in 1956, a special forces unit initially led by Lieutenant Colonel A. O. Mitha that could fight the Soviets should they invade and occupy the country. It was trained to fight a guerrilla war, and Pakistani officers were brought to Fort Bragg and other facilities in the United States.[8] Pakistani professional military journals also began exploring "low-intensity conflict," a concept and vernacular that Pakistanis still use in place of *counterinsurgency*. Case studies were written

---

6 As numerous writers have noted, Pakistan agreed to the terms of the anti-Soviet alliance out of a dire need to rebuild its armed forces after partition in which Pakistan did not receive its fair share of movable assets. Moreover, most of the fixed assets remained with India as they were located there. India was supposed to pay Pakistan to compensate it for these lost assets and it was to provide other financial resources. However, India soon reneged. The few trainloads of supplies that India did dispatch was full of obsolete equipment or other materials deemed undesirable by Pakistan. Because of British recruitment policies after the 1857 mutiny, there were no all-Muslim units. Given the logic of partition and the distribution of the armed forces, Pakistan received no unit in full strength and suffered a severe shortage of officers. Thus the haphazard process of partition gave rise to the intractable security competition that persists. Given that Pakistan and India came into being as adversaries, Pakistan felt an urgent need to build its weaker armed forces. Given India's alliance with Russia, Pakistan concluded that a formal military alliance with Washington was an expeditious means of doing so. See Pervaiz Iqbal Cheema, *The Armed Forces of Pakistan*, Karachi: Oxford University Press, 2002; Stephen P. Cohen, *The Pakistan Army*, Berkeley: University of California Press, 1984; Hassan Askari Rizvi, *The Military and Politics in Pakistan: 1947–1997*, Lahore: Sang-e-Meel, 2000; Hassan Askari Rizvi, *Military, State and Society in Pakistan*, London: Palgrave, 2000; Dennis Kux, *The United States and Pakistan, 1947–2000: Disenchanted Allies*, Baltimore: Johns Hopkins University Press, 2001; and Nawaz, *Crossed Swords*.

7 Stephen P. Cohen, *The Idea of Pakistan*, Washington, D.C.: Brookings, 2004, p. 105.

8 Nawaz, *Crossed Swords*, p. 133.

on Yugoslavia, North Vietnam, Algeria, and China. Many of these studies concluded that guerilla warfare could be a "strategic weapon," a "slow but sure and relatively inexpensive" strategy that was "fast, overshadowing regular warfare."[9] Maoist doctrine in particular was appealing because of Pakistan's close ties to China and its perceived applicability for Kashmir. Pakistan concluded that the key conditions for a successful guerilla war in Kashmir were in place: a worthy cause, challenging terrain, a resolute and warlike people (referring to Pakistanis), a sympathetic local population, the ready availability of weapons and equipment, and a "high degree of leadership and discipline to prevent [the guerillas] from degenerating into banditry" unlike what had happened in 1947.[10]

Pakistan launched Operation Gibraltar in 1965, named after Tariq bin Ziad's conquest of Spain in 711 with 10,000 Moroccans. Pakistan's military leaders may have been motivated by their study of asymmetric warfare and by U.S. military assistance to India during its 1962 war with China. In addition, India was relatively weak following its defeat in the 1962 war, and the Pakistani military appeared confident of victory following a 1965 skirmish with India in the Rann of Kutch, along the Indo-Pakistani border. Pakistani planners sought to ensure plausible deniability that regular forces were involved. The bulk of each company of about 120 men comprised *razakars* and mujahideen. Recruited from Pakistan-administered Jammu and Kashmir, they were given special training. Officers and a component of men from two paramilitary organizations, the Northern Light Infantry and the Azad Kashmir Rifles, accompanied the irregulars, as did a small number

---

[9] Cohen, *The Idea of Pakistan*, p. 342. Cohen cites a few illustrative examples of these Pakistan military studies of low-intensity conflict. S. A. El-Edroos (Major, Frontier Forces regiment), "A Plea for a People's Army," *Pakistan Army Journal*, Vol. 4, June 1962, pp. 19–25; S. A. El-Edroos, "Afro Asian Revolutionary Warfare and Our Military Thought," *Pakistan Army Journal*, Vol. 4, December 1962, pp. 35–41; Major Mohammad Shafi, "The Effectiveness of Guerilla War," *Pakistan Army Journal*, Vol. 5, June 1963, pp. 4–11.

[10] Cohen, *The Idea of Pakistan,* p. 105. Cohen cites Shafi, "The Effectiveness of Guerilla War," p. 11.

of elite Special Services Group commandos.[11] Groups of four to six companies were combined into units commanded by an officer with the rank of a major. Many of the locations where Pakistan trained the irregular fighters were later used to train mujahideen for the Kashmir jihad launched in 1989.[12]

In total, Pakistan dispatched approximately 30,000 infiltrators during Operation Gibraltar into Indian-administered Kashmir to set up bases, carry out sabotage, and create conditions that would foment a wider indigenous insurrection and facilitate the induction of regular troops into the conflict. While Operation Gibraltar failed to ignite the desired indigenous rebellion against India, it did succeed in precipitating the second conventional Indo-Pakistani conventional conflict, the 1965 war, which ended in a stalemate.[13]

In the early 1970s, Pakistan began to provide covert aid to Islamist militant groups in Afghanistan, including those led by Gulbuddin Hekmatyar. Pakistan's assistance was modest, most likely to minimize punitive action from the Soviet Union, whose military and civilian presence in Afghanistan grew during the 1970s.[14] Especially alarming to the Pakistanis was the desire of senior Afghan government officials, including President Daoud Khan, to unite Pashtuns on both sides of the Afghanistan-Pakistan border.[15] Contrary to conventional wisdom,

---

[11] The Northern Light Infantry was inducted into the regular army in 1999 in part to reward it for its participation in the 1999 Kargil War and in part to properly compensate families for their losses in that conflict. See Tellis et al., *Limited Conflicts Under the Nuclear Umbrella*.

[12] The most detailed account of this is given by Praveen Swami, *India, Pakistan and the Secret Jihad: The Covert War in Kashmir, 1947–2005*, London: Routledge, 2007. Swami used a number of classified Indian documents, which were subsequently declassified, that he obtained in his capacity as a journalist.

[13] Swami, *India, Pakistan and the Secret Jihad*.

[14] See Barnett R. Rubin, *The Fragmentation of Afghanistan*, New Haven: Yale University Press, 2002; and Rizwan Hussain, *Pakistan and the Emergence of Islamic Democracy in Afghanistan*, Burlington, Vt.: Ashgate, 2005.

[15] Afghanistan rejects the de facto and de jure border, the Durand Line, that separates Pakistan from Afghanistan. The Durand Line was demarcated by the British in a treaty signed by the Afghan ruler, Abdur Rahman Khan, in 1893. Afghanistan argues that the treaty was signed under duress and furthermore that Pakistan was not a successor state to the British Raj. As such, Afghans argue that the treaty is void. International law does not support the

Pakistan's support to Afghan militants did not commence with the December 1979 Soviet invasion of Afghanistan. Some argue that Pakistan was a victim of U.S. exploitation during the Soviet occupation and U.S. abandonment of Pakistan once the Soviets withdrew.[16] But Pakistani assistance began at least five years before the Soviet invasion.

Pakistan intensified these activities with active support from the United States, Saudi Arabia, and others following the Soviet invasion. U.S. officials, including National Security Adviser Zbigniew Brzezinski, were particularly concerned about Soviet designs in the region. Brzezinski told President Jimmy Carter that the Soviets might not stop at Afghanistan. "I warned the President that the Soviets would be in a position, if they came to dominate Afghanistan, to promote a separate Baluchistan, which would give them access to the Indian Ocean while dismembering Pakistan and Iran," he noted.[17] During this period, Pakistan dramatically expanded its armed forces, adding U.S. weapon systems. Pakistan also expanded the capabilities of its premier intelligence agency, ISI. In the service of the jihad, Pakistan employed religious institutions and parties, such as the Jamaat-e-Islami and the Jamiat-e-Ulema Islami, to establish Pakistan-based militant groups that could operate in Afghanistan.

Pakistan preferred Afghan militant factions that were Sunni Islamist, rather than Shia or secular, and that were ethnically Pashtun. This appeared to be a deliberate effort to ensure that Pashtun political aspirations would be channeled through religious—not ethnic—terms. Much as during the 1970s, Pakistan was concerned about Kabul's irre-

---

Afghan position. See, among others, Rubin, *The Fragmentation of Afghanistan*, and Hussain, *Pakistan and the Emergence of Islamic Democracy in Afghanistan*.

[16] This narrative is deeply flawed. As noted, Pakistan had already begun pursuing such policies in Afghanistan. Pakistan benefited from its alliance with the United States in that it received weapons, cash, and training of the military and ISI. Moreover, Pakistan was allowed to continue receiving this support even though it had passed key nuclear redlines which would have precipitated arms cut off had the Press Amendment not been passed. This is explained in considerable detail in C. Christine Fair, "Time for Sober Realism: U.S.-Pakistan Relations," *The Washington Quarterly*, Vol. 32, No. 2, April 2009.

[17] Zbigniew Brzezinski, *Power and Principle: Memoirs of the National Security Adviser, 1977–1981*, New York: Farrar, Straus, and Giroux, 1983, p. 427.

dentist claims to Pakistan's Pashtun areas and about Pashtun demands for a separate Pashtun state. With massive international support, the mujahideen forced the Soviets to withdraw in 1989. In addition, Pakistan used Pashtuns from the regular Pakistan Army to infiltrate into Afghanistan to assist mujahideen groups. These soldiers were under strict instructions not to reveal their identity. If they were captured, Pakistan would deny they were from the army. "It was part of my job to select the individuals, and brief them as to their tasks," noted a senior ISI official. "Their mission was to accompany Mujahedeen on special operations, they acted as advisers, assisting the Commander in carrying out his task."[18]

Expanding Support to Militants

By the late 1980s, several factors increased Pakistan's desire to expand the scale and scope of its support to militant groups. First was the success of the anti-Soviet war in Afghanistan. If mujahideen in Afghanistan could defeat a nuclear-armed superpower, why could not a similar force succeed in Indian-administered Kashmir? While Pakistan's interest in launching a guerilla war with India began as early as the 1950s, the Afghan success buoyed Pakistan's confidence in using a similar approach in Kashmir. In the 1980s, Pakistan had also provided extensive assistance to the Sikh ethnonationalist insurgency in the Punjab.[19]

Second was Pakistan's burgeoning nuclear weapon program. By the 1980s, U.S. intelligence indicated that Pakistan had developed a nuclear weapon capability. Military aid to Pakistan could only be supplied through a presidential certification called the Pressler Amendment. It banned most economic and military assistance to Pakistan unless the U.S. president certified, on an annual basis, that "Pakistan does not possess a nuclear explosive device and that the proposed United States military assistance program will reduce significantly the

[18] Yousaf and Adkin, *Afghanistan the Bear Trap*, p. 113.

[19] This is important to note because this insurgency had nothing to do with Muslim interests. Pakistan also stands accused of supporting ethnic insurgents in India's restive northeast.

risk that Pakistan will possess a nuclear explosive device."[20] In 1990, President George H. W. Bush declined to issue this certification, which triggered U.S. sanctions.[21]

A third factor was the surplus of battle-hardened jihadis from the Afghan conflict and the sprawling infrastructure to train new militants that Pakistan had developed to support the Afghan effort. With the withdrawal of the Soviet Union from Afghanistan, Pakistan redeployed many of the Afghan mujahideen to the Kashmir front and established training camps in Pakistan and Afghanistan.

The Kashmir insurgency had initially developed for a number of reasons, including India's mismanagement of the state. Several indigenous Kashmiri militant groups formed in response. Some of these groups began to lobby for independence, rather than union with Pakistan, and some turned from violence toward political activism. A new group of Pakistan- and Afghanistan-based groups directly competed with these older, more ethnically Kashmiri groups. When Pakistan began to introduce fighters from the Afghan jihad, the Pakistan-based groups, such as Lashkar-e-Taiba, Harkat-ul-Mujahideen, and Harkat-ul-Jihad Islami, eliminated many indigenous and proindependence insurgents. By the mid-1990s, Pakistan-based militant groups that were prosecuting Pakistan's agenda of weakening India and seizing Kashmir had overrun the conflict.[22]

The most lethal of these militant groups were adherents of the Deobandi and Ahl-e-Hadith interpretative traditions. They were hostile to the heterodox Sufi Islam practiced by Kashmiris in the valley. These groups were motivated to fight Indian forces on behalf of Islam-

---

[20] Committees on International Relations and Foreign Relations of the U.S. House of Representatives and the Senate, *Legislation on Foreign Relations Through 2002*, Washington, D.C., U.S. Government Printing Office, 2003, p. 316.

[21] See discussion in Fair, "Time for Sober Realism."

[22] See inter alia Swami, *India, Pakistan and the Secret Jihad;* Alexander Evans, "The Kashmir Insurgency: As Bad as It Gets," *Small Wars and Insurgencies*, Vol. 11, No. 1, Spring 2000, pp. 69–81; Ahmed Rashid, *Descent into Chaos*, New York: Viking Penguin, 2008. See also Sumit Ganguly, "A Mosque, A Shrine, and Two Sieges," in Christine C. Fair and Sumit Ganguly, eds., *Treading on Hallowed Ground: Counterinsurgency Operations in Sacred Spaces*, New York: Oxford University Press, 2008, pp. 66–88.

abad, but they also aimed to convert Kashmiris to more orthodox interpretations of Islam. While indigenous Kashmiri militant groups were unwilling to destroy their sacred shrines, these foreign militants were much more inclined to do so.[23] They demanded strict adherence to their interpretations of Islam and used violence to enforce them. For example, they attacked newspapers that declined to publish their propaganda or that employed women, threw acid on women's faces, discouraged families from sending their girls to school, and insisted that females abandon traditional Kashmiri veiling practices in favor of the burqa (a loose enveloping garment that covers the face and body) and use of the niqab (face covering).[24] These developments created significant dissatisfaction among many Kashmiris with Pakistan, as illustrated by a poll conducted by A.C. Nielson in the urban areas of Srinagar and Anantnag (in the Muslim-dominated district of Kashmir) and in the cities of Jammu and Udhampur (in the Hindu-dominant district of Jammu). The poll found almost no support in Kashmir, much less in Jammu, for unification with Pakistan.[25]

While Pakistan became ever more embroiled in its proxy war in Kashmir, Pakistan supported an array of Pashtun Islamist groups in Afghanistan well after the Soviet Union and United States withdrew. In the early 1990s, Afghan state authority collapsed and governance fractured among a range of warlords and local commanders.[26] Pakistan initially provided most of its support to Gulbuddin Hekmatyar and his Pashtun militant faction, Hezb-e-Islami, to achieve a reasonably stable Afghanistan whose leadership was positively disposed toward Islam-

---

[23] See inter alia Swami, *India, Pakistan and the Secret Jihad;* Evans, "The Kashmir Insurgency; Rashid, *Descent into Chaos*. See also Ganguly, *The Crisis in Kashmir*; Ganguly, "A Mosque, A Shrine, and Two Sieges," pp. 66–88.

[24] Fair fieldwork in Kashmir in fall 2002. Also see Human Rights Watch, "'Everyone Lives in Fear': Patterns of Impunity in Jammu and Kashmir," Human Rights Reports, Vol. 18, No. 11, September 11, 2006. That report details the atrocities of both the Indian security forces as well as the militant groups.

[25] "Kashmiris Don't Want to Join Pak: Survey," *The Times of India*, September 27, 2002.

[26] See, for example, Antonio Giustozzi, *Empires of Mud: Wars and Warlords in Afghanistan*, New York: Columbia University Press, 2009.

abad.[27] But Hekmatyar failed to deliver. According to classified U.S. government assessments at the time, ISI and other Pakistani military leaders concluded that Hekmatyar's Hezb-i-Islami could not conquer and hold Kabul.[28] Pakistan began to shift its support to the Taliban, a group largely composed of madrassa students, or *talibs,* that emerged in southern Afghanistan.[29]

Pakistan's intelligence services provided significant assistance, according to U.S. government documents. U.S. State Department officials assessed that ISI was "deeply involved in the Taliban take over in Kandahar and Qalat."[30] ISI officers were deployed to such Afghan cities as Herat, Kandahar, and Jalalabad—and stationed in Pakistani consulates—to provide assistance and advice.[31] A U.S. intelligence assessment contended that the ISI was "supplying the Taliban forces with munitions, fuel, and food," and "using a private sector transportation company to funnel supplies into Afghanistan and to the Taliban forces."[32] The ISI often masked its activities effectively. One example is its use of private-sector transportation companies to funnel supplies to Taliban forces, including ammunition, petroleum, oil, lubricants, and food. These companies operated vehicle convoys that departed Pakistan late in the evening and, especially if carrying weapons and ammunition aboard, concealed the supplies beneath other goods loaded onto the trucks. There were several major supply routes. One began in Peshawar, Pakistan, and passed through Jalalabad in eastern Afghani-

---

[27] During the Soviet jihad, Pakistan backed seven Pakistan-based militant groups, six of which were Pashtun dominated. Burhanuddin Rabbani's Tajik-dominated Jamiat-i-Islami was the only non-Pashtun group supported by Pakistan. See Rubin, *The Fragmentation of Afghanistan*, 81–110.

[28] Ron McMullen, Afghanistan Desk, U.S. Department of State, "Developments in Afghanistan," cable, December 5, 1994. Released by the National Security Archive.

[29] Abdul Salam Zaeef, *My Life with the Taliban*, London: Hurst and Company, 2009.

[30] McMullen, "Developments in Afghanistan."

[31] U.S. Embassy, Islamabad, "Afghanistan: [Excised] Criticizes GOP's Afghan Policy; Says It Is Letting Policy Drift," cable, June 16, 1998. Released by the National Security Archive.

[32] [Excised] to Defense Intelligence Agency (DIA) Washington, D.C., Cable, "Pakistan Interservice Intelligence/Pakistan (PK) Directorate Supplying the Taliban Forces," October 22, 1996. Released by the National Security Archive.

stan on its way to Kabul. Another left Quetta and passed through Kandahar before ending in Kabul. Yet another began in Miramshah, Pakistan, and continued through Khowst and Gardez before entering the Afghan capital.[33]

In some ways, however, the Taliban failed to deliver much of what Islamabad had hoped to accomplish. While able to establish a semblance of order, the Taliban government lacked international legitimacy and gradually became an international pariah. The Taliban destroyed the Buddha statues in Bamiyan Province, which Abdul Salam Zaeef, the Taliban Ambassador to Pakistan, later described as "unnecessary and a case of bad timing."[34] In addition, the Taliban allowed Osama bin Laden and his al Qa'ida network to establish a sanctuary in Afghanistan, despite Pakistan's repeated requests that bin Laden be handed over to Pakistani authorities.

Over time, some Pakistani policymakers—including senior diplomats—began to see the Taliban as more of a political liability than an asset, fearing growing criticism about the Taliban's human rights violations and alliance with al Qa'ida. This was particularly apparent in 1998 when al Qa'ida, which was headquartered in Afghanistan, organized the simultaneous attacks on two American embassies in Kenya and Tanzania. The United States retaliated by conducting cruise missile strikes in Afghanistan, targeting al Qa'ida facilities near Khowst Province. The strikes helped consolidate Mullah Mohammad Omar's commitment to Osama bin Laden, despite earlier reservations about his guest's connections to international jihadists. Bin Laden had arrived in Afghanistan with the support of Mullah Omar in 1996 after spending time in Sudan and had installed many of the senior Arab fighters in residential complexes near Kandahar and Jalalabad.

---

[33] [Excised] to DIA Washington, D.C.; U.S. Consulate, Peshawar, Cable, "Afghan-Pak Border Relations at Torkham Tense," October 2, 1996. Released by the National Security Archive.

[34] Zaeef, *My Life with the Taliban*, p. 128.

During the Khowst attack, the Pakistani militant group Harkat-ul-Mujahideen reported that five of its members were killed.[35]

After September 11, 2001, however, Pakistan abruptly changed its policy and assisted the United States in overthrowing the Taliban government, although some Taliban officials later acknowledged that the "ISI had even advised Mullah [Omar] to find a safe haven."[36] Pakistan faced the stark option of abandoning the Taliban and supporting the United States or becoming the target of an American war.[37] As the next chapter will discuss in more detail, Pakistan helped overthrow the Taliban regime and captured a range of al Qa'ida militants and other foreign fighters.

Yet Pakistan's U-turn on the Taliban appeared to be short lived.[38] Support from individuals within the Pakistani government to the Taliban and other Afghan insurgent groups appeared to increase by around 2006.[39] Among the Pakistani concerns were that too many Tajik and Uzbek leaders were filling key Afghan government positions and that Pashtuns were not securing desirable levels of representation in the government, police force, and army. Some senior U.S. officials, including LTG David Barno, argued that another reason Pakistan provided aid to the Taliban was that the United States was discussing downsizing forces in Afghanistan.[40] In July 2006, the United States turned over southern Afghanistan to NATO. NATO deployed 12,000 soldiers to six southern provinces: Helmand, Kandahar, Nimroz, Uru-

---

35 This discussion draws from C. Christine Fair, "Pakistan's Relations with Central Asia: Is Past Prologue?" *Journal of Strategic Studies*, Vol. 31, No. 2, April 2008, pp. 201–227. Also see Chidanand Rajghatta and Kamal Siddiqui, "Pak Cries Foul over US Revenge Strike," *Indian Express*, August 22, 1998.

36 Zaeef, *My Life with the Taliban*, p. 152.

37 See account in Pervez Musharraf, *In the Line of Fire*, New York: Free Press, 2006. Also see in Fair, *The Counterterror Coalitions;* Fair, "Pakistan's Relations with Central Asia."

38 Seth G. Jones, *In the Graveyard of Empires: America's War in Afghanistan*, New York: W.W. Norton, 2009.

39 See, for example, Rashid, *Descent into Chaos*.

40 See, for example, Lieutenant General David W. Barno, Testimony Before the Committee on Foreign Affairs, U.S. House of Representatives, February 15, 2007, p. 21.

zgan, Zabol, and Day Kundi. The largest contingent in this force was British, which included 3,600 soldiers based in Helmand Province. Canada and the Netherlands also deployed sizable contingents. Yet Pakistani government officials appeared to interpret this shift as a signal that the U.S. commitment to Afghanistan was waning.[41]

After September 11, 2001, India provided several hundred million dollars in financial assistance to Afghanistan. It helped fund construction of the new Afghan parliament building and provided financial assistance to elected legislators.[42] India built roads near the Pakistani border, which were run by the Indian state-owned Border Roads Organization.[43] India also established several consulates in such Afghan cities as Jalalabad, Kandahar, and Herat. Pakistan accused India of using these consulates for "terrorist activities" inside Pakistan, especially in Baluchistan Province.

Asymmetric Conflict Under the Nuclear Umbrella

One possible reason for Pakistan's ability to sustain support for militant campaigns over six decades is that jihad is religiously sanctioned.[44] Ayesha Jalal contends that Balakot, located in the district of Mansehra in Pakistan's NWFP, is the "epicenter of jihad" in South Asia. It was there that Sayyid Ahmad of Rai Bereilly (1786–1831) and Shah Ismail (1779–1831), both "quintessential Islamic warriors in South Asian Muslim consciousness," were slain fighting the Sikhs in May 1831. Some scholars consider this the only genuine jihad to establish Muslim supremacy in South Asia. Ahmad and Ismail's grave sites have since

---

[41] Author interviews with Pakistani government officials, Washington, D.C., January 2006.

[42] David C. Mulford, U.S. Ambassador to India, *Afghanistan Has Made a Remarkable Transition*, New Delhi: U.S. Department of State, February 2006; Amin Tarzi, "Afghanistan: Kabul's India Ties Worry Pakistan," *Radio Free Europe/Radio Liberty*, April 16, 2006.

[43] Border Roads Organization, *Vision, Mission, Role*, Delhi, 2010.

[44] This section is drawn from Fair's reworking and updating sections of an earlier RAND publication, Tellis et al., *Limited Conflicts Under the Nuclear Umbrella*.

become sacred sites that are intertwined with both jihad and colonial resistance:

> To this day Balakot where the Sayyid lies buried is a spot that has been greatly revered, not only by militants in contemporary Pakistan, some of whom have set up training camps near Balakot, but also by anticolonial nationalists who interpreted the movement as a prelude to a jihad against the British in India.[45]

The association of Balakot with the jihad in the 1990s was cemented when Pakistan established militant training camps there for groups operating in Kashmir and the rest of India.[46]

More generally, popular consciousness in Pakistan is strewn with "collective myths and legends of jihad based on selective representation of history."[47] The Pakistani state itself has nurtured a public discourse that is anti-India, anti-Hindu, and pro-jihad using Pakistani public and military schools, a variety of media, and public celebrations of national events.[48] Thus, one reason that Pakistan has successfully sustained proxy wars may be that it has marketed them as jihad, which enjoys considerable legitimacy in Pakistan and elsewhere in South Asia.[49]

While Pakistan already had a long history of using Islamist militants as proxies, it began to expand the jihad in scale, scope, and territorial range in the late 1980s when it became an overt nuclear power. Pakistan's status as a nuclear state increased the confidence of some

---

[45] Ayesha Jalal, *Partisans of Allah*, Lahore: Sang-e-Meel, 2008, p. 61.

[46] Jalal, *Partisans of Allah*, pp. 1–2.

[47] Jalal, *Partisans of Allah*, p. 20.

[48] K. K. Aziz, *Murder of History: A Critique of History Textbooks Used in Pakistan*, Lahore: Vanguard Books, 1998; A. H. Nayyar and Ahmed Salim, *The Subtle Subversion: The State of Curricula and Textbooks in Pakistan—Urdu, English, Social Studies and Civics*, Islamabad: Sustainable Development Policy Institute, 2003; Iftikhar Ahmed, "Islam, Democracy and Citizenship Education: An Examination of the Social Studies Curriculum in Pakistan," *Current Issues in Comparative Education*, Vol. 7, No. 1, December 15, 2004.

[49] Jacob N. Shapiro and C. Christine Fair, "Why Support Islamist Militancy? Evidence from Pakistan," *International Security*, Vol. 34, No. 3, Winter 2009/2010.

officials that India would respond extremely cautiously to attacks from militant groups in Kashmir. Consequently, Pakistani jihad groups spread in larger numbers to Kashmir.

Pakistan became even more aggressive following the 1998 Indian and Pakistani nuclear tests. It launched a limited incursion into Indian-administered Kashmir to seize a small amount of territory in Kargil District. Many analysts have argued that such a brazen incursion would have been unlikely before Pakistan had attained its overt nuclear status.[50] In the Kargil conflict, Pakistan employed the Northern Light infantry disguised as civilian irregular fighters. It is likely that Gen Pervez Musharraf, the Chief of Army Staff at the time, began planning for this operation in fall 1998, when Pakistani Prime Minister Nawaz Sharif and Indian Prime Minister Atal Bihari Vajpayee undertook the historical "Lahore Peace Process." That process culminated in Vajpayee's visit to Lahore in February 1999. He surprised the populations of both countries when he accepted the legitimacy of the Pakistani state at an important landmark commemorating Pakistan's independence, the Minar-e-Pakistan in Lahore.

While Pakistan had limited territorial aims, its use of army officers as irregular fighters caused some analysts to reconsider whether nuclearization of the subcontinent would create long-term stability, as some nuclear theorists had predicted.[51] Kargil exemplified what has been called the "stability-instability paradox."[52] It holds that nuclear weapons can reduce the possibility of a conventional war between

---

[50] See Tellis et al., *Limited Conflicts Under the Nuclear Umbrella;* Paul S. Kapur, *Dangerous Deterrent: Nuclear Weapons Proliferation and Conflict in South Asia*, Stanford: Stanford University Press, 2007; C. Christine Fair, "Militants in the Kargil Conflict: Myths, Realities, and Impacts," in Peter Lavoy, ed., *Asymmetric Warfare in South Asia: The Causes and Consequences of Kargil*, Cambridge, U.K.: Cambridge University Press, December 2009.

[51] For a discussion of proponents of this view, see Neil Joeck, *Maintaining Nuclear Stability*, New York: Oxford University Press for the International Institute for Strategic Studies, Adelphi Paper, 0567-932X, 1997.

[52] See Glenn Snyder, "The Balance of Power and the Balance of Terror," in Paul Seaburry, ed., *The Balance of* Power, San Francisco: Chandler, 1964; Robert Jervis, *The Meaning of the Nuclear Revolution*, Ithaca, N.Y.: Cornell University Press, 1989.

nuclear states but at the same time increase the possibility of minor or limited war.[53]

Kargil underscored the importance of nuclear weapons for Pakistan's strategy in Kashmir and India and illustrated the destabilizing aspects of nuclearization of the subcontinent. In particular, Pakistan's possession of these weapons was a critical *precondition* that enabled the planning and execution of Kargil because nuclear weapons provided security against a full-scale Indian retaliation.[54] This immunity had two dimensions. First, Pakistan's nuclear weapons deterred a conventional and nuclear Indian response. Second, Pakistan used the possibility of nuclear escalation to galvanize international intervention on its behalf when the crisis intensified. India publicly acknowledged that Pakistan's strategic assets enabled the possibility of low-intensity conflict.[55] So did Pakistan. In April 1999, General Musharraf noted that, even though nuclearization rendered large-scale conventional wars obsolete, proxy wars were still possible.[56]

Pakistan reportedly "brandished" various nuclear threats during the Kargil crisis, although the threats from senior policymakers were ambiguous. Pakistan activated at least one missile base. Bruce Reidel, who served as a special assistant to the U.S. President and was Senior Director for Near East and South Asia Affairs at the National Security Council at the time, noted that U.S. intelligence indicated the Paki-

---

[53] Michael Krepon and Chris Gagné, "Introduction," in Michael Krepon and Chris Gagné, eds., *The Stability-Instability Paradox: Nuclear Weapons and Brinkmanship in South Asia*, Washington, D.C.: Stimson Center, June 2001.

[54] Tellis et al., *Limited Conflicts Under the Nuclear Umbrella.*

[55] Timothy D. Hoyt, "Kargil: The Nuclear Dimension," in Peter R. Lavoy, ed., *Asymmetric Warfare in South Asia: The Causes and Consequences of the Kargil Conflict*, Cambridge: Cambridge University Press, 2009; Tellis et al., *Limited Conflicts Under the Nuclear Umbrella.*

[56] "Pak Defence Strong, Says Army Chief," April 19, 1999, cited in Timothy Hoyt, "Politics, Proximity and Paranoia: The Evolution of Kashmir as a Nuclear Flashpoint," *The India Review*, Vol. 2, No. 3, July 2003, pp. 117–144. See also statement of Musharraf in April 1999 cited in the Kargil Review Committee, *From Surprise to Reckoning: The Kargil Review Committee Report*, New Delhi: SAGE Publications, December 15, 1999, p. 77.

stanis were preparing their nuclear arsenal for possible deployment.[57] Some of Pakistan's threats were difficult to discern. For example, Pakistan's Religious Affairs Minister, Raja Zafarul Haq, warned that Pakistan could resort to the nuclear option and had legitimate authority from the army to do so. Similar ambiguity surrounds Reidel's assertion because the movement of nuclear assets could have been a defensive step to protect them from a preemptive Indian strike. However, the utility—and danger—of such signaling during a crisis lies in the multiple interpretations adversaries may draw from them.[58]

While Kargil may have been the first conventional conflict under the nuclear umbrella, the most brazen uses of proxy warfare happened after 1998. These instances add credibility to the argument that nuclearization emboldened Pakistan's use of militant groups. They include, for example, the 1999 Lashkar-e-Taiba attack on a security force establishment collocated with New Delhi's tourist attraction, the Red Fort; the 2001 Jaish-e-Mohammad attack on the Indian Parliament; the 2002 Lashkar-e-Taiba massacre of army wives and children in Kaluchak; and a range of bombings Lashkar-e-Taiba and affiliated groups have conducted throughout India, including the 2006 and 2008 attacks in Mumbai.[59]

While some disaggregate the nuclear and militant threats in Pakistan, the two are inextricably linked. With the development of a covert and then an overt nuclear capability, Pakistan could support militant groups with limited concern about retaliation. In short, Pakistani lead-

---

[57] Bruce Riedel, "American Diplomacy and the 1999 Kargil Summit at Blair House," Center for the Advanced Study of India, University of Pennsylvania Policy Paper Series, 2002; Tellis et al., *Limited Conflicts Under the Nuclear Umbrella.*

[58] Hoyt, "Kargil: The Nuclear Dimension."

[59] C. Christine Fair advanced this argument in Angel Rabasa, Robert D. Blackwill, Peter Chalk, Kim Cragin, C. Christine Fair, Brian A. Jackson, Brian Michael Jenkins, Seth G. Jones, Nathaniel Shestak, and Ashley J. Tellis, "The Lessons of Mumbai," Santa Monica, Calif.: RAND Corporation, OP-249-RC, 2009. See also Fair, "Leader-Led Jihad in Pakistan."

ers banked on the fear of escalation, which some nuclear experts have long argued can be a strong deterrent.[60]

Pakistan's Militant Landscape

Prior to September 2001, Pakistan's militant landscape could be organized according to each group's sectarian orientation, theater of operation, and ethnic constitution.[61] For example, there were *askari tanzeems* (militant groups) that traditionally focused on Kashmir, including the Deobandi groups Jaish-e-Mohammad and Harkat-ul-Mujahideen, as well as Ahl-e-Hadith organizations such as Punjab-based Lashkar-e-Taiba. While these are often referred to as "Kashmiri groups," this is a misnomer because they include few ethnic Kashmiris and most do not operate exclusively in Kashmir. Indeed, Lashkar-e-Taiba and Jaish-e-Mohammad have long operated throughout India, and Deobandi groups have begun operating in Pakistan in recent years. Lashkar-e-Taiba and some Deobandi militant groups have also been operating in Afghanistan against U.S., NATO, and Afghan forces.[62] Other "Kashmiri groups" are operating under the influence of the Islamist political party Jamaat-e-Islami, such as al-Badr and Hizbul Mujahideen, which tend to comprise ethnic Kashmiris.

---

60 See, for example, Kenneth Waltz's arguments in Scott D. Sagan and Kenneth Waltz, *The Spread of Nuclear Weapons: A Debate*, New York: W.W. Norton, 1995. Also see Jervis, *The Meaning of the Nuclear Revolution*.

61 This section draws from C. Christine Fair, "Pakistani Attitudes Towards Militancy and State Responses to Counter Militancy," written while the author was a Luce Fellow at the University of Washington in 2009. This paper is forthcoming in an edited volume by James Wellman. C. Christine Fair, "Who Are Pakistan's Militants and Their Families?" *Terrorism and Political Violence*, 2008, and C. Christine Fair, "Militant Recruitment in Pakistan: Implications for Al-Qaeda and Other Organizations, *Studies in Conflict and Terrorism*, Vol. 27, No. 6, November/December 2004.

62 See C. Christine Fair, "Antecedents and Implications of the November 2008 Lashkar-e-Taiba Attack upon Mumbai," testimony presented before the House Homeland Security Committee, Subcommittee on Transportation Security and Infrastructure Protection on March 11, 2009.

Many *askari tanzeems* have traditionally been sectarian; these include the anti-Shia Lashkar-e-Jhangvi and Sipah-e-Sahaba Pakistan.[63] Both groups are under the sway of the Deobandi organization Jamiat-e-Ulema Islami (JUI) and are funded by wealthy Arab individuals and organizations. These sectarian tanzeems also have overlapping memberships with other Deobandi militant groups, including the Afghan and Pakistani Taliban, which have strong connections to the JUI.[64] In the past, Shia sectarian groups were also active. These groups targeted Sunni Muslims and obtained funding from Iran, although they have largely disappeared.[65]

Since 2006 and possibly earlier, Pakistani militant groups have successfully established an archipelago of microemirates imposing sharia across large swaths of the Pashtun belt. These militant groups are best understood as a series of loose networks.[66] Networked groups tend to be dispersed, but different nodes can communicate and coordinate their campaigns to some degree. Individual groups may be hierarchically structured, but there is little or no overall command across groups. A range of transnational terrorist, criminal, and insurgent groups have adopted networked strategies and organizational structures. As John Arquilla and David Ronfeldt argued,

---

63 Many of these groups have been proscribed numerous times, only to reemerge. Many now operate under new names. This book uses the names that are likely to be most familiar to readers.

64 Mariam Abou Zahab and Olivier Roy, *Islamist Networks: The Afghan-Pakistan Connection*, London: C. Hurst, 2004; Fair, "Militant Recruitment in Pakistan."

65 Since the onset of sanguinary sectarian violence in Iraq and Iran's 2006 victory in Lebanon, it is possible that Iran may once again have become involved in inciting anti-Sunni violence in Pakistan. Indeed, sectarian violence increased sharply in Pakistan in 2007 from 2006 and previous years. However, anti-Shia militias perpetrated the overwhelming majority of these attacks. Thus, allegations about Iran's involvement so far lack empirical support.

66 On networked groups, see, for example, John Arquilla and David Ronfeldt, eds., *In Athena's Camp: Preparing for Conflict in the Information Age*, Santa Monica, Calif.: RAND Corporation, MR-880-OSD/RC, 1997; Ian O. Lesser, Bruce Hoffman, John Arquilla, David Ronfeldt, Michele Zanini, and Brian Michael Jenkins, *Countering the New Terrorism*, Santa Monica, Calif.: RAND Corporation, MR-989-AF, 1999; John Arquilla and David Ronfeldt, eds., *Networks and Netwars: The Future of Terror, Crime and Militancy*, Santa Monica, Calif.: RAND Corporation, MR-1382-OSD, 2001.

> The organizational structure is quite flat. There is no single central leader or commander; the network as a whole (but not necessarily each node) has little to no hierarchy. There may be multiple leaders. Decision-making and operations are decentralized and depend on consultative consensus-building that allows for local initiative and autonomy. The design is both acephalous (headless) and polycephalous (Hydra-headed)—it has no precise heart or head, although not all nodes may be "created equal."[67]

The rise of the Tehreek-e-Taliban-e-Pakistan (TTP) network seems to coincide with—or was precipitated by—Pakistani military operations in FATA, as well as U.S. unmanned aerial vehicle (UAV) strikes in FATA.[68] The 2006 U.S. conventional ground and air strikes in Damadola, Bajaur, intended to eliminate Ayman al-Zawahiri and the October 2006 drone strike against an al Qa'ida–affiliated madrassa in Chingai, a village in Bajaur, were widely seen as the catalysts for the suicide attacks against Pakistani security forces in FATA and NWFP. The madrassa in Chingai was run by Tehreek-e-Nafaz-e-Shariat-e-Mohammadi (TNSM), a Sunni militant group founded by Sufi Mohammad. In support of the Taliban, Sufi Mohammad dispatched 8,000 volunteers into Afghanistan to fight the Americans and Northern Alliance during Operation Enduring Freedom. While Sufi Mohammad was jailed, his militant son-in-law, Maulana Fazlullah, took over the organization. Sufi Mohammad's deputy, Maulvi Liaquat, died in the Chingai attack.

As Figure 2.1 illustrates, examples of these networks include Maulvi Nazir (South Waziristan), Abdullah Mehsud (South

---

[67] John Arquilla and David Ronfeldt, "The Advent of Netwar," in Arquilla and Ronfeldt, *In Athena's Camp*, p. 280.

[68] While drone strikes were at first infrequent, they have become more routine. Between August 2008 and April 1, 2009, there were at least 30 drone strikes which may have killed as many as 300 people. While the political leadership complain about this, it is widely believed that the targeting of militants in FATA is done with the tacit knowledge and input from the Pakistan Army, public displays of outrage notwithstanding. See "Many Killed in 'U.S. Drone Attack,'" BBC News, April 1, 2009. Also see Tom Coghlan, Zahid Hussain, and Jeremy Page, "Secrecy and Denial as Pakistan Lets CIA Use Airbase to Strike Militants," *The Times* (London), February 2009.

Figure 2.1
Example of Militant Networks in FATA and NWFP

RAND *MG982-2.1*

Waziristan), Hafiz Gul Bahadur (North Waziristan), the Haqqani network (North Waziristan), Mangal Bagh (Khyber), TNSM (Swat, Dir, Malakand), and Faqir Mohammad (Bajaur). Several foreign-fighter networks were also active, such as al Qa'ida. In addition, a stream of Uzbek, Tajik, Chechen, Uighur, and other fighters cycled through Kashmir and Pakistan's tribal areas, including such groups as the Islamic Jihad Union and the Islamic Movement of Uzbekistan. Other groups remained entrenched in Pakistan, such as Lashkar-e-Taiba and Jaish-e-Mohammad.

In late 2007, several of the commanders coalesced under the TTP banner, led by Baitullah Mehsud. He was eventually killed by a U.S. UAV strike in 2009. Baitullah Mehsud claimed many allies, all of whom sought to establish their radical interpretation of sharia across the Pashtun belt. In late February 2008, two commanders, Mullah Nazir and Hafiz Gul Bahadur, appeared to set aside their differences with Baitullah Mehsud temporarily and forged the Shura Ittehad-ul-Mujahideen, though this alliance was mostly a facade.[69]

Many of these networks had an important Pashtun tribal component. Gul Bahadur, for example, was a tribal elder from the Madda Khel section of the Ibrahim Khel clan of the Utmanzai Wazir tribe. The TTP gained support from the Alizai clan of the Mehsud tribe, though some elements of the Shaman Khel and Bahlolzai clans opposed the TTP. One of the Haqqani network's strongest support bases was the Mezi subtribe of the Zadran tribe. The Haqqani network also co-opted a range of *kuchis*, nomadic Pashtun tribes, and developed a close relationship with Mullah Nazir's group, which had a significant support base among the Kaka Khel subtribe of the Ahmadzai Waziris.[70]

While the "Talibanization" of the tribal areas was initially limited to North and South Waziristan, the phenomenon next spread to Bajaur. A range of networks allied with the TTP pushed into areas that had previously been peaceful, such as the Mohmand, Orakzai, and Kurram Agencies. Networks also emerged in the frontier areas of Bannu, Tank, Kohat, Lakki Marwar, Dera Ismail Khan, and Swat. Throughout summer 2007, the Frontier Corps and Frontier Constabulary battled the Pakistani militants associated with TNSM, which

---

[69] See Hassan Abbas, "Increasing Talibanization in Pakistan's Seven Tribal Agencies," *Terrorism Monitor* Vol. 5, No. 18, September 27, 2007, pp. 1–5; Hassan Abbas, "A Profile of Tehrik-i-Taliban Pakistan," *CTC Sentinel*, Vol. 1, No. 2, January 2008, pp. 1–4; Syed Shoaib Hasan, "Profile: Baitullah Mehsud," BBC News, December 28, 2007. Pakistan has considered Maulvi Nazir an ally because he helped oust or kill numerous Uzbeks in South Waziristan. He is considered to be a dedicated foe of U.S. and NATO forces as he dispatches fighters to Afghanistan. Gul Bahadar has had a number of differences with Baitullah Mehsud. It is not clear what this alliance means for Pakistan or for the United States and allies in Afghanistan. See Saeed Shah, "Taliban Rivals Unite to Fight U.S. Troops Surge," *The Guardian*, March 3, 2009.

[70] Thomas Ruttig, "Loya Paktia's Insurgency: The Haqqani Network as an Autonomous Entity," in Antonio Giustozzi, ed., *Decoding the New Taliban: Insights from the Afghan Field*, New York: Columbia University Press, 2009, pp. 57–101.

seized the Swat Valley in late October.[71] The valley was wrestled from the militants when elements from Pakistan's 11th Corps entered the fray, and Pakistan's armed forces remained engaged in Swat until the early 2009 peace deal. This deal ceded sovereignty to the TNSM and sanctioned the imposition of sharia (via the Nizam-e-Adil regulations) in Swat and Malakand.[72]

How did these groups expand? One of their most successful methods was to exploit local grievances: socioeconomic concerns among local Pakistanis; Pakistani governance failures, including inadequate security and justice; and frustration with government corruption. Local militant commanders in FATA pressured political agents to provide services. They established functional—and draconian—police functions and dispute resolution. The courts established in Swat, run by *qazis*, or Islamic jurists, required adding new *qazis* when the caseload of a given court exceeded 150 cases. No such provision existed in the mainstream courts. TTP-linked groups also established "love marriage bureaus" to solemnize "love marriages." This had the advantage of appealing to youth who resented forced marriages and ameliorated the economic requirement for young men to pay large bride prices.[73]

Also enabling the expansion of TTP-linked groups were the state's failure to provide security to those who resisted the Taliban and the Pakistan Army's excessive use of force. Indeed, local populations were

---

[71] C. Christine Fair, "Pakistan Loses Swat to Local Taliban," *Terrorism Focus*, Vol. 4, No. 37, 2007.

[72] There is very little scholarly literature on this phenomenon, with most coverage taking place in the popular press or security publications. See, inter alia, Rahimullah Yusufzai, "The Emergence of the Pakistani Taliban," *Jane's Information Group*, December 11, 2007. See also Fair, "Pakistan Loses Swat to Local Taliban," p. 8; Hassan Abbas, "Is the NWFP Slipping out of Pakistan's Control?" *Terrorism Monitor*, Vol. 5, No. 22, November 26, 2007; Abbas, "Increasing Talibanization"; Idrees Bakhtiar, "Between the Lines," *The Herald* (Karachi), July 2007; Ghafar Ali Khan, "The Lost Frontier," *The Herald* (Karachi), July 2007; Owais Tohid, "The New Frontier," *Newsline* (Karachi), April 2004; Owais Tohid, "The Warrior Tribes," *Newsline* (Karachi), April 2004; Zahid Hussain, "Al-Qaeda's New Face," *Newsline* (Karachi), August 2004. For a recent article, see Anand Gopal, "Pakistani Taliban in Swat Refuse to Give Up Arms: The Militants Had Struck a Deal to Relinquish Their Weapons in Return for Islamic Law in the Region," *Christian Science Monitor*, April 16, 2009.

[73] Author fieldwork in Pakistan in February and April 2009.

more likely to acquiesce to the Taliban because of the benefits they conferred and the high cost of confronting or opposing them. Many Pakistanis who refused to be co-opted simply fled and joined the swelling ranks of internally displaced persons. By 2009, the situation was grave. Fears that the TTP and its allies would reach Islamabad were misplaced, partly because various TTP allies had already established a presence there. Indeed, TTP supporters were ensconced in the Lal Masjid until Pakistani security forces launched Operation Silence in July 2007.[74] Since many of the students in the associated madrassas were from Swat and Chitral, there was a backlash from this operation in those areas.

In April 2009, news reports asserted the arrival of the "Punjabi Taliban," referring to the various militant groups in the Punjab, Pakistan's most populated province.[75] While it is tempting to view this as a new theater—or even as a future locus of Talibanization—these areas are interrelated. Punjab-based groups have links with the TTP and at least two of them, Lashkar-e-Jhangvi and Jaish-e-Mohammad, have conducted suicide attacks in Pakistan. Jaish-e-Mohammad leader Masood Azhar was close to the Taliban. Jaish-e-Mohammad, which shares considerable membership and infrastructure with Lashkar-e-Jhangvi, was the first South Asian Islamist group to use suicide attacks in the region. Mohammad Bilal, a British Pakistani, attacked Indian Army headquarters in Srinagar.[76]

The leadership structure of Mullah Omar's Afghan Taliban is also located in Pakistan, with shuras in Baluchistan, Peshawar, Karachi, and North Waziristan.[77] By 2010, a growing number of senior Taliban

---

[74] Zahid Hussain, "The Battle for the Soul of Pakistan," *Newsline* (Karachi), July 2007.

[75] See Sabrina Tavernise, Richard A. Oppel, Jr., and Eric Schmitt, "United Militants Threaten Pakistan's Populous Heart," *New York Times,* April 13, 2009.

[76] Author interviews with Pakistani journalists and terrorism analyst in February 2009. Also see Emma Brockes, "British Man Named as Bomber Who Killed 10," *The Guardian,* December 28, 2000.

[77] See, inter alia, Senator Carl Levin, "Opening Statement of Senator Carl Levin, Senate Armed Services Committee Hearing on Afghanistan and Pakistan," February 26, 2009; Ian Katz, "Gates Says Militant Sanctuaries Pose Biggest Afghanistan Threat," *Bloomberg News,*

officials—including Mullah Abdul Ghani Baradar—fled to such cities as Karachi because of concerns about U.S. Predator and Reaper strikes in Baluchistan. The Afghan Taliban focused on ousting foreign forces in Afghanistan, overthrowing the Karzai regime, and restoring the Taliban role in governing Afghanistan. Al Qa'ida also used Pakistani territory, housing operatives in North Waziristan, South Waziristan, Bajaur, and other areas. Moreover, many al Qa'ida operatives, such as Abu Zubaidah and Khalid Sheikh Mohammad, were arrested in Pakistani cities.[78]

Since late 2001, many of Pakistan's militant groups—particularly those of Deobandi background—splintered or altered their strategies and tactics. Some of these groups, especially the TTP, began to target military, intelligence, and civilian leaders in the Pakistani government. Al Qa'ida leaders, including Ayman al-Zawahiri and Abu al-Yazid, continue to operate and plan attacks from the tribal areas. Recent attacks and plots—such as the successful July 2005 attack in London, the transatlantic plot foiled in 2006, the plot to attack U.S. and German targets in 2007, Najibullah Zazi's plot to conduct an attack in New York City in 2009, and the May 2010 attempt to bomb Times Square—had connections back to Pakistan. Since 2006, militants have launched suicide attacks against Pakistan's national security establishment, including the Frontier Corps, intelligence services, and the army. While the actual number of suicide attacks dramatically increased in 2007, the change in targeting seems to have occurred in 2006, perhaps in response to U.S. attacks on sites in Bajaur.[79]

March 1, 2009; Barnett R. Rubin, "Saving Afghanistan," *Foreign Affairs*, January/February 2007.

[78] See comments made by National Intelligence Director John Negroponte cited in "Al-Qaeda 'Rebuilding' in Pakistan," BBC News, January 12, 2007; K. Alan Kronstadt, *U.S.-Pakistan Relations*, Washington, D.C.: Congressional Research Service, 2008.

[79] For example, on November 5, 2007, a suicide attacker assaulted army recruits doing exercises in northwest Pakistan, killing at least 41 soldiers and wounding dozens. This attack was reportedly in retaliation for the U.S. strike on a purported madrassa on October 30, 2007, which killed 82 persons. See Pamela Constable and Kamran Khan, "Suicide Bombing Kills 41 Troops at Pakistani Army Base: Attack Called Reprisal for Strike on School," *Washington Post*, November 9, 2006.

In 2007 and 2008, public opinion polls indicated that Pakistanis supported peace deals with militants and believed they would help end the fighting. In addition, Pakistanis were opposed to army combat operations against militants in Pakistan. Public opinion began to change in the late spring 2009, when the Taliban broke its "sharia-for-peace" deal in Swat and overran Buner. Polling results in May 2009 and July 2009 suggested that the public was opposed to peace deals and was increasingly supportive of military action.[80] Without political support, Pakistan's leadership will be unable to wage a sustained and effective counterinsurgency campaign.

While militant groups in Pakistan pose a threat to the state, the region, and the international community more broadly, Pakistan may be unable to conduct an effective campaign as long as it uses some groups as assets. It has been willing to tolerate near-term risks associated with using militants in India and Afghanistan. Pakistan's delicate efforts to maintain a relationship with some groups—while targeting others—have become particularly challenging because many Deobandi groups have overlapping memberships.[81] Pakistan's decision in 2010 to capture senior Taliban leaders, such as inner shura member Mullah Abdul Ghani Baradar and Kunduz leader Mullah Salam, marked a significant change from its pattern of supporting the Taliban. But terminating links with the panoply of militant networks in Pakistan will be a long-term effort.

---

[80] Christine C. Fair, "Pakistan's Own War on Terror: What the Pakistani Public Thinks," *Journal of International Affairs*, Vol. 63, No. 1, 2009, pp. 39–56.

[81] Thinking of Lashkar-e-Jhangvi and Sipah-e-Sahaba Pakistan as solely sectarian groups would be misleading. They fought in Afghanistan in support of the Taliban and share much of the Deobandi infrastructure with the Taliban. See Mariam Abou Zahab, "The Regional Dimension of Sectarian Conflicts," in Cristopher Jafferlot, ed., *Pakistan: Nationalism Without a Nation?* London: Zed Books, 2002, pp. 115–128, and S. V. R. Nasr, "Islam, the State and the Rise of Sectarian Militancy in Pakistan," in Jaffrelot, ed., *Pakistan: Nationalism Without a Nation,* pp. 85–114.

Conclusion

This chapter has argued that Pakistan's use of militant groups as a tool of foreign policy is not new and, in fact, dates back to the early weeks of statehood. Pakistan's ability to conduct sustained militant campaigns with public support is likely tied to the historical and social milieus of jihad, which has long been viewed as a legitimate mode of conflict. Husain Haqqani, who later became the Pakistani ambassador to the United States, noted that the reliance on militancy "is not just the inadvertent outcome of decisions by some governments (beginning with that of Gen Zia ul-Haq in 1977), as is widely believed."[82] While Pakistan had long used Islam to strengthen Pakistan's identity, he continued, the state "gradually evolved into a strategic commitment to jihadi ideology."[83]

The acquisition of nuclear weapons enabled and emboldened Pakistan to pursue such strategies with increasing confidence. Indeed, nuclear weapons were an important enabling condition for Pakistan's continued reliance on jihad in the region. In contrast, U.S. policymakers have tended to view the issues of nuclear proliferation and militant support as distinct problems. During the 1980s, for example, the United States largely ignored Pakistan's nuclear program because it needed support against the Soviet Union in Afghanistan. During the 1990s, however, Pakistan faced numerous sanctions because of its nuclear program. After September 2001, the United States again pushed its nuclear concerns to the background and increased cooperation with Pakistan to target al Qa'ida.

Pakistan's support to militant groups, which its nuclear program emboldened, began to backfire not long after September 2001, when the TTP and other groups conducted terrorist attacks in Pakistan. In response, Pakistani forces conducted a series of military campaigns. The next chapter examines the effectiveness of these efforts.

---

82 Husain Haqqani, *Pakistan: Between Mosque and Military*, Washington, D.C.: CEIP, 2005, p. 2.

83 Haqqani, *Pakistan: Between Mosque and Military*, p. 3.

CHAPTER THREE

Pakistani Operations Against Militants

In the aftermath of the September 11, 2001, terrorist attacks, Pakistani President Pervez Musharraf helped target al Qa'ida and other foreign fighters operating in the country as part of the U.S.-led Operation Enduring Freedom. Pakistan provided extensive land, air, and seaport accessibility, as well as a host of other logistical and security-related provisions. In early 2002, Pakistan's security forces began conducting operations against foreign militants and their support networks in FATA. But as the war in Afghanistan spiraled, several indigenous insurgencies began to develop on the Pakistani side of the border. When Pakistan expanded its scope of operations, local insurgencies continued to develop across FATA and adjoining areas. In late 2007, several local militant groups nominally gathered under the TTP umbrella, under the leadership of the South Waziristan–based Baitullah Mehsud. Mehsud and allied militants responded to Pakistani incursions with a brutal suicide bombing campaign throughout Pakistan.[1]

Despite the importance of Pakistan's efforts to contend with its domestic militancy, there have been few systematic analyses of these operations. The purpose of this chapter is to redress this gap. This analysis does not offer a comprehensive assessment of *all* Pakistani operations since 2001, but rather briefly examines some of the most important campaigns:

[1] C. Christine Fair, and Seth G. Jones, "Pakistan's War Within," *Survival*, Vol. 51, No. 6, December 2009–January 2010, pp. 161–188.

- Operation Enduring Freedom (2001–2002)
- Operation Al Mizan (2002–2006)
- Operation Zalzala (2008)
- Operations Sher Dil, Rah-e-Haq, and Rah-e-Rast (2007–2009)
- Operation Rah-e-Nijat (2009–2010).

Figure 3.1 shows the locations of these operations. The chapter uses a comparative case study methodology to assess how effectively these campaigns achieved their goals—and why.[2] These cases vary across geography (from FATA to NWFP) and instruments (from military force to peace settlements).

Our analysis found that Pakistan's operations have generally been unsuccessful in holding territory, although they appear to have improved over time. Some intelligence assessments indicate that militant control of territory *increased* during this period. In several engagements, the Pakistan Army prosecuted peace deals with militants, often as ratifications of Pakistan's defeat on the ground. The deals called for the military to withdraw from forward locations, compensated the militants for their losses, and allowed them to retain their small arms. This process of engaging the government also endowed local militants with a degree of political legitimacy that they did not previously have. In return, the militants promised not to harbor foreign fighters or to set up parallel governments. The deals did not have adequate verification or enforcement mechanisms and were usually broken quickly.

As these cases illustrate, Pakistan has not established a *counterinsurgency* doctrine that focuses on using security forces—including

2 See Alexander L. George, "Case Studies and Theory Development: The Method of Structured, Focused Comparison," in Paul Gordon Lauren, ed., *Diplomacy: New Approaches in History, Theory, and Policy*, New York: Free Press, 1979, pp. 43–68; Collier, "The Comparative Method," pp. 7–31; Ragin, "Comparative Sociology and the Comparative Method," pp. 102–120; Van Evera, *Guide to Methods for Students of Political Science,* pp. 49–88. As George and McKeown argue, case studies are useful in uncovering "what stimuli the actors attend to; the decision process that makes use of these stimuli to arrive at decisions; the actual behavior that then occurs; the effect of various institutional arrangements on attention, processing, and behavior; and the effect of other variables of interest on attention, processing, and behavior." (George and McKeown, "Case Studies and Theories of Organizational Decision Making," p. 35.)

Figure 3.1
Examples of Pakistani Operations, 2001–2010

RAND *MG982-3.1*

police forces—to protect the local population.[3] Instead, its military doctrine has concentrated on conventional operations against India in response to India's "Cold Start" doctrine, which involved the swift penetration of Pakistan to isolate, destroy, or capture vital points, such as nuclear stores and other installations.[4] When Pakistan has conducted

---

3 Author interactions with Pakistani senior military officers about their low-intensity force doctrine. In bilateral forums, Pakistani officers will often adopt the language of "population-centered" counterinsurgency, at least in part because it is expected and in part to defuse the accumulating U.S. concerns about Pakistani efficacy, about which Pakistani military leadership has become very defensive. See for example, "Pak Army Needs No Foreign Training: COAS," *The Nation*, May 16, 2009.

4 Cyril Almeida, "Kayani Spells Out Threat Posed by Indian Doctrine," *Dawn* (Karachi), February 4, 2010.

operations on its own soil, the army has tended to use punishment strategies more in line with the Russian army's approach in Grozny, Chechnya. "Russian units sought to crush organized resistance and reestablish control of the capital and all other major towns and transportation routes," concluded one assessment of Russian operations. "The fighting caused extensive bloodshed on both sides and inflicted enormous damage on Chechen cities, particularly Grozny, which was almost completely leveled by Russian air and artillery forces."[5]

The remainder of this chapter is organized as follows: The first section describes the various military, paramilitary, and police forces that have been used. The second assesses the campaigns as comparative case studies. The third draws several lessons across the cases and examines public opinion data. The final section outlines key conclusions.

Pakistani Forces

Pakistan has generally employed three kinds of forces in these operations: the regular army, the paramilitary Frontier Corps, and the Frontier Constabulary. Each of these forces is discussed below. A robust accounting of security operations is not publicly available. However, according to data the authors obtained, somewhat fewer than 120,000 regular army, Frontier Corps, and Frontier Constabulary troops were located in FATA and NWFP between March 2008 and March 2009. Because many of these were garrisoned in these areas, it would be inaccurate to say they were all "deployed." These troops accounted for between four and five infantry divisions drawn from headquarters (HQ) 9 Division, HQ 7 Division, HQ 14 Division, and HQ 17/23 Division. These divisions draw, in turn, from XI Corps (Peshawar), X Corps (Rawalpindi), II Corps (Multan), and I Corps (Mangla). Organizationally, there were approximately 17 infantry brigades,

[5] Mark Kramer, "Counterinsurgency in Chechnya," *International Security*, Vol. 29, No. 3, Winter 2004/05, p. 8.

45 infantry battalions, and some 58 Frontier Corps wings.[6] *Wing* is the term used to describe a formation in the Frontier Corps that is roughly equivalent to a battalion.[7]

Pakistan Army

The Pakistan Army has an end-strength of approximately 550,000 active-duty personnel and another 500,000 reservists. It has nine corps headquarters in addition to the Army Strategic Forces Command, which commands all of Pakistan's land-based strategic assets. This is sometimes called Pakistan's "tenth corps." Table 3.1 lists the locations of the corps headquarters.[8] The Pakistan Army is a conventional force that is primarily geared toward a conflict with India, although that has begun to change. Past conflicts with India have involved high-altitude operations, as well as operations across the plains and desert. The army has traditionally configured its forces to fight a conventional war with India. In the early months of Gen Ashfaq Kayani's tenure as chief of army staff, there was some optimism that Pakistan would formally adopt a counterinsurgency strategy. Those hopes largely dissipated as Pakistan remained reluctant to develop such a doctrine. In fact, General Kayani often stated that the Pakistan Army would not become a counterinsurgency force; rather, the bulk of the army would remain deployed along the Indian border, ready to defend Pakistan in the event of an Indo-Pakistan war.[9]

---

6 This information was obtained from a variety of sources, including personal information from Pakistani officers. Also See Gurmeet Kanwal, "Losing Ground: Pak Army Strategy in FATA and NWFP," New Delhi: Institute of Peace and Conflict Studies, Issue Brief No. 84, October 2008.

7 Note that XII Corps, based in Baluchistan, has *not* been involved in these operations. We thank Jack Gill for pointing this out.

8 Each corps has either two or three divisions and is commanded by a lieutenant general. Each division holds three brigades and is commanded by a major general. A brigade is commanded by a brigadier and has three or more battalions. A battalion has roughly 600 to 900 soldiers under the command of a lieutenant colonel. See International Institute for Strategic Studies, *The Military Balance 2009*, London: Routledge, 2009; Federation of Atomic Scientists, "Pakiston [sic]: Total Military Force," 2008.

9 Ahmed Rashid, "Pakistan's Worrisome Pullback," *Washington Post*, June 6, 2008, p. A19.

Table 3.1
Corps and Locations

Corps	Headquarters City	Province
I	Mangla	Kashmir
II	Multan	Punjab
IV	Lahore	Punjab
V	Karachi	Sindh
X	Rawalpindi	Punjab
XI	Peshawar	NWFP
XII	Quetta	Baluchistan
XXX	Gujranwala	Punjab
XXXI	Bahawalpur	Punjab

In addition to the regular army, Pakistan deployed the Special Services Group during many of its key operations. This group, created in 1956 with active support from U.S. Special Operations Forces (SOF), is an elite special operations force within the Pakistan Army.[10] Unlike most of Pakistan's other security units, the Special Services Group has been involved in low-intensity operations throughout its history. During the 1980s, for example, the Special Services Group engaged in covert activities in Afghanistan against the Soviet Union.

Frontier Corps

The Frontier Corps is a federal paramilitary force that belongs to the Ministry of Interior but may be under control of the army command during specific operations. It consists of two separate forces, Frontier Corps NWFP and Frontier Corps Baluchistan, with separate inspectors general controlling each; the combined end-strength is 80,000. Frontier Corps officers are seconded from the Pakistan Army and are rotated in and out of the Frontier Corps. Frontier Corps NWFP has security duties for FATA and NWFP, is headquartered in Peshawar, and comes under operational command of XI Corps. Frontier Corps

[10] See, for example, Nawaz, *Crossed Swords*, pp. 133, 267.

Baluchistan is responsible for Baluchistan, is headquartered in Quetta, and comes under the operational command of XII Corps. While Frontier Corps NWFP is overwhelmingly Pashtun, Frontier Corps Baluchistan includes many who are not ethnically Baluch.[11]

Over the last several years, some have argued that the Frontier Corps should be the force of choice in FATA. This has some appeal, since Frontier Corps cadres are recruited from FATA and therefore have local knowledge, language skills, and a refined sense of the human terrain. But there are questions about using the Frontier Corps in this way. Some elements of the Frontier Corps have facilitated insurgent movement across the Durand Line (the de facto border between Pakistan and Afghanistan). David Kilcullen, who served as special adviser for counterinsurgency to U.S. Secretary of State Condoleezza Rice, argued that infiltrators into Afghanistan "have typically taken little trouble to disguise their movement or activity, in some cases infiltrating in broad daylight under the noses of Pakistan Army checkpoints, or even with direct assistance from Pakistani Frontier Corps troops."[12] There have also been some concerns that the Frontier Corps includes some militant sympathizers. Since at least 2004, there have been consistent reports that elements of the Frontier Corps have been helping the Taliban.[13]

Frontier Constabulary and Frontier Police

The Frontier Constabulary provides law and order in the settled areas outside FATA and border protection along the Pakistan-Afghanistan border. However, the Frontier Constabulary also provides static secu-

---

[11] See Hassan Abbas, "Transforming Pakistan's Frontier Corps," *Terrorism Monitor*, Vol. 5, No. 6, March 30, 2007.

[12] David Kilcullen, *The Accidental Guerrilla: Fighting Small Wars in the Midst of a Big One*, New York: Oxford University Press, 2009, p. 57.

[13] For an account from 2004 involving the Tochi Scouts, see M. Ilyas Khan, "Mixed Signals," *The Herald*, March 2004, pp. 63–65. For recent revelations about Frontier Corps complicity and a recent U.S. attack on Frontier Corps positions firing on U.S. troops in Afghanistan, see Peter Beaumont and Mark Townsend, "Pakistan Troops 'Aid Taliban': New Classified U.S. Documents Reveal That Mass Infiltration of Frontier Corps by Afghan Insurgents Is Helping Latest Offensive," *The Observer*, June 22, 2008.

rity duties in Islamabad and throughout the Punjab.[14] While personnel are generally recruited from the Pashtun belt, the officers are derived from the Pakistani police.[15] Until 2009, the Frontier Constabulary had taken the brunt of the violence in settled Pashtun areas, such as Swat. The Frontier Constabulary outposts in the capital and throughout the Pashtun belt are targeted systematically by insurgents. Similarly, Frontier Corps outposts in FATA have sustained insurgent assaults. The Frontier Constabulary is generally ill-prepared for this fight because its forces are poorly trained and inadequately equipped, with outdated arms and little personal-protection equipment. Its members have been killed in large numbers or have simply deserted the force, fearing that they would be killed.[16]

In addition to the Frontier Constabulary, NWFP has a provincial police force, the Frontier Police. This force, like all Pakistan's police forces, is in dire need of better training, equipment, and compensation reform.[17]

Case Studies

This section examines several Pakistani campaigns since 2001. We do not offer a comprehensive assessment of all Pakistani operations, but rather of some of the most important campaigns since 2001. Figure 3.2 highlights the operations and the general geographic areas where they occurred.

---

[14] International Crisis Group, *Reforming Pakistan's Police*, Asia Report No. 157; July 14, 2008; U.S. Embassy Press Release, "U.S. Embassy Teams Up with the Ministry of Interior to Bolster Frontier Constabulary Capacity in Frontier Regions: MOU Signed Worth US $2.7 Million," August 3, 2006.

[15] An excellent set of resources on policing in Pakistan is available from this website: Dominique Wisler, maintainer, "Pakistan," World Database on Policing, Geneva, Switzerland: COGINTA, undated.

[16] Author fieldwork in Pakistan in February and April 2009.

[17] Hassan Abbas, *Police & Law Enforcement Reform in Pakistan: Crucial for Counterinsurgency and Counterterrorism Success*, Report of the Institute for Social Policy and Understanding, April 2009.

Support to Operation Enduring Freedom

After the September 11, 2001, terrorist attacks, the United States initiated Operation Enduring Freedom to overthrow the Taliban regime in Afghanistan and to target al Qa'ida.[18] Pakistan's strategic location next to Afghanistan and its historical involvement there made it a key player.

Pakistan agreed to assist U.S. efforts in Afghanistan and to capture some militants—especially al Qa'ida and other foreign fighters—that escaped into Pakistan. These objectives were ironed out during negotiations in September 2001. In the end, Pakistan participated in Operation Enduring Freedom in two major ways. First, it permitted overflight and landing rights for U.S. military and intelligence units, allowed access to some Pakistani bases, provided intelligence and immigration information, cut off most logistical support to the Taliban, and broke diplomatic relations with the Taliban.[19] The United States used several bases, such as those near Jacobabad, Dalbandin, and Shamsi; set up a joint Pakistan-American facility in the U.S. embassy in Islamabad for deconflicting U.S. aircraft flying through Pakistan; and shared intelligence on key Taliban and al Qa'ida leaders.[20] The U.S. military also installed radar facilities in Pakistan, which provided extensive coverage of Pakistani airspace.[21]

Second, Pakistan deployed units from the regular army, Special Services Group, Frontier Corps, and ISI to the Afghanistan-Pakistan border to conduct operations along infiltration routes from Afghanistan to Pakistan (Figure 3.2). The Pakistani regular army had two brigades of infantry forces from 9th Division, XI Corps deployed for

---

[18] Operation Enduring Freedom also included U.S. counterterrorist efforts in other locations, including the Philippines and the Horn of Africa. But this section focuses only on militants fleeing Afghanistan into Pakistan.

[19] See, for example, the negotiations as outlined in Bob Woodward, *Bush at War*, New York: Simon and Schuster, 2002, p. 59. Also see Musharraf, *In the Line of Fire*, pp. 201–207.

[20] Author interview with Wendy Chamberlin, U.S. Ambassador to Pakistan, August 27, 2008.

[21] K. Alan Kronstadt, *Pakistan-U.S. Anti-Terrorism Cooperation*, Washington, D.C.: Congressional Research Service, March 2003, p. 12.

Figure 3.2
Pakistani Deployments to FATA, 2002

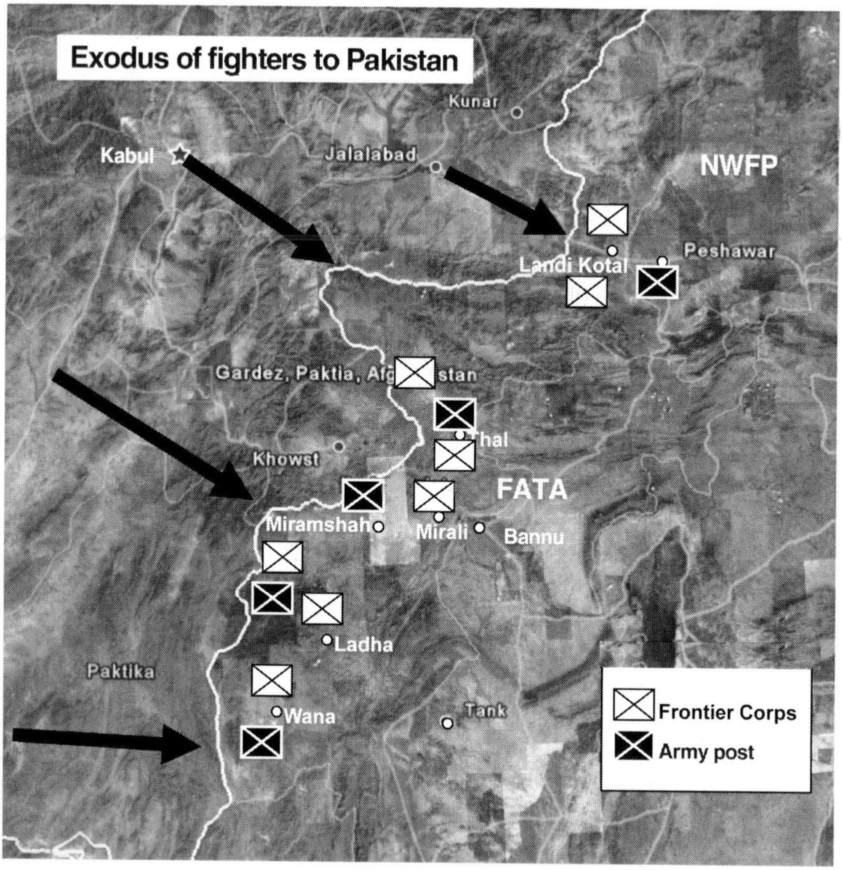

RAND *MG982-3.2*

border and internal security operations for much of 2001 and 2002. Pakistan also established two quick-reaction forces from the Special Services Group in Kohan and Wana to provide local Pakistan commanders the ability to deploy troops quickly. In addition, a force of approximately 4,000 Frontier Corps personnel conducted operations in Pakistan's FATA.[22]

---

[22] Gary Berntsen and Ralph Pezzullo, *Jawbreaker: The Attack on bin Laden and Al-Qaeda: A Personal Account by the CIA's Key Field Commander*, New York: Crown Publishers, 2005,

Pakistan security forces conducted operations against militants crossing into Pakistan. In October 2001, for example, Frontier Corps forces clashed with militants crossing the border around Nawa Pass in Bajaur agency. In December 2001, Pakistan deployed a mixture of forces to Khyber and Kurram tribal agencies during U.S. operations at Tora Bora and helped capture a number of al Qa'ida and other foreign fighters.[23] In March 2002, Pakistan increased force levels in North and South Waziristan to target militants during U.S.-led Operation Anaconda, which took place in the Shah-i-Kot Valley of Paktia Province in Afghanistan.[24] In May, Pakistani Tochi Scouts raided a suspected cache in Miramshah, netting mortar rounds, antipersonnel mines, and ammunition. In June, soldiers from the Special Services Group, Frontier Corps, and regular army conducted an assault against al Qa'ida operatives during Operation Kazha Punga in the Azam Warsak region of South Waziristan. In July, Pakistani troops entered the Tirah Valley in the Khyber Agency and Parachinar in Kurram Agency to capture al Qa'ida fighters coming from Afghanistan.[25] And in August, Pakistani military, police, and intelligence forces conducted operations against militants in Baluchistan Province. Al Qa'ida and foreign fighters were turned over to the ISI, and many were handed over to the U.S. government and were temporarily housed in prisons in Kandahar, Bagram, and other locations. In most cases, however, Pakistan retained the Afghans or Pakistanis that it captured.[26]

---

p. 305. Berntsen commanded the CIA team in Afghanistan in late 2001, taking over from Gary Schroen.

[23] Rahimullah Yusufzai, "Fall of the Last Frontier?" *Newsline* (Karachi), June 2002.

[24] On Operation Anaconda see, for example, U.S. Air Force, Office of Lessons Learned, *Operation Anaconda: An Air Power Perspective*, Washington, D.C.: Headquarters U.S. Air Force, February 2005; Paul L. Hastert, "Operation Anaconda: Perception Meets Reality in the Hills of Afghanistan," *Studies in Conflict and Terrorism*, Vol. 28, No. 1, January–February 2005, pp. 11–20; and Sean Naylor, *Not a Good Day to Die: The Untold Story of Operation Anaconda*, New York: Berkley Books, 2005.

[25] International Crisis Group, *Pakistan's Tribal Areas: Appeasing the Militants*, Brussels, Islamabad, December 2006, p. 14.

[26] Author interview with Robert Grenier, CIA Station Chief in Islamabad, Washington, D.C., November 6, 2007.

How effective were these operations? Pakistan's security forces had limited experience in waging sustained operations in FATA prior to Operation Enduring Freedom, despite some experience in other areas. Pakistan's operations in Eastern Pakistan (Bangladesh) to put down rebelling Bengals failed and resulted in the 1971 conflict with India. That war resulted in the independence of Bangladesh. In addition, the Pakistani military was used in Baluchistan between 1973 and 1977. Pakistani operations in Baluchistan since 2005 have resulted in the deaths of key insurgent leaders and effectively diminished the local insurgency.[27] Campaigns in East Pakistan and Baluchistan relied heavily on firepower and inflicted significant collateral damage. But fighting "counterinsurgency" had not been a major focus of the Pakistan Army; its training was largely geared toward a conventional war with India.

Despite these drawbacks, one of the most significant objectives of Operation Enduring Freedom—to overthrow the Taliban regime in Afghanistan—was achieved, and Pakistan played an important role. "Musharraf became an international hero," remarked Ambassador Wendy Chamberlin. "Money was flowing into Pakistan. And Pakistan was no longer a pariah state. The situation was euphoric. Musharraf was on the cover of every magazine and newspaper."[28] Over the course of 2002, Pakistan's security agencies picked up thousands of militants, although many were eventually released.[29] In March 2002, a joint Pakistani-U.S. raid in Faisalabad captured Abu Zubaidah, a senior al Qa'ida commander. In September 2002, Pakistan and Central Intelligence Agency (CIA) operatives captured Ramzi bin al-Shibh, a key figure in planning the September 2001 terror attacks in the United

[27] Peter Patchell, "Pakistan's Secret War in Baluchistan," *The Guardian*, December 21, 2007.

[28] Author interview with Wendy Chamberlin, former U.S. Ambassador to Pakistan, August 27, 2008.

[29] In some cases, the militants were released at the cutoff period for detention under the Maintenance of Public Order law, or by the relevant courts on bail. But Pakistan has selectively observed such detention cutoffs. The state has held numerous persons without filing charges against them well beyond this legal period, including President Asif Zardari. Zaffar Abbas, "Operation Eyewash," *The Herald* (Karachi), August 2005, p. 64.

States, and Sharib Ahmad, the alleged organizer of the June 2002 car bomb attack on the U.S. consulate in Karachi.[30]

Yet Pakistan was not asked to target all—or even most—militant groups. The Pakistani campaign focused primarily on al Qa'ida and foreign fighters, whom U.S. policymakers were most interested in capturing.[31] Deputy Secretary of State Richard Armitage later noted that "Musharraf did not push hard against the Taliban" but was "only cooperative in targeting some key al Qa'ida militants."[32] To the degree that the United States was interested in Pakistan, it focused on al Qa'ida operatives as well. "The ISI worked closely with us to capture key al Qa'ida leaders such as Khalid Sheikh Mohammad, Ramzi bin al-Shibh, Abu Faraj al-Libbi, and Abu Zubeida," recalled Robert Grenier, the CIA's station chief in Pakistan. "But they made it clear that they didn't care about targeting the Taliban." Neither did the CIA or the U.S. government more broadly. "The U.S. government was focused on al Qa'ida," Grenier continued, "not on capturing or killing Taliban leaders. The U.S. considered the Taliban a spent force."[33]

In sum, Operation Enduring Freedom was partially successful in its objectives of overthrowing the Taliban regime and capturing some al Qa'ida militants crossing the border. The United States and Pakistan failed to capture some senior al Qa'ida figures, including Osama bin Laden and Ayman al-Zawahiri, who crossed into Pakistan. Over the long run, however, the United States and Pakistan ignored the growing number of Taliban and other militants using Pakistan as a safe haven, which would eventually undermine Pakistan's own stability.

---

[30] On the capture of Abu Zubaidah and Ramzi bin al-Shibh see George Tenet, with Bill Harlow, *At the Center of the Storm: My Years at the CIA*, New York: HarperCollins, 2007, pp. 240–243; Musharraf, *In the Line of Fire*, pp. 237–240.

[31] Ashley J. Tellis, *Pakistan and the War on Terror: Conflicted Goals, Compromised Performance*, Washington, D.C.: Carnegie Endowment for International Peace, 2008, p. 7.

[32] Author interview with Richard Armitage, former Deputy Secretary of State, Arlington, Va., October 17, 2007.

[33] Author interview with Robert Grenier, former CIA Station Chief in Islamabad, Washington, D.C., November 6, 2007.

Operation Al Mizan

In 2002, Pakistan commenced Operation Al Mizan (Justice), which targeted militants in FATA, with a focus on South Waziristan. The collapse of the Taliban regime triggered a flow of fighters into Pakistan, many of whom settled near the Afghanistan-Pakistan border. In June 2002, for example, al Qa'ida militants conducted a lethal attack on the Pakistan Army in Azam Warsak, near Wana in South Waziristan, killing nearly a dozen Pakistani soldiers.[34] U.S. policymakers pressured Pakistan to conduct operations because most senior al Qa'ida leaders—including those involved in the September 11 terrorist attacks—were still loose in Pakistan and because militants had begun to attack U.S. firebases, such as Shkin on the Afghanistan-Pakistan border.

Pakistan's primary objective during Operation Al Mizan was to kill or capture militants—especially foreign militants—that threatened the Pakistani government. This meant clearing notable portions of South Waziristan of foreign fighters.[35] President Musharraf also had a personal reason for supporting Operation Al Mizan: He had survived several assassination attempts from networks operating in the tribal areas, including South Waziristan. Indeed, al Qa'ida's deputy leader, Ayman al-Zawahiri, had issued a fatwa calling for the death of Musharraf.[36] For the United States, the primary objectives continued to be killing or capturing senior al Qa'ida leaders in Pakistan and curbing attacks on U.S. firebases along the border. U.S. efforts to persuade Pakistan involved massive financial assistance. The U.S. government gave over $2 billion per year to Pakistan's key national security agencies to conduct operations against militants, including the army, Frontier Corps, and ISI.[37]

During Operation Al Mizan, Pakistan employed between 70,000 and 80,000 forces in FATA. Major units included the following:

---

[34] M. Ilyas Khan, "Descent into Anarchy," *The Herald* (Karachi), March 2004, p. 62.

[35] Pakistan Army, General Headquarters, Military Operations Directorate, *Record on Pakistan's War on Terror*, December 28, 2006.

[36] Rashid, *Descent into Chaos*, p. 270.

[37] Craig Cohen and Derek Chollet, "When $10 Billion Is Not Enough: Rethinking U.S. Strategy Toward Pakistan," *Washington Quarterly*, Vol. 30, No. 2, Spring 2007, pp. 7–19.

- two division headquarters
- eight brigade headquarters
- 20 infantry battalions
- six engineer battalions
- one Special Services Group battalion
- two signals battalions
- 39 Frontier Corps wings.[38]

Pakistan also used army aviation units to assist operations and artillery, transportation, and logistics units to support forward-deployed units. The Pakistan Army began to infiltrate South Waziristan in early 2002. Previously, one wing of the Frontier Corps in each of the two agencies—the Tochi Scouts and the South Waziristan Scouts—was available for operations. Units of the Special Services Group and command units of the quick reaction force were flown in regularly to carry out operations. Two army brigades also set up checkpoints along the border in Waziristan. In mid-2003, the Pakistani government formally asked South Waziristan's political administration to identify locals harboring foreign militants. The administration conducted several shuras, consulted maliks, and examined intelligence from local informants to identify over 70 Ahmadzai Wazir tribesmen that were supporting foreign fighters.[39] In October, the Pakistan Army dispatched 2,500 soldiers to the village of Baghar in South Waziristan to capture militants. On January 8, 2004, the army conducted a similar operation in South Waziristan but was ambushed on its way back. Later that night, the Pakistan Army camp in Wana came under rocket attack from three sides. Over the next several nights, militants fired more rockets on the army camps in Wana and a military check post in Shulama, west of Wana.[40]

The situation in South Waziristan continued to deteriorate in early 2004. Pakistan's intelligence services collected reports of al Qa'ida activities in the Wana Valley of South Waziristan. In March,

---

[38] Author interview with Pakistani government officials, Pakistan, May 2009.

[39] International Crisis Group, *Pakistan's Tribal Areas*, p. 14.

[40] Khan, "Descent into Anarchy," p. 62.

Pakistani forces launched Operation Kalosha II, partly in response to the ambush of Frontier Corps personnel in the area and the need to mount a rescue operation (Figure 3.3). The operation involved a 13-day cordon-and-search effort across a 36-km^2 area west of Wana. The area had come under the command of several militants—including Nek Mohammad Wazir, Noor-ul-Islam, Haji Mohammad Sharif, Maulvi Abbas, and Maulvi Abdul Aziz—who were suspected of harboring foreign fighters.[41] During Operation Kalosha II, Pakistan employed the Frontier Corps and the XI Corps, based out of Peshawar and under the command of Lt Gen Muhammad Safdar Hussain.

On March 16, Frontier Corps forces surrounded the three fortress-like houses of Nek Mohammad Wazir, Haji Mohammad Sharif, and Noor-ul-Islam in Kalosha village, 15 km west of Wana. At 6:30 am, they burst in. Militants from the Ahmadzai Wazir tribe had thrown a siege around the Frontier Corps' outer cordon, and fighting ensued. By the end of the day, 15 Frontier Corps and one Pakistan Army soldiers

Figure 3.3
Map of Operation Kalosha II, 2004

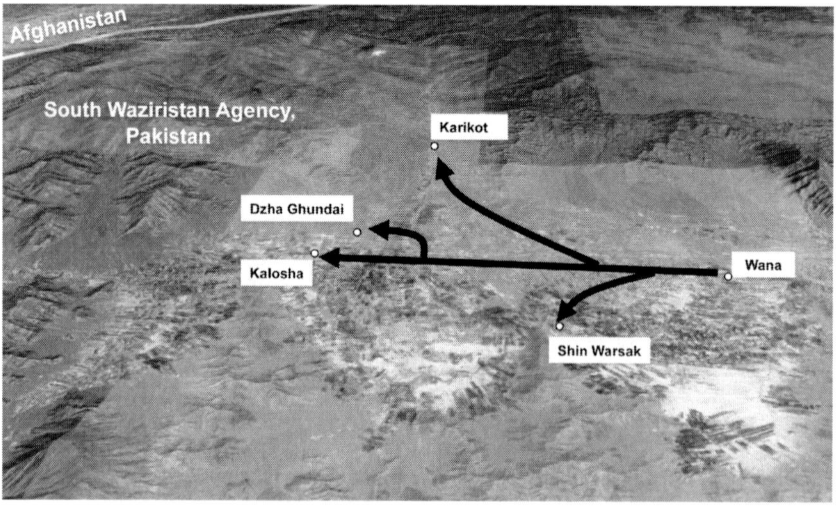

RAND *MG982-3.3*

---

[41] Amir Mohammad Khan, "Spiralling into Chaos," *Newsline* (Karachi), March 2004, pp. 34–36.

had been killed, and 14 others had been taken hostage. The militants also immobilized, destroyed, or burned roughly a dozen army trucks, as well as pickups, armored personnel carriers, and light artillery. Pakistani forces also faced tough resistance in the villages of Dzha Ghundai, Shin Warsak, and Karikot. The cordon drawn around Kalosha and the surrounding villages failed to retard the mobility of militants, some of whom dispersed through a network of tunnels. The operation was launched with 700 personnel, but by March 19, roughly 7,000 army and Frontier Corps troops were battling the militants at several locations in a 50-km^2 stretch southwest of Wana. The operation also involved more than a dozen Cobra helicopters and Pakistan Air Force fighter jets. On March 26, General Hussain declared victory: "We have accomplished the mission that was given to us."[42]

During Operation Kalosha II, Pakistani forces killed a number of local and foreign fighters, disrupted a major al Qa'ida command and control center, and raided a network of tunnels containing sophisticated electronic equipment and supplies. But the operation also triggered attacks against Pakistan Army and Frontier Corps bases in such places as Shah Alam, Bermal, Sarwekai, Angoor Adda, Laddha, Tiarza, and Wana.[43] Some locals were enraged at Pakistan's scorched-earth tactics; the Pakistan Army demolished a number of houses and used private residences as fortifications and barracks.[44] As one local lamented, "[t]he army took away everything from my house: jewelry, clothes, toiletries, even pillow covers and shoe polish."[45]

In June 2004, Pakistani forces conducted operations in the Shakai Valley after an alarming series of U.S. and Pakistani intelligence reports indicated that a force of more than 200 Chechens and Uzbeks, some Arabs, and several hundred local supporters was gathering in the area. On June 10, the Pakistani government deployed 10,000 army troops and U.S.-trained Special Operations Task Force and Frontier

---

[42] M. Ilyas Khan, "Who Are These People?" *The Herald* (Karachi), April 2004, pp. 60–68.

[43] Khan, "Spiralling Into Chaos," pp. 34–36.

[44] Khan, "Who Are These People?" pp. 60–68; Sailab Mahsud, "Caught in the Crossfire," *The Herald* (Karachi), April 2004, pp. 66–67.

[45] Mahsud, "Caught in the Crossfire," pp. 66–67.

Corps forces.[46] Nearly 3,000 soldiers established an outer cordon. The Pakistan Air Force struck at dawn, using precision weapons against nine compounds. Pakistan Army forces used indirect artillery fire and rocket attacks from helicopter gunships. Helicopters dropped off Special Operations Task Force troops to search the compounds, and infantry troops initiated a simultaneous operation to clear the valley. Later, 3,000 additional troops were brought in to help clear the valley. During the operation, four soldiers were killed and 12 were injured, while over 50 militants were killed. The Pakistani military, with intelligence assistance from U.S. SOF and CIA operatives, partially eliminated a major propaganda base and militant stronghold, which included a facility for manufacturing improvised explosive devices. The haul from a large underground cellar in one of the compounds included two truckloads of TV sets, computers, laptops, disks, tape recorders, and tapes.[47]

Throughout 2004 and 2005, the United States and Pakistan conducted a range of precision strikes against targets, many of which were in North and South Waziristan Agencies. Examples included attacks in the Madakhel Wazir area of North Waziristan in March 2004, Dhog village near Wana in June 2004, the Lawara Mandi area of North Waziristan in July 2004, and Asoray village in North Waziristan in December 2005 (which killed Hamza Rabia, a senior al Qa'ida operative).[48] But as Frontier Corps and army casualties mounted, the army pursued "peace deals" with the local militants. The Pakistan Army tried to depict these deals as part of a long-standing precedent in the region, noting that the British negotiated with local Pashtun tribes in NWFP during their rule. However, these deals differed in many ways from those of the British.[49] One of the most egregious differences

46 The Special Operations Task Force was a U.S.-trained unit consisting of a battalion from Special Services Group that was helicopter mobile.

47 Musharraf, *In the Line of Fire*, pp. 269–270.

48 Rahimullah Yusufzai, "Whose Country Is It Anyway?" *The Herald* (Karachi), February 2006, pp. 27–32; "Hit and Run," *The Herald* (Karachi), February 2006, p. 58; Intikhab Amir, "Waziristan: No Man's Land?" *The Herald* (Karachi), April 2006, p. 78.

49 See, for example, Christian Tripodi, "Peacemaking Through Bribes or Cultural Empathy? The Political Officer and Britain's Strategy Towards the North-West Frontier, 1901–

was the British use of "butcher and bolt," in which British forces killed unruly tribesmen and then moved quickly to pacify new areas. The British used "butcher and bolt" as a stick against local tribes that violated peace deals.[50]

One of the first major deal-making efforts came in the aftermath of Pakistani operations in Kalosha in March 2004, and it produced the Shakai Agreement. The government helped cobble together a 50-member jirga, an assembly of tribal elders, with the help of NWFP governor Syed Iftikhar Hussain Shah and reportedly with the assistance of important leaders from the Islamist political party, JUI.[51] JUI held the provincial government in NWFP from 2002 to 2008 and governed in a coalition with Musharraf's Pakistan Muslim League–Qaid in Baluchistan during the same period. The JUI had longstanding ties to a range of Deobandi militant groups, including Jaish-e-Mohammad, Sipah-e-Sahaba e Pakistan, Lashkar-e-Jhangvi, and the Taliban.

The Pakistani government demanded the unconditional surrender of foreign militants and their local supporters, as well as over a dozen individuals taken hostage in the Kalosha area on March 16. During subsequent negotiations, the militants presented the jirga with three counterconditions: lift the army's siege, pay compensation for the 83 houses demolished during the fighting, and release 163 people arrested during the operation. On March 27, Nek Mohammad Wazir and Haji Mohammad Sharif held final negotiations with 18 members of the jirga—which also included local *ulema* (Muslim scholars) affiliated with the JUI and some elders from the Zalikhel tribe—at a Deobandi madrassa near Wana.[52] This was an important signal. Traditionally, jirgas are held in public places—not in mosques or madrassas—and

---

1945," *Journal of Strategic Studies*, February 2008, Vol. 31, No. 1, pp. 123–151.

[50] See, for example, David Loyn, *Butcher and Bolt: Two Hundred Years of Foreign Engagement in Afghanistan*, London: Hutchinson, 2008.

[51] Author discussions in Pakistan.

[52] Khan, "Who Are These People?" pp. 60–68; Tohid, "The New Frontier"; Ismail Khan, "Five Militants Pardoned for Peaceful Life: Aliens Asked to Surrender by 30th," *The Dawn*, April 25, 2004.

religious leaders have had little role in this process.[53] Conducting this jirga in a madrassa signaled the growing role of religious actors.

The deal included several provisions: Pakistan Army troops would not interfere in the internal tribal affairs and would stay in their cantonment areas; local insurgents would not attack Pakistani government personnel or infrastructure; and all foreigners would have to register with the government.[54] There were several problems with this deal. It compensated the militants for their losses but did not require them to compensate their victims. The militants were also allowed to keep their arms. Weapons were not "surrendered" but rather "offered" to the military as a token, ceremonial gesture. As Mariam Abou Zahab noted, the militants described the deal as a "reconciliation," which was understood as tacit acceptance that they were as powerful and legitimate as the army. By forging this reconciliation with the militants, the army bestowed previously unearned political legitimacy on them and permitted them to consolidate their hold over South Waziristan.[55]

However, the most egregious problem was how the army reached the deal. Pakistan Army officials met Nek Mohammad Wazir at a Deobandi madrassa, the Jamia Arabia Ahsanul Madaris. This was viewed by locals as a tacit surrender of the army. As Mariam Abou Zahab argued: "In tribal tradition, surrender means that you approach the rival group and meet them on their territory . . . . In Shakai, the army came to meet Nek Mohammad."[56] Pakistani journalist Rahimullah Yusufzai came to a similar conclusion when he noted that

> this is very important in the tribal context because an army general [General Safdar Hussain] is going to [Nek Mohammad Wazir's] place. Instead of the militants coming to the army, the

[53] See discussion of traditional jirga practices in Mariam Abou Zahab, "Changing Patterns of Social and Political Life Among the Tribal Pashtuns in Pakistan," draft paper, 2007.

[54] Locals denied the existence of the last clause and argued that they did not agree to register all foreigners with the government.

[55] Zahab, "Changing Patterns of Social and Political Life.""

[56] Zahab, "Changing Patterns of Social and Political Life." As noted previously, weapons were not surrendered but rather "offered" and, after the recent deal, "exchanged."

> army is going to their place, which means they recognize their strength and their influence. Then you go to a madrassa, which was in a way one of the headquarters of the militants.[57]

General Safdar Hussain, in his uniform, actually bestowed a garland on Nek Mohammad Wazir, exchanged gifts with him, and called him a "brother."[58] Worse yet, donning a tribal headdress, General Hussain addressed the assembled tribesmen and condemned U.S. operations in Afghanistan, noting that no Afghan pilots were involved in the September 11, 2001, attacks.[59]

Nek Mohammad Wazir also characterized the transaction as an army surrender. He proclaimed that "I did not go to them, they came to my place. That should make it clear who surrendered to whom."[60] The deal fortified Nek Mohammad Wazir's confidence in his ability to contend with the Pakistani state, and he soon violated the agreement. In June 2004, he was killed by a U.S. missile strike near Wana, and the agreement broke down entirely.[61] In November 2004, the Pakistani government reached agreements with Ahmadzai Wazir leaders, but that deal lasted only six weeks.

How successful was Operation Al Mizan? Pakistan military, police, and intelligence services did capture or kill several senior al Qa'ida leaders, such as Khalid Sheikh Mohammad, Abu Faraj al-Libbi, Abu Zubaidah, and Abu Talha al-Pakistani.[62] As CIA Director George Tenet later recalled, the relationship between the CIA and Pakistani police and intelligence officials was critical.[63] A range of U.S. military

---

57 Rahimullah Yusufzai interview with Frontline about Nek Mohammad, October 3, 2006.

58 Rahimullah Yusufzai interview with Frontline.

59 See the comments General Safdar made during the peace accords in Shakai. Frontline. *Return of the Taliban*, October 2006.

60 Iqbal Khattak, "I Did Not Surrender to the Military, Says Nek Mohammad," *Friday Times*, April 30–May 6, 2004.

61 Ismail Khan and Dilawar Khan Wazir, "Night Raid Kills Nek, Four Other Militants," *Dawn* (Karachi), June 19, 2004; Khattak, "I Did Not Surrender."

62 Musharraf, *In the Line of Fire*, p. 240; Tenet, *At the Center of the Storm*, pp. 251–255.

63 Tenet, *At the Center of the Storm*, pp. 252–253.

officials praised Pakistan's activities. "Musharraf was very helpful," noted Dov Zakheim, U.S. Undersecretary of Defense and Comptroller and an adviser to Secretary of Defense Donald Rumsfeld. "He was definitely opposed to radicalization in Pakistan. On basic fundamental issues, the Pakistani government was part of the solution."[64]

However, Operation Al Mizan ultimately failed to clear South Waziristan of foreign militants. With the aid of foreigners, local militant groups made significant inroads in usurping the power of tribal maliks and increasing the importance of mullahs who espoused a Taliban worldview. In addition, Pakistan's operations were not sustained over time. Pakistani efforts were marked by sweeps, searches, and occasional bloody battles, but none of these employed enough forces to hold territory. Further, the government's initiatives were hindered by religious conservative parties operating in the tribal areas. These groups considered the Pakistani government's efforts against al Qa'ida and other militants to be an "American war." The peace deals also failed to achieve their objectives. As President Musharraf eventually acknowledged,

> we thought if we reached an agreement, that would be the end of it; they will suppress it to peaceful means.
>
> Well, it proved wrong, because the people who got involved on the other side, they double-crossed. While they carried on with their own activities, the army, in fact, became a little complacent that we have reached an agreement. Then we reactivated the same process again. With hindsight one can see, well, that didn't prove to be correct.[65]

Indeed, the tribal deals appeared to have the opposite effect. The power of the Taliban and other militants in the tribal areas appeared to *increase*. A Pakistan Ministry of Interior document, which was briefed

---

[64] Author interview with Dov Zakheim, U.S. Undersecretary of Defense and Comptroller, January 30, 2008.

[65] Pervez Musharraf, interview conducted for "Return of the Taliban," Frontline, transcript, June 8, 2006.

to President Musharraf and discussed at a Pakistan National Security Council meeting, noted that

> Talibanisation has not only unfolded potential threats to our security, but is also casting its dark shadows over FATA and now in the settled areas adjoining the tribal belt. The reality is that it is spreading.

The document concluded by noting: "There is a general policy of appeasement towards the Taliban, which has further emboldened them."[66] A DIA assessment also warned that

> Pakistan's border with Afghanistan remains a haven for al-Qaida's leadership and other extremists. In a September accord with the Pakistan government, North Waziristan tribes agreed to curtail attacks into Afghanistan, cease attacks on Pakistani forces and expel foreign fighters. However, the tribes have not abided by most terms of the agreement.[67]

Local militants gradually became a parallel government in the tribal areas and a sanctuary for insurgent groups operating in Afghanistan. The traditional jirga was formally banned. In its place, aggrieved parties had to seek intervention from the Taliban representative in their village, who performed the functions of police officer, administrator, and judge. Local militants, inspired by Mullah Mohammad Omar and the Afghan Taliban, banned music stores, videos, and televisions and issued edicts that men had to grow beards. They also continued to target progovernment tribal elders, forcing many to flee.[68] This was clearly the intent of local militants, as they repeated in public state-

---

[66] Pakistan Ministry of Interior, *The Talibanisation Problem*, Islamabad: Ministry of Interior, 2007. The document was subsequently leaked to the press. See, for example, Ismail Khan, "Talibanisation Imperils Security, NSC Warned: Immediate Action Urged," *Dawn* (Karachi), June 22, 2007.

[67] LTG Michael D. Maples, *Current and Projected National Security Threats to the United States, Statement for the Record, Senate Select Committee on Intelligence Committee*, Washington, D.C.: DIA, January 2007, p. 12.

[68] Intikhab Amir, "Whose Writ Is It Anyway," *The Herald* (Karachi), Vol. 37, No. 4, April 2006, pp. 80–82.

ments. In one public statement, for example, they argued that "the situation is augmenting and the Taliban in Waziristan are capturing hearts and minds. We see the tribes who were struggling for tens of years accepting arbitration by Taliban scholars."[69]

As Mariam Abou Zahab argued, Pakistani operations further weakened the power of tribal leaders:

> The military raids have weakened the already eroded power of the tribal elders who, locked in negotiations with the political administration, saw it as a betrayal and a violation of the traditions and lost whatever influence they still had on tribes.[70]

U.S. officials also remained focused on capturing or killing al Qa'ida leaders, not on significantly undermining the militant sanctuary in the tribal areas. Some U.S. policymakers, such as Zalmay Khalilzad, who served on the National Security Council and then became U.S. Ambassador to Afghanistan, repeatedly voiced concerns about the growing sanctuary in Pakistan but were rebuffed by senior U.S. policymakers.[71]

Operation Zalzala

Over the next few years, Pakistan continued to broker peace deals in the tribal areas. In September 2006, for example, the governor of the NWFP, Lt Gen (ret.) Ali Mohammad Jan Orakzai, reached an agreement with a tribal grand jirga in Miramshah, North Waziristan. As part of the agreement, militants promised that they would not use the area to attack the Afghan or Pakistani governments, would stop targeted killings of progovernment tribal *maliks*, and would not impose their lifestyle on others by force. Like many previous efforts, however, the deals had an effect opposite to the one intended: Militant groups used them to increase their power and control in the tribal areas, including in North Waziristan: "There have been more kidnappings, robberies and murders since then as the Khasadar force—a ragtag,

---

[69] Taliban Statement on Waziristan, April 13, 2006.

[70] Zahab, "Changing Patterns of Social and Political Life."

[71] Author interview with Ambassador Zalmay Khalilzad, February 22, 2008. Also see Jones, *In the Graveyard of Empires*, pp. 256–278.

untrained tribal force left to man the posts—has neither the teeth nor the wherewithal to rein in the militants or control crime, area residents point out," noted one assessment. "There is growing evidence that militants are now more assertive than they were before the September 5 agreement."[72]

The same challenges existed in South Waziristan, where the Pakistan Army launched Operation Zalzala (Earthquake). The operation's goal was to clear areas in South Waziristan held by militants loyal to Baitullah Mehsud. The operation came on the heels of a series of troubled peace deals. In February 2005, the government had signed the Sararogha Agreement with Baitullah Mehsud after a month of negotiations. Under the terms of the agreement, the army agreed to pull out troops from Baitullah Mehsud's areas and deploy only Frontier Corps personnel at the five forts there. In reality, the peace agreement virtually handed over control of the area to Baitullah Mehsud because roadside checkpoints were removed and because Mehsud and his fellow tribesmen were compensated for human and material losses as a result of military operations. The agreement was effectively terminated in early August 2007 after tension began growing between Baitullah Mehsud and Pakistani security forces.[73]

In May 2007, Frontier Corps and units from the Special Services Group raided a foreign fighter training camp in Zarga Khel, North Waziristan Agency. In August 2007, over 200 Pakistani security forces were abducted in South Waziristan Agency. In addition, Pakistan Army and intelligence units covertly supported Taliban commander Mullah Nazir—a bitter rival of Baitullah Mehsud—against Uzbek militants in South Waziristan. Nazir's Ahmadzai tribal rivals had offered *melmastia*, the Pashtun word for hospitality, to the Uzbeks in 2001 but the Uzbek militants had become unpopular among locals for their criminality and viciousness. In past decades, *melmastia* did have

---

72 Ismail Khan, "Why the Waziristan Deal Is a Hard Sell," *Dawn* (Karachi), October 14, 2006.

73 "Accord in Bajaur to Curb Terrorists," *Dawn* (Karachi), May 31, 2005; "The Bajaur Massacre," *Dawn* (Karachi), November 1, 2006; Mohammad Ali, "Peace Deal in Bajaur Soon, Says Aurakzai," *Dawn* (Karachi), February 24, 2007.

some limits.[74] In some of these areas, however, it had become a "stay as you pay system," allowing many in the tribal areas to enrich themselves while providing food and shelter to various foreign and domestic militants.[75] Consequently, *Pashtunwali*, the Pashtun code of conduct, became increasingly flexible and adaptive and was used to legitimize the symbiotic relationship between foreign and domestic militants.

Pakistani support to Mullah Nazir against Uzbek militants was supposed to be covert, but it was well covered in the Pakistani media.[76] As with other militant groups, individuals within the Pakistani government likely provided support to Mullah Nazir for a range of reasons, including to help balance against the Tehreek-e-Taliban-e-Pakistan in South Waziristan and to ensure some Pakistani oversight over Nazir's group. While the Pakistan Army largely stayed out of the fighting, it eventually sent military and paramilitary forces into the area to seize strategic hilltops and ridges, and to help establish law and order once the fighting stopped. In the end, Mullah Nazir temporarily evicted some Uzbek fighters from Wana in South Waziristan after a month of fighting.[77]

Yet the security situation in Pakistan continued to deteriorate. Popular anger grew over the government's handling of the July 2007 military operation against militants ensconced in Islamabad's Red Mosque, referred to as Operation Silence.[78] In addition, Baitullah Mehsud conducted a relentless suicide bombing campaign in cooperation with allied Pashtun and Punjabi militants. Some U.S. and Pakistani intelligence assessments concluded that Baitullah Mehsud's network

---

[74] For a discussion of this concept and its limits, see C. Christine Fair and Peter Chalk, *Fortifying Pakistan: The Role of U.S. Internal Security Assistance*, Washington, D.C.: United States Institute of Peace, 2006.

[75] Zahab, "Changing Patterns of Social and Political Life."

[76] Ismail Khan and Alamgir Bhittani, "442 Uzbeks Among 58 Dead: Fierce Clashes in S. Waziristan," *Dawn* (Karachi), March 21, 2007.

[77] Rahimullah Yusufzai, "Eviction or Safe Passage?" *Newsline* (Karachi), May 2007.

[78] Operation Silence is not treated here because it was not a sustained campaign per se. For an excellent account of this operation, see Manjeet Singh Pardesi, "Battle for the Soul of Pakistan at Islamabad's Red Mosque," in Fair and Ganguly, eds., *Treading on Hallowed Ground*, pp. 88–116.

was responsible for the assassination of Benazir Bhutto in December 2007.[79] Tensions between Baitullah Mehsud and the Pakistani government became acute again in January 2008. The most important precipitant of tensions, which ultimately culminated in Operation Zalzala, was the militant's capture of Sararogha Fort in South Waziristan, which resulted in the deaths of some Pakistani security forces. According to a Pakistan Army account, "About 200 militants charged the fort from four sides . . . They broke through the fort's wall with rockets."[80] As Baitullah Mehsud explained in a public interview, the Pakistan Army "uses the weapons it has against the people and against Muslims. Pakistan should protect Muslims with these weapons and defy enemies with them. However, the army has harmed the people and Muslims with its weapons."[81] Militants in Sarawakai, Splitoi, and Ladha in South Waziristan began assaulting a number of additional forts in their vicinities. In January 2008, the Pakistan Army began dropping leaflets urging locals in South Waziristan to vacate the area as the government prepared to launch Operation Zalzala.

On January 24, the Pakistan Army then used the 14th Division to attack Baitullah Mehsud's militants in several parts of South Waziristan, including Spinkai and Kotkai. The goal was not to target groups engaged in attacks in Afghanistan or Kashmir, or even foreign fighters, but to capture or kill key individuals in Baitullah Mehsud's network. One was Qari Hussain Mehsud, who was believed to be leading a campaign of suicide bombings. Pakistan Army forces destroyed his house in Kotkai but failed to capture or kill him.[82] During the operation, the army employed infantry, artillery, tanks, bulldozers, and fighter jets and used a range of more-sophisticated equipment to try to disrupt insurgent responses, including electronic jamming devices to

---

[79] Joby Warrick, "CIA Places Blame for Bhutto Assassination," *Washington Post*, January 18, 2008, p. A01.

[80] "Militants Overrun Pakistan Fort," BBC News, January 17, 2008. Also see "Pakistani Troops 'Flee Border Post,'" Al Jazeera, January 17, 2008.

[81] "Al-Jazeera TV Interviews Pakistan Taliban Chief," BBC, May 29, 2008.

[82] "Taliban Chief Ideologist Survives 'Zalzala,'" *Daily Times* (Lahore), May 26, 2008.

thwart improvised explosive devices.[83] In response, forces loyal to Baitullah Mehsud fought back and engaged in a fairly sophisticated propaganda effort to discredit the Pakistani military, even uploading videos to YouTube.[84] Militants also told locals that the army was composed of non-Muslims and was fighting on behalf of the United States.[85] This became an important issue because some clergy would not do last rites for slain security force personnel. Over the next several months, the army cleared most of Spinkai and captured a few other villages and small towns.[86]

By May 2008, the Pakistan Army began to withdraw, claiming victory. The 14th Division was directed to allow the reopening of road networks and to consolidate tactical outposts into forward operating bases on the eastern side of South Waziristan. The army's intent was apparently to stay in the Mehsud tribal area, continue to dominate key terrain, and retain the capability to redeploy into tactically dominant positions within 48 hours, should the security situation dictate.[87]

How successful was Operation Zalzala? Pakistani security forces cleared parts of South Waziristan—at least temporarily—and disrupted some suicide bombing efforts. According to Major General Tariq Khan, who commanded the 14th Division, the army cleared a "factory that had been recruiting 9- to 12-year-old boys and turning them into suicide bombers."[88] The army also seized computers, weapons, improvised explosive devices, and propaganda material. Indeed, Major General Khan boasted: "I have made the entire area from D. I.

---

83 "Taliban Chief Ideologist Survives 'Zalzala'"; Iqbal Khattak, "Army in Waziristan Better Equipped, More Relaxed," *Daily Times* (Lahore), May 21, 2008.

84 Iqbal Khattak, "Pakistan: Mehsud Says Local Taliban to Begin Media War; Slams Reporter's Murder," *Daily Times* (Lahore), May 27, 2008.

85 Khattak, "Army in Waziristan."

86 Zaffar Abbas, "Taliban Ousted, But Spinkai Is Now a Ghost Town," *Dawn* (Karachi), May 19, 2008.

87 Author interview with Pakistan and British government officials, Islamabad, April 2009.

88 Abbas, "Taliban Ousted."

Khan up to Jhandola weapon free, and need be, I can do it in the rest of the area too."[89]

But there were significant costs. According to a Pakistani investigation of the operation led by senior military, political, intelligence, and tribal officials, Pakistani forces destroyed over 4,000 houses in South Waziristan in January alone, especially in the towns of Spinkai, Cheg Malai, Nawazkot, and Kotkai. In addition, Operation Zalzala displaced roughly 200,000 locals, which caused significant animosity.[90] As one assessment noted, "[n]ot a single shop [in Spinkai] . . . is now intact. Even petrol stations and local factories have been razed to the ground."[91] The Pakistan Army applied collective punishment in several Pakistani villages, authorized under the colonial-era governance structure, the Frontier Crimes Regulation (FCR), which governs FATA. When the army discovered bomb factories, detonation-ready suicide jackets, and schools for teenage suicide bombers in a village, they punished it for harboring the Taliban and allowing them to operate there. Bulldozers and explosives experts turned Spinkai's bazaar into a mile-long pile of rubble; gas stations, shops, and even parts of the hospital were leveled or blown up.

This notion of collective punishment is based on an understanding that tribes and families are collectively responsible for the misdeeds of their members. While collective responsibility and collective punishment apply to residents of FATA, the government can also target their tribe and family members *outside* FATA. In June 2009, for example, the senior political official in South Waziristan, Shahab Ali Shah, ordered the

> seizure, where they may be found, of all members of the Mehsud tribe and confiscation of movable/immovable property belong-

---

[89] Abbas, "Taliban Ousted."

[90] Zulfiqar Ali, "Over 4,000 Houses Destroyed in Waziristan Operation: Report," *Dawn* (Karachi), November 8, 2008; Iqbal Khattak, "Deserted Town Shows Human Cost of Operation Zalzala," *Daily Times* (Lahore), May 20, 2008.

[91] Abbas, "Taliban Ousted." Also see Declan Walsh, "Demolished by the Pakistan Army: The Frontier Village Punished for Harboring the Taliban," *The Guardian* (U.K.), May 20, 2008.

> ing to them in the North-West Frontier Province and the arrest and taking into custody of any person of the tribe wherever he is found.[92]

This order resulted in the closure of dozens of businesses in Dera Ismail Khan, Tank, and Peshawar in NWFP.

In sum, Pakistani security forces failed to hold key territory during Operation Zalzala. Not long after the Pakistan Army withdrew from such villages as Spinkai, Pakistani and Western intelligence assessments concluded that militants loyal to Baitullah Mehsud reinfiltrated many of the areas.[93] Pakistani authorities discovered that after the Army's withdrawal, Qari Hussain Mehsud eventually reactivated the Spinkai Ragzai suicide training camp that the Pakistan Army had dismantled.[94] Pakistan's harsh collective-punishment practices also created animosity among locals and failed to secure support. As one shopkeeper from Spinkai noted, "[h]atred against the army will increase if they destroy homes of common people."[95]

Operations Sher Dil, Rah-e-Haq, and Rah-e-Rast

Given their limited success in the southern parts of the tribal areas, Pakistan security forces focused on operations against militants elsewhere in Pakistan. There were significant differences among many of these operations, but this section focuses on Bajaur and Swat, which were part of a broader Pakistan campaign to stem the spreading insurgency in the northern parts of FATA and the NWFP. There was some cooperation among militant networks operating in these areas, including those led by Faqir Mohammad, Maulana Fazlullah, and Sufi Muhammad. In addition, Baitullah Mehsud provided some fighters and assistance to militants in Bajaur and Swat as part of his strategy

---

[92] See Joshua Partlow and Haq Nawaz Khan, "Tribe Members Held Accountable: Pakistani Order Says Mehsuds Can Be Targeted Over Taliban Leader's Crimes," *Washington Post*, July 21, 2009.

[93] Author interview with Pakistan and British government officials, Pakistan, April 2009.

[94] Amir Mir, "Story Behind Manawan Fidayee Attack," *The News* (Pakistan), April 1, 2009.

[95] Stephen Graham, "Ghost Village Haunts Pakistani Plans to Make Peace with Tribal Militants," *Associated Press*, May 19, 2008.

to better coordinate the insurgencies through his Tehreek-e-Taliban-e-Pakistan.

Operation Sher Dil. Operation Sher Dil (Lion Heart), which took place in Bajaur Agency, was one of the largest operations (Figure 3.4). Pakistan's primary objective during Sher Dil was to target militant groups that threatened Pakistan and to clear and hold Bajaur's population centers and main arteries against a range of militants, including foreign fighters. Attacks against government agencies, including ISI, Frontier Corps, and army personnel, created a strong incentive to strike back. In March 2007, for example, a senior ISI officer, his subordinate, and two tribesmen were killed when their vehicle was ambushed

Figure 3.4
Operation Sher Dil, 2008

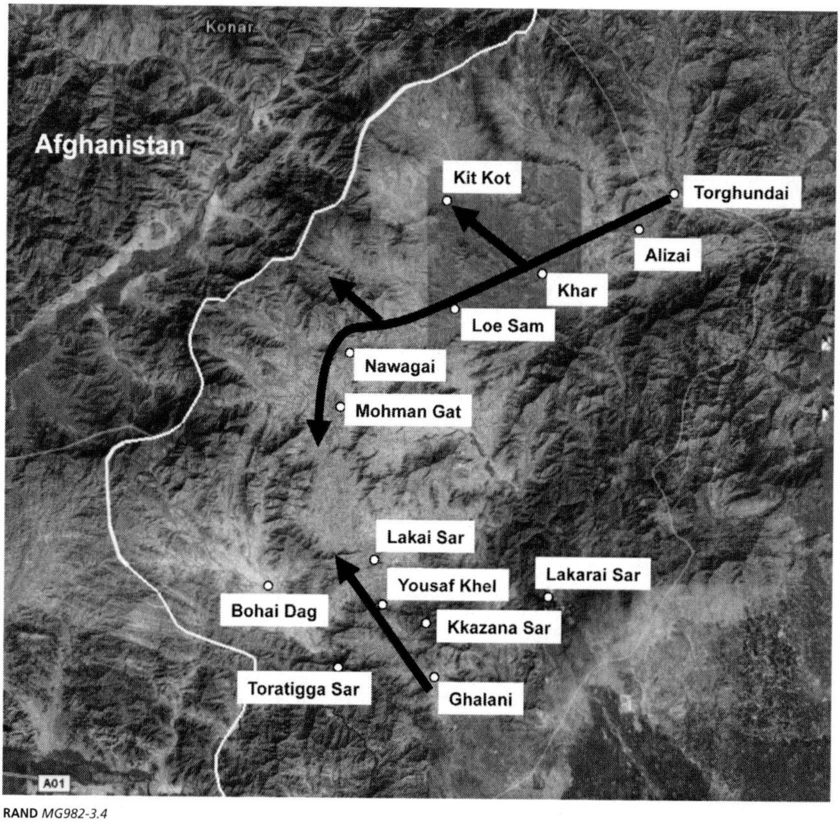

RAND *MG982-3.4*

in Bajaur Agency.[96] In September 2007, militants conducted a suicide attack against a bus carrying ISI employees. And in November, two simultaneous suicide attacks targeted the heart of Pakistan's military establishment in Rawalpindi. One bomber drove a car packed with explosives into a bus carrying up to 90 ISI employees, and a second attacker blew himself up after driving his car into a checkpoint outside the army headquarters.

By early 2008, local militants led by such individuals as Qari Zia Rahman, had pushed government-supported tribal forces, referred to as *levees*, out of their checkpoints at Loe Sam. By June, they had destroyed more than half of the 72 checkpoints in Bajaur and disrupted the civilian government by conducting suicide bombings against officials and robbing a major bank. On September 9, 2008, Pakistan Army and Frontier Corps units launched Operation Sher Dil in Bajaur, not long after a Pakistani security convoy was ambushed by local militants in Loe Sam.[97] Pakistan employed a brigade headquarters, four infantry battalions, one squadron, the headquarters of the Bajaur Scouts, and seven Frontier Corps wings. They were under the control of the XI Corps Commander, General Hussain, with the assistance of the Frontier Corps Commander, General Khan. Ground forces moved southwest from Torghundai through such towns as Alizai, Khar, Loe Sam, and Nawagai, since Pakistani intelligence assessments indicated that several of these villages, including Loe Sam, had become major hubs of militant activities.[98]

The operation was heavy handed and relied on aerial bombing sorties, bulldozers, and tanks, which rolled through Bajaur villages. In the village of Loe Sam, Pakistani forces discovered an extensive tunnel system and razed virtually every house connected to a tunnel. Militants were armed with heavy weapons and were reinforced by fighters

---

[96] Anwarullah Khan, "ISI Official, Three Others Killed in Bajaur Ambush," *Dawn* (Karachi), March 28, 2007.

[97] Mukhtar A. Khan, "A Profile of Militant Groups in Bajaur Tribal Agency," *Terrorism Monitor*, Vol. 7, No. 6, March 19, 2009, p. 1.

[98] Author interview with British and Pakistani government officials, April and May 2009.

from Afghanistan and other parts of FATA and NWFP. As one Pakistani military official remarked,

> [t]hey have good weaponry and a better communication system [than ours] . . . . Their tactics are mind-boggling and they have defenses that would take us days to build. It does not look as though we are fighting a rag-tag militia; they are fighting like an organized force.[99]

The fighting caused a significant exodus of locals to other parts of Pakistan and Afghanistan. By early December 2008, over 1,000 militants and 63 security officials had been killed. Pakistani forces were successful in clearing a range of key villages and arteries in Bajaur, especially along the main north-south corridor. They found tunnel complexes used for hiding people and storing materials, such as weapons, ammunition, radio frequency lists, guerrilla warfare manuals, propaganda, and bomb-making instructions.[100]

To facilitate army and Frontier Corps efforts, Pakistani commanders sought the aid of local tribes to help secure major roads, some of whom created lashkars (local defense forces). In addition, on November 4 and 5, Pakistani authorities dropped leaflets in some areas of Mohmand Agency calling for people to follow the example of tribes in Bajaur, Darra Adam Khel, and Orakzai, and to raise lashkars against militants. The Salarzai tribe was one of the first to raise a lashkar against militants, as was the Utmankhel tribe. But the Salarzai suffered a serious blow on November 6, when a tribal jirga in the area was attacked and more than 20 people were killed, including several of the tribe's senior leaders. Four Charmang tribal elders were beheaded by militants while returning home from a tribal jirga. After completing Operation Sher Dil, Pakistan Army and Frontier Corps forces moved to Mohmand agency, where they conducted additional operations.

Operation Rah-e-Haq. The next series of operations took place in Swat District, NWFP. Swat had been one of Pakistan's prized tourist

---

99 Ismail Khan, "Battle to Be Won or Lost in Bajaur," *Dawn* (Karachi), September 21, 2008.

100 Anthony Lloyd, "Captured Battle Plan Shows Strength and Training of Taleban Forces," *The Times* (London), November 11, 2008.

destinations, with ski resorts and majestic mountains. But the TNSM, a militant group led by Sufi Mohammad, had been steadily building military and political power in Swat.

Pakistan commenced the first phase of Operation Rah-e-Haq (Path of Truth) in late November 2007.[101] Local police led cordon-and-search operations to clear militants operating in the valley, but militants gradually reinfiltrated key cities. TNSM militants controlled several key areas around Mingora and, in July, surrounded a security post and abducted 29 police and paramilitary forces. The second phase began in July 2008 and continued through the remainder of the year. Pakistan utilized a range of forces, including two division headquarters, five brigades, 17 infantry battalions, five artillery regiments, and aviation assets (including Mi-17s, Bell 412s, and Cobra helicopters).[102] Fighting was initially heavy in the northern part of the Swat Valley, and the army responded to militant attacks in Sar Banda and Wainai with Cobra attack helicopters and artillery strikes. Fighting then spread to southern areas as well.[103] In January 2009, the Pakistan Army launched a third phase of Operation Rah-e-Haq and established "shoot-on-sight" curfews in major cities of Swat. Militant forces retaliated by destroying schools and attacking security forces.

The fighting ended with a peace agreement known as the Malakand Accord. The accord institutionalized a framework of Islamic laws. Cases would be heard by religious authorities, or *qazis*, and decided in accordance with Islamic injunctions in Malakand Division (which compromises the districts of Swat, Buner, Shangla, Upper Dir, Lower Dir, Chitral, and Malakand) and the Kohistan district of Hazara

---

[101] The Pakistan government signed an agreement with the Muttahida Majlis-e-Amal government and the TNSM in May 2007. The government agreed to let Mullah Fazlullah continue broadcasts through his FM radio stations, while Fazlullah agreed to support government efforts to maintain law and order in the districts, education for girls, and polio vaccination. Akhtar Amin, "Government Moves Additional Army Contingents to Swat," *Daily Times* (Lahore), October 19, 2007.

[102] Author interview with Pakistani and British government officials, Islamabad, April and May 2009.

[103] Khashnud Ali Khan, "Why and How Did the Operation Commence in Mohmand Agency and Bajaur Agency?" *Jinnah* (Pakistan), September 30, 2008.

Division.[104] But by late April 2009, militant networks began to occupy shops and government buildings in Mingora, the largest city in Swat, and moved into a range of areas in Swat and neighboring districts, such as Buner. They also attacked police stations, ambushed Frontier Constabulary personnel, robbed government and NGO offices, destroyed several schools, and set up checkpoints along key roads.[105]

Operation Rah-e-Rast. In May 2009, Pakistan launched Operation Rah-e-Rast (Path of Righteousness). The objective was to clear areas in Swat and capture or kill key militants, such as Muslim Khan, Mahmmod Khan, and a range of other commanders loyal to Maulana Fazlullah, Sufi Mohammad, and Baitullah Mehsud.[106] Pakistani security forces used helicopter gunships, fighter jets, artillery (including 130-mm field gun batteries), and infantry advances to target militants.

Fighting commenced in the largest city, Mingora, between Special Services Group commandos and about 300 militants positioned in deserted buildings. Amid heavy street fighting, the Pakistan Army captured large parts of the city, including several key intersections and squares. On May 24, the Pakistan Army announced that it had retaken large parts of Mingora. Pakistani soldiers continued to engage militants in street fighting and to search buildings for fighters. Pakistani troops also retook several nearby towns previously under militant control. On May 30, the Pakistani military announced that it had regained control of all of Mingora, although small pockets of resistance still remained in the city's outskirts. It also announced that it had destroyed concrete

---

[104] Nizam e Adl Regulation, 2009. A copy of the text can be found at "Text of Pakistan's Shari'ah Law 2009," BBC Monitoring South Asia, April 14, 2009.

[105] Abdur Rehman Abid, "Taliban Ambush FC Convoy, Foil Buner Deployment," *Dawn* (Karachi), April 24, 2009; Daud Khattak and Delawar Jan, "Operation Against Taliban on Government Mind," *The News* (Pakistan), April 24, 2009; "Taliban Turn Troops Back from Mingora," *The News* (Pakistan), April 26, 2009; Abdur Rehman Abid, "Buner Falls to Swat Taliban," *Dawn* (Karachi), April 22, 2009; Ghulam Farooq, "Taliban Step into Shangla as Buner Showdown Looms," *Daily Times* (Lahore), April 24, 2009.

[106] Zahid Hussain, "From Much Sought After to 'Most Wanted,'" *Dawn* (Karachi), May 31, 2009.

bunkers and confiscated arms, ammunition, and explosives hidden in caves.[107]

The heavy fighting in Swat, Buner, and Lower Dir, as well as Pakistan's scorched-earth practices, triggered a significant flood of internally displaced persons. Refugee organizations estimated that nearly three million people were displaced because of the fighting, making it one of the largest population migrations since Rwanda in 1994.[108] Some went to camps, but many found refuge with host families, rented accommodations, and makeshift shelters across Pakistan. Local militants took advantage of the displacement to enlist popular support, provide assistance to internally displaced people, and recruit locals.

Other Operations. In addition to Operations Sher Dil, Rah-e-Haq, and Rah-e-Rast, Pakistan conducted a range of operations in FATA and NWFP over the course of 2008 and 2009. As Figure 3.5 illustrates, examples included Operation Sirat-e-Mustaqeem (Khyber Agency), Operation Eagle Swoop (Kohat District), Operation Mountain Scanner (North Waziristan Agency), and Operation Mountain Sweep II (South Waziristan Agency). Overall, Pakistan engaged approximately 74,000 troops as part of these operations, including four infantry divisions, one task force, 17 brigades, 54 battalions, one Special Services Group battalion, and 58 Frontier Corps Wings.

Effectiveness of the Operations. How successful were Operations Sher Dil, Rah-e-Haq, and Rah-e-Rast? Figure 3.5 offers some insights into these and the other operations referred to above. In Operation Sher Dil, Pakistani security forces were successful in temporarily clearing some areas under militant control, such as Loe Sam. The operation involved much better cooperation along two fronts: between the Frontier Corps and the army, and between Pakistan and the United

---

[107] Iftikhar A. Khan, "Security Forces Advance on Strategic Kamber Bridge," *Dawn* (Karachi), May 21, 2009; Iftikhar A. Khan, "Army Takes 'Complete Control' over Mingora," *Dawn* (Karachi), May 30, 2009.

[108] Author interviews with nongovernmental organizations in Pakistan, May 2009; International Committee of the Red Cross, *Pakistan: ICRC and Pakistan Red Crescent Substantially Expanding Operations,* news release, Islamabad, June 2009; Office of the United Nations High Commissioner for Refugees, *Newly Displaced Pakistani Civilians Report Grim Conditions in Swat Valley*, Islamabad, June 2009.

Figure 3.5
Pakistani Operations, 2008–2009

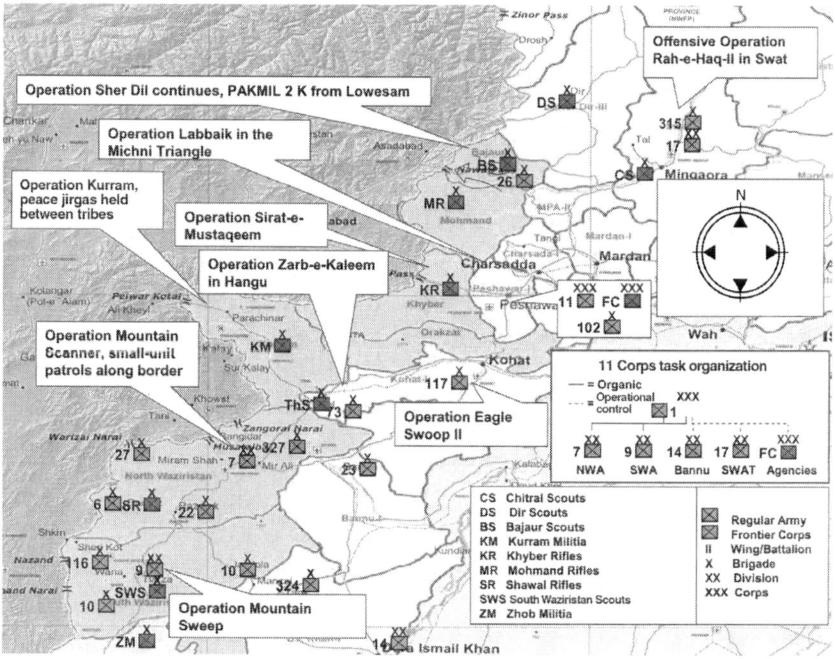

NOTES: Approximately 74,000 troops were in FATA: four infantry divisions, one task force, 17 brigades, 54 battalions, one Special Services Group battalion, and 58 Frontier Corps wings.
RAND *MG982-3.5*

States. U.S.-Pakistani cooperation appeared to be much better than in previous operations. The Frontier Corps commander, Major General Tariq Khan, regularly briefed U.S. officials on the operations. The U.S. Agency for International Development's Office of Transition Initiatives provided development assistance, including relief supplies for internally displaced persons and reconstitution assistance. The U.S. military also provided information to Pakistani forces along the Afghanistan-Pakistan border, where the United States conducted intelligence, surveillance, and reconnaissance operations along major passes, such as Nawa and Torkham.

A number of Pakistani civilians, however, considered U.S. assistance heretical. Maulana Abdul Khaliq Haqqani, patron-in-chief of the madrassa Gulshan-i-Uloom in Miramshah, responded that he would meet Pakistani or U.S. operations with force: "We will hit them with suicide bombers and remote-controlled bombs." Furthermore, he noted that U.S. "attacks were carried out in the presence of the Pakistan Army; we cannot ignore our army's cooperation with foreign forces in actions that kill innocent people."[109] In addition, a range of local tribes—such as the Salarzai—supported the operation and raised lashkars to help patrol roads, even though militants established a lethal campaign of assassination and intimidation against them. But Pakistan was not successful in holding territory over the long run, and the practice of razing villages and collective punishment (as in FATA) contributed to growing frustration with the army. There was a significant displacement of locals from their villages, a number of which were razed by Pakistani forces.

During Operations Rah-e-Haq and Rah-e-Rast, Pakistani security forces temporarily cleared parts of Swat and surrounding districts, such as Buner. But holding territory remained a challenge. Militant networks had tapped into a range of political, social, and economic grievances to co-opt or coerce locals, none of which were adequately addressed.

Operation Rah-e-Nijat

The failure of Operation Zalzala and other Pakistani efforts in South Waziristan became increasingly apparent as Baitullah Mehsud and his TTP network escalated violence across Pakistan in 2008 and 2009 from their base in South Waziristan.[110] TTP violence was part of a much broader trend across Pakistan. There were 2,148 terrorist, insurgent, and sectarian attacks in 2008 in Pakistan—a 746-percent increase from 2005.[111]

Pakistan had several objectives during Operation Rah-e-Nijat (Path of Salvation) (Figure 3.6). The most significant were to secure

[109] Interview with Maulana Abdul Khaliq Haqqani in *The Herald* (Karachi), July 2007, pp. 66–67.

[110] Author interview with Pakistani and British government officials, Pakistan, May 2009.

[111] Pakistan Institute for Peace Studies, *Pakistan Security Report 2008*, Islamabad, 2009, p. 3.

Figure 3.6
Map of Operation Rah-e-Nijat, 2009–2010

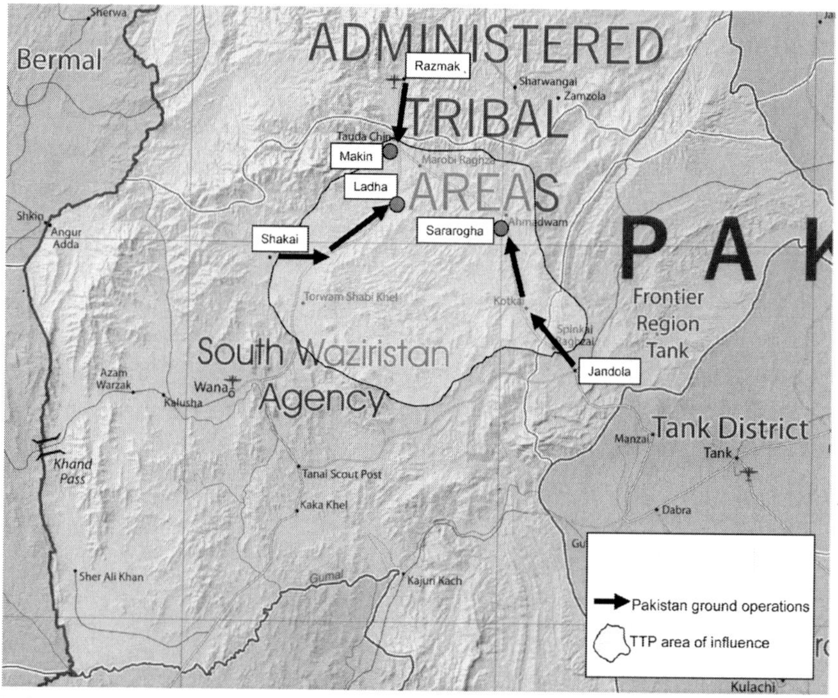

RAND *MG982-3.6*

key lines of communication (LOCs) and weaken the TTP and its infrastructure in South Waziristan, including its support base within the Mehsud tribe, one of the largest Pashtun tribes in South Waziristan. LOCs refer to land, water, and air routes that connect an operating military force with a base of operations, and along which supplies and reinforcements move. Baitullah Mehsud had gained support from the Alizai clan of the Mehsud tribe, while some elements of the Shaman Khel and Bahlolzai clans opposed the TTP. In a formal letter to Mehsud tribal leaders, Chief of the Army Staff General Ashfaq Kayani explained that the operation was aimed at foreign fighters and "cruel terrorists" in South Waziristan, not the Mehsud tribe.[112] To prepare for

112 General Ashfaq Parvez Kayani, Chief of the Army Staff, letter to Mehsud Tribes, October 2009. Also see, for example, Iftikhar A. Khan, "Kayani Writes to Mehsuds, Seeks Tribe's

Operation Rah-e-Nijat, the Pakistan Army and Air Force conducted initial targeting operations in South Waziristan during summer 2009, with some assistance from the U.S. military and CIA.

But TTP militants struck back. On June 30, militants ambushed a Pakistani military convoy near the Afghan border, killing 12 Pakistani soldiers. On August 5, a CIA drone killed Baitullah Mehsud in South Waziristan. He was replaced by Hakimullah Mehsud, who was later killed by a drone strike, in January 2010. On October 5, a suicide bomber dressed in a Frontier Corps uniform attacked the World Food Program office in Islamabad, killing five staff members. On October 9, a suicide attack in Peshawar killed over 50 civilians. On October 10, nearly a dozen militants dressed in army uniforms stormed Pakistan Army General Headquarters in Rawalpindi, taking over 40 hostages.[113]

In the midst of escalating violence, the Pakistani military initiated ground operations in South Waziristan on October 17, 2009, with support from Pakistani helicopter gunships and fixed-wing aircraft.[114] The 11th Corps was in overall command, with three divisions: the 7th, based in Miramshah; the 9th, in Wana; and the 14th, forward deployed to Jandola. In addition, two Special Services Group battalions and two infantry brigades were deployed from the eastern border with India, as well as Frontier Corps and other units. Pakistan utilized armor units with main battle tanks, as well as infantry units that conducted foot patrols and were equipped with heavy artillery and mortars. Pakistan's operations focused on clearing the TTP strongholds of Ladha, Makin, and Sararogha. As one Pakistani official noted: "The command and control structure of the Taliban exists in Sararogha, Makin and Laddah. It's going to be a tough fight for these places."[115] Pakistan ground units began by conducting search-and-clearance

---

Support," *Dawn* (Karachi), October 20, 2009.

[113] See, for example, Massoud Ansari, "Security: A Series of Unfortunate Events," *The Herald* (Karachi), November 2009.

[114] Sailab Mehsud, "Army Embarks on Rah-i-Nijat Finally," *Dawn* (Karachi), October 18, 2009.

[115] "Street Battles Rage in Uzbek Militants' Stronghold," *Dawn* (Karachi), November 2, 2009. Also see Mehsud, "Army Embarks on Rah-i-Nijat Finally."

operations along several key roads in South Waziristan, such as the Central Waziristan Road and the road running through Ahmadwam and Ragha.

On November 12, the Pakistani military encountered stiff resistance, and casualties were heavy in the Alizai Mehsud village of Kaniguram. But the following week, the 7th Division advanced into the village of Makin with little opposition. On November 19, the 14th Division entered Janata with apparent impunity, again indicating little resistance. As in other operations, Pakistani units leveled parts of some villages in South Waziristan.[116] One report described the devastation in Sararogha as significant: "Heaps of mud bricks and twisted iron were all that was left of the town after the forces seized it."[117] In addition to combat operations, Pakistan attempted to broker deals with neighboring militant organizations, such as Mullah Nazir's group in South Waziristan. Pakistan asked Mullah Nazir and his Wazir tribal allies to refuse to provide support, sanctuary, or safe passage to TTP militants in exchange for aid and a ceasefire agreement. Pakistan reached a similar deal with Hafiz Gul Bahadur in North Waziristan.[118] And Pakistani military and intelligence units encouraged a range of communities to establish lashkars.

By December 2009, Pakistani ground forces controlled most of Ladha, Makin, and Sararogha.[119] They had met little resistance in many areas, suggesting that the TTP strategy was to conduct a hasty withdrawal, temporarily relocate to other areas, and eventually return to continue the insurgency. TTP official Qari Hussain Mehsud noted that its strategy was "aimed at saving manpower and weapons for . . . guerrilla war against [the Pakistani military] in South Waziristan" over

---

[116] "Five More Militants Killed in South Waziristan: ISPR," *Dawn* (Karachi), December 10, 2009.

[117] Zahid Hussain, "Laddah, Sararogha Cleared; Street Fighting in Making," *Dawn* (Karachi), November 18, 2009.

[118] Author interview with senior Pakistan officials, December 2009.

[119] "Fifteen Militants Killed in Waziristan Operation: ISPR," *Dawn* (Karachi), December 28, 2009.

the long run.[120] Some militants fled to neighboring Afghanistan, to such provinces as Paktika, which borders South Waziristan.[121] Others fled to Orakzai, Khyber, Kurram, and North Waziristan (including the Shawal Valley), where Pakistani security forces conducted operations. In Orakzai Agency, for example, Frontier Corps units backed by gunships and artillery hit insurgent targets, destroying a number of hideouts and making several arrests. In addition, Pakistan continued to target militants in South Waziristan throughout the winter of 2010, even though the maneuver phase had concluded.

How successful was Operation Rah-e-Nijat? Pakistan appeared to disrupt TTP command, control, and logistics in key Mehsud areas of South Waziristan, especially in the short term. Pakistani forces also temporarily secured several key LOCs in South Waziristan, including those around Sararogha, Makin, and Ladda. In addition, the Pakistan Army deployed seven combat brigades from the Indian border, for a total of 15 brigades to support operations in—or near—South Waziristan. The shift of some resources from the Indian border was notable, indicating that the Pakistan Army viewed the operation as strategically significant. By January 2010, Pakistani forces had cleared several key villages in South Waziristan and recovered a range of weapon caches.[122]

But the operation did not destroy the TTP or its ability to attack the government, and numerous TTP militants evaded 11th Corps forces by temporarily leaving South Waziristan. In December 2009, militants with support from the TTP lobbed grenades and opened fire on worshippers, many of whom were active and retired military officials, at a mosque in Rawalpindi. At least 36 people—including several high-ranking military officials—were killed, and more than 45 were wounded.[123] In addition, the Pakistan Army continued to use

---

[120] "Pakistan Taliban to Increase Suicide Attacks," *Xinhua General News Service*, November 14, 2009.

[121] Author interview with Afghan and NATO officials, December 2009.

[122] "Four Militants Killed in Waziristan Operation," *Dawn* (Karachi), January 2, 2010; Hussain, "Laddah, Sararogha Cleared."

[123] "TTP Claims Peshawar Suicide Bombing," *The News* (Pakistan), December 27, 2009.

scorched-earth tactics in key population centers, including in Sararogha. As with previous operations, key challenges included holding territory once it had been cleared; dealing with disenchanted refugees and internally displaced persons; and failing to ameliorate some of the social, political, and economic root causes of the insurgency. By the end of 2009, there were several hundred thousand internally displaced persons and refugees from South Waziristan, and many settled in the neighboring districts of Tank and Dera Ismail Khan.[124]

Across Pakistan, violence reached an all-time high in 2009, with a total of 3,816 attacks that killed 12,632 people and injured 12,815. These figures represented a 32-percent increase in the number of attacks, a 37-percent increase in the number killed, and a 25-percent increase in the number injured from 2008. Indeed, the number of Pakistani civilians killed in militant attacks exceeded the number of civilian deaths in Afghanistan. In addition, there was a 28-percent increase in the number of suicide attacks.[125]

Effects on the Military

Beginning in 2001, Pakistani security forces conducted the first systematic operations in FATA since independence.[126] Table 3.2 provides a brief qualitative overview and assessment of several key operations. Pakistan lost well over a thousand forces during these operations. The table suggests that Pakistan's operations had varying degrees of success. Operation Enduring Freedom led to the capture of several key al Qa'ida operatives and the overthrow of the Taliban regime, and Pakistani operations in South Waziristan, North Waziristan, Bajaur, and Swat successfully cleared some territory. However, Pakistani secu-

[124]Qaiser Khan Afridi, *UNHCR Helps South Waziristan's Displaced in Neighbouring Districts*, Geneva: Office of the United Nations High Commissioner for Refugees, December 2009.

[125]Pakistan Institute for Peace Studies, *Pakistan Security Report 2009*, Islamabad: Pakistan Institute for Peace Studies, 2010.

[126]The army previously conducted some limited operations, such as in Bajaur in 1960, but not to the extent that it did beginning in 2001.

Table 3.2
Summary of Key Operations

Operation	Dates	Goals	Summary of Operation	Effectiveness
Enduring Freedom	2001–2002	Capture or kill key al Qa'ida fighters; help overthrow Taliban regime	Allowed U.S. access to Pakistan; deployed forces along infiltration routes	Medium success. Some al Qa'ida fighters captured or killed; Taliban regime overthrown
Al Mizan	2002–2006	Capture or kill key foreign fighters, as well as target local support networks	Deployed between 70,000 and 80,000 forces into FATA	Low success. Several al Qa'ida leaders captured or killed; but failed to clear and hold territory, especially in South Waziristan
Zalzala	2008	Clear key towns in South Waziristan held by networks loyal to Baitullah Mehsud	Deployed 14th Division to several areas in South Waziristan	Low success. Failed to hold territory; collective punishment alienated many locals
Sher Dil	2008–2009	Clear Bajaur's population centers	Deployed forces to Loe Sam, other key villages, and along roads	Medium success. Cleared villages but failed to hold territory in some areas, and collective punishment created some animosity
Rah-e-Haq	2007–2009	Clear key parts of Swat District from TNSM; negotiate peace agreement	Deployed forces to Mingora and other key villages, as well as along roads	Low success. Malakand Accord collapsed and Pakistani forces failed to hold territory in Swat
Rah-e-Rast	2009	Clear key parts of Swat District from TNSM	Deployed forces to Mingora and other key villages, as well as along roads	Medium success. Cleared some key areas, including Mingora, but failed to address local grievances, and collective punishment alienated some locals
Rah-e-Nijat	2009–2010	Clear parts of South Waziristan from TTP	Deployed forces to Ladha, Makin, Sararogha, and other key villages	Medium success. Temporarily cleared several key areas (including Ladha, Makin, and Sararogha) but failed to hold some territory

rity forces faced considerable challenges in holding that territory and addressing key political, social, and economic grievances. These challenges have plagued numerous counterinsurgency operations, including Afghan, U.S., and broader NATO operations in Afghanistan.

The operations took a significant toll on the Pakistan Army. In 2007, Musharraf issued a temporary order to military personnel not to wear their uniforms off base because of threats received and because of the abuse they were sustaining from the population. In April 2008, one officer explained that he disliked killing Pakistanis and that he joined the Pakistan Army to kill Indians.[127] While some of this opposition was due to the widening unpopularity of Musharraf, some of it was also due to the deep ambivalence that Pakistanis held toward the offensives in FATA and NWFP.

Several surveys were conducted to illuminate the opinions of Pakistanis toward their government's handling of the security situation. In 2007, one of the authors conducted a nationally representative survey of nearly 1,000 urban Pakistanis to probe their support for government actions in FATA and other areas, under the auspices of the U.S. Institute of Peace (USIP) in partnership with the Program on International Policy Attitudes (PIPA).[128] As the data in Table 3.3 demonstrate with respect to FATA, there was considerable ambivalence toward Pakistan's operations, with 48 percent approving either strongly or somewhat and 34 percent disapproving somewhat or strongly. Support for the government's handling of the Lal Masjid situation was even lower, with 31 percent lending some degree of support while a majority disapproved.

Given the international pressure on Pakistan to halt the insurgencies, the poll sought to obtain a more granular understanding of public preferences for FATA. Thus the USIP/PIPA team offered respondents

---

[127]Author interviews in Pakistan in July 2007, February 2008, April 2008, February 2009, and April 2009. Also see various polls on the army's popularity and that of President Musharraf conducted by IRI.

[128]For more information about this poll, see C. Christine Fair, Clay Ramsay, and Steve Kull, "Pakistani Public Opinion on Democracy, Islamist Militancy, and Relations with the U.S.," Washington, D.C.: USIP/PIPA, January 7, 2008.

Table 3.3
Pakistani Support for Government Policies (in percent)

	Approve		Disapprove		Refused or Do Not Know
Policy	**Strongly**	**Somewhat**	**Some**	**Strongly**	
The situation in the FATA	14	34	22	12	18
Religious extremism, such as the Lal Masjid	12	19	27	29	13

three statements about FATA and asked which "comes closer to your view?"

Statement A: Pakistan's government should exert control over FATA, even if it means using military force to do so

Statement B: The government should not try to exert control over FATA but should try to keep the peace through negotiating deals with local Taliban

Statement C: The government should withdraw its forces from FATA and leave the people alone.

The plurality (46 percent) believed that "B" (keep peace through negotiating) best represented their view. Nearly 25 percent believed that "A" (military force if needed to control FATA) best accorded with their preference. A small minority (12 percent) identified "C" (withdraw forces and leave the people alone). Only 18 percent declined to provide an answer. This seemed to suggest that the least objectionable aspect of Pakistan's approach to FATA was negotiating deals brokered with the militants.

The USIP/PIPA team found that Pakistanis were somewhat more accepting of Pakistani military action when the target was al Qa'ida. Respondents were asked whether they favored or opposed the Pakistan Army entering FATA to pursue and capture al Qa'ida fighters. While 44 percent said they favored the policy, 36 percent said they opposed it.[129] The results were similar when the USIP/PIPA team asked about

[129] Fair, Ramsay, and Kull, "Pakistani Public Opinion on Democracy."

hot pursuit of Taliban insurgents who crossed over from Afghanistan. Nearly half (48 percent) favored allowing the Pakistan Army to pursue and capture Taliban insurgents who crossed into Pakistan. However, more than one in three (34 percent) opposed it.[130] The USIP/PIPA team found nearly universal opposition (80 percent) to allowing U.S. or other foreign troops to enter Pakistan to pursue and capture al Qa'ida and similar levels of opposition (77 percent) for those troops to engage in hot pursuit of Taliban fighters crossing into Pakistan from Afghanistan.[131]

The International Republican Institute (IRI), using a different series of questions and a nationally representative sample of rural and urban Pakistanis, found similar results, which are detailed in Figure 3.7.[132] Most Pakistanis initially did not support the army fighting extremists in NWFP and FATA. While a majority opposed this as late as July 2009, an IRI poll released in October 2009 indicated that 69 percent supported the army fighting extremists in Malakand Division.[133] Attitudes toward the peace deals fluctuated. Until March 2009, a majority supported the army's peace deal with the militants. By March 2009, in the wake of the controversial peace deal in Swat, a majority (72 percent) supported the peace deals. Despite the much-touted resistance to the controversial deal in Swat, IRI found that a majority (74 percent) polled in March 2009 believed that the peace deal would bring peace to the region compared to 20 percent who did not have such confidence. Six percent declined to answer.[134] However, following the fall of Buner to the Taliban, Pakistani opinion switched

---

[130] Fair, Ramsay, and Kull, "Pakistani Public Opinion on Democracy."

[131] Fair, Ramsay, and Kull, "Pakistani Public Opinion on Democracy."

[132] IRI, "IRI Releases Survey of Pakistan Public Opinion," press release linking to survey data for October 15–30, 2008, December 18, 2008.

[133] IRI, "IRI Releases Survey of Pakistan Public Opinion," press release linking to survey data for July 15–August 7, 2009, October 1, 2009.

[134] IRI, "IRI Releases Survey of Pakistan Public Opinion," press release linking to survey data for March 7–30, 2009, May 11, 2009.

Figure 3.7
Pakistani Views of Military Approaches Against Militant Groups

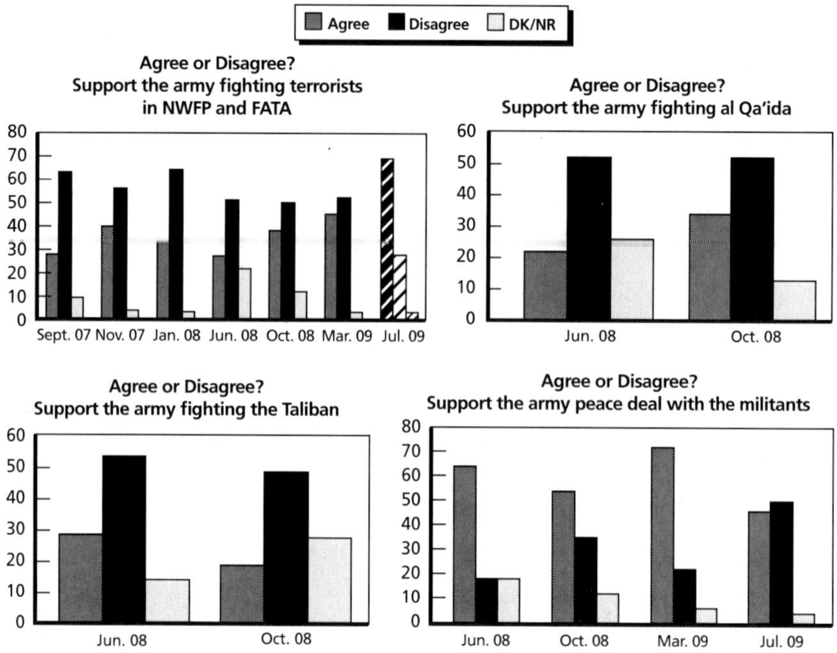

SOURCES: IRI public opinion survey data, various dates.
RAND *MG982-3.7*

sharply. By July 2009, IRI polls suggested that a majority of Pakistanis rejected these peace deals.[135]

While the military component of Pakistan's policy may be unpopular, another USIP/PIPA survey found that Pakistanis support political reform for FATA. When asked whether they supported leaving the draconian colonial-era FCR unchanged, modifying it "slowly over time such that the people there should have the same rights and responsibilities as all other Pakistanis," or abolishing it such that the people there

[135]IRI, "IRI Releases Survey of Pakistan Public Opinion," press release linking to survey data for October 15–30, 2008, December 18, 2008; IRI, "IRI Releases Survey of Pakistan Public Opinion," press release linking to survey data for March 7–30, 2009, May 11, 2009; IRI, "IRI Releases Survey of Pakistan Public Opinion," press release linking to survey data for July 15–August 7, 2009, October 1, 2009.

should have the same rights and responsibilities as all other Pakistanis," only a slim minority (8 percent) favored leaving the FCR intact. The largest percentage (46 percent) favored modification, and more than 25 percent favored abolishing it altogether. These surveys underscored the challenging environment in which Pakistani armed forces operated. This environment included a deep ambivalence about the government's policy of military action and cooperation with the United States; at the same time, appeasement of the militants and political reform seems quite palatable.

Conclusion

Several factors may explain Pakistan's mixed performance since 2001. First, Pakistan's army and Frontier Corps demonstrated an uneven ability to conduct operations, including clearing and holding territory. As Shuja Nawaz concluded in his study of Pakistani operations in the tribal areas: "Both the [Frontier Corps] and the army operated with severe handicaps: poor training for counterinsurgency warfare and poor equipment for the highly mobile war against the militants."[136] Prior to 2001, Pakistan had limited experience in counterinsurgency operations. Even after 2001, Pakistan continued to focus on a war against India rather than against substate actors. Its performance during Operation Al Mizan—especially in South Waziristan—demonstrated serious deficiencies in conducting cordon-and-search operations and holding territory. By Operations Sher Dil, Rah-e-Rast, and Rah-e-Nijat, Pakistan's performance had somewhat improved. Frontier Corps and army forces were better able to clear territory, integrate operations with local tribes, and add a development component. Recognizing these challenges, the United States provided significant assistance to Pakistan's security forces to improve their competence. During Operation Sher Dil, for example, the United States even provided intelligence,

---

[136] Shuja Nawaz, *FATA—A Most Dangerous Place: Meeting the Challenge of Militancy and Terror in the Federally Administered Tribal Areas of Pakistan*, Washington, D.C.: Center for Strategic and International Studies, January 2009, p. 34.

surveillance, and reconnaissance assistance during the fighting, as well as aid from the U.S. Agency for International Development.

Yet Pakistan's doctrine does not focus on population-centric approaches more in line with recent innovations in counterinsurgency warfare. Instead, it has often forced local inhabitants out of areas it is attacking, sometimes fostering unnecessary resentment. Pakistan's commitment to its conventional orientation and demands for hardware that is most appropriate for fighting India has ill-equipped it to contend with the burgeoning domestic threat. The army has long contended that it alone is the sole institution that can protect Pakistan. During successive military and civilian regimes, Pakistan's police institutions have languished. Moreover, the United States has disproportionately provided aid to the army while paying scant regard to the police.[137] Yet the counterinsurgency literature consistently finds that police-led—not army-led—approaches ultimately prevail.[138] Pakistan's federal and provincial bureaucracies have also failed to provide development and other aid to conflict-afflicted areas, offer adequate assistance to internally displaced persons, or engage in other efforts to secure the support of locals for the government and military operations. The lack of government capability to provide immediate relief has exacerbated the army's reliance on scorched-earth policies in such places as South Waziristan, Bajaur, and Swat, which have alienated some locals and fostered anger throughout Pakistan.

Some in Pakistan began to worry about using the army for internal security operations. A committee that reviewed the Armed Forces Special Powers Act argued that

> the armed forces of the Union should not be so deployed, since too frequent a deployment, and that too long for periods of time, carries with it the danger of such forces losing their moorings and

---

[137] C. Christine Fair, "From Strategy to Implementation: The Future of the U.S.-Pakistan Relationship," Testimony presented before the House Foreign Affairs Committee on May 5, 2009; Abbas, "Police & Law Enforcement Reform"; and Fair and Chalk, *Fortifying Pakistan*.

[138] Seth G. Jones and Martin C. Libicki, *How Terrorist Groups End: Lessons for Countering al-Qa'ida*, Santa Monica, Calif.: RAND Corporation, 2008; Fair and Ganguly, eds., *Treading on Hallowed Ground*.

> becoming, in effect, another police force, prey to all the temptations such exposures involve. Such exposures for long periods of time may well lead to the brutalization of such forces—which is a danger to be particularly guarded against.[139]

U.S. intelligence assessments also questioned Pakistan's capabilities. As one DIA assessment concluded:

> This new focus, however, is unlikely to displace India as Pakistan's perceived traditional, preeminent threat over the near term . . . Pakistan has added more border posts, begun counter-insurgency training, fenced portions of the border and seeks to obtain counter-insurgency equipment while also expanding para-military forces. Pakistan lacks the transport and attack helicopters and upgraded communication gear needed to prosecute more effective and sophisticated counter-insurgency operations. Much of the Pakistani army also lacks the knowledge and language skills required to successfully operate across the tribal frontier's complicated cultural terrain. While Frontier Corps troops understand the culture and region better and speak the local language, they have even less equipment and less training than the military.[140]

Second, Pakistan's challenges are due as much to political will as to deficiencies in capability. Pakistan has continued to distinguish among militant groups operating in FATA and NWFP and to use the tribal areas for training proxy groups destined for Afghanistan, Kashmir, India, or other fronts. Not only did Pakistan refuse to target some militant organizations, but some elements in the ISI, Frontier Corps, and military continued to back some of them. This practice of supporting some proxy organizations, including their broader religious, political, and financial networks, created an environment conducive to militancy and undermined the government's ability to estab-

---

[139] Ayesha Siddiqa, "In the Line of Fire," *The Herald* (Karachi), December 2006, p. 60.

[140] LTG Michael D. Maples, *Annual Threat Assessment: Statement Before the Committee on Armed Services United States Senate,* Washington, D.C.: DIA, February 2008, p. 22. Also see LTG Michael D. Maples, *Annual Threat Assessment: Statement Before the Committee on Armed Services, United States Senate,* Washington, D.C.: DIA, March 2009, p. 12.

lish law and order. Ironically, few militant leaders were captured or killed during Pakistani operations.

Third, U.S. strategy focused far too much on carrots and too little on sticks. As will be discussed later, successful persuasion requires a mixture of carrots and sticks. The United States secured President Musharraf's cooperation in 2001 precisely because its strategy included carrots (waiving U.S. sanctions and providing military and nonmilitary aid) and sticks, which caused Musharraf to war-game the United States. As the war in Afghanistan spiraled, U.S. and Pakistani interests began to diverge. Pakistani operations focused primarily on groups that threatened the government, even though the United States urged Pakistan to target groups that threatened the U.S. homeland and its regional interests. In some cases, such as with al Qa'ida and TTP, U.S. and Pakistani interests converged. But in other cases, such as the Haqqani network and Mullah Mohammad Omar's Taliban, they diverged.

Fourth, as demonstrated by the consistent findings of polls in Pakistan, the army and the government have not been successful in mobilizing the country against the militant threat. There is, however, some evidence that this temporarily changed following the Taliban's seizure of Buner in the wake of the 2009 peace deal with militants in Swat. Unless the government and the army can mobilize the population to support military operations, a sustained commitment to "holding" territory and rebuilding conflict-affected areas is unlikely. With over 3 million internally displaced persons seeking shelter and assistance across Pakistan, the Pakistan public's aversion may even worsen. The wholesale displacement of Pashtuns is likely to exacerbate longstanding ethnic and sectarian fissures in Pakistan's social fabric. Until Pakistan finds a way to redress these critical issues, its success in staving off the militant threat remains dubious.[141]

---

[141] Khan, "Descent into Anarchy," p. 61.

CHAPTER FOUR

Counterinsurgency and Persuasion

Pakistan's operations against militants have been deeply affected by the capabilities and political will of its national security agencies. The army and Frontier Corps have at times struggled to clear and hold territory, as well as to secure local support in FATA and NWFP. In addition, Pakistan has been willing to target some militant groups but not others. These realities have enormous implications for the United States and its interests in Pakistan and the broader region. Some U.S. policymakers have expressed frustration that, despite giving the Pakistan government billions of dollars in assistance since September 2001, they cannot persuade Pakistan to do more. As U.S. Senator Carl Levin noted, "I don't have a lot of confidence that the Pakistani government has the will or the capability to take on the violence."[1]

This chapter therefore asks two questions. First, what factors have historically contributed to the success of counterinsurgency operations? While Pakistani officials have usually shied away from using the term counterinsurgency—and have often resorted to a much more punitive strategy—a wide body of research on counterinsurgency has identified several factors that have contributed to the success (and failure) of efforts. Second, under what conditions is persuasion likely to be effective? Persuasion, as used here, involves efforts to change the behavior of a state by affecting its costs and benefits. It is distinguished from deterrence, which includes efforts to maintain the status quo by discouraging another state from changing its behavior.

---

[1] Andrew Gray, "U.S. Senator Doubts Pakistan, Blasts 'Pitiful' NATO," Reuters, March 31, 2009.

Counterinsurgency and persuasion are different concepts, but they are deeply interlinked in the case of Pakistan's struggle against insurgents. One involves prosecuting a war against militants trying to overthrow a government or take territory from it, while the other involves influencing the behavior of another state. Yet outside powers involved in an insurgency or counterinsurgency regularly try to influence the behavior of the local government or opposition groups. As Daniel Byman argues, states frequently support one side in an insurgency to "increase local or regional influence" and "especially as a means of applying pressure on a rival."[2] France supported different sides in francophone African wars to influence behavior and pursue its national security interests. Iran has supported insurgent groups, such as Lebanese Hezbollah and Palestinian Hamas, to influence the Palestinian-Israeli peace negotiations and leverage groups adjacent to its enemy, Israel.[3] Outside powers regularly try to affect the preferences of their allies, including during counterinsurgencies, using a range of political, economic, and other instruments. In fact, persuasion is more likely to be effective with allies because they are less concerned than adversaries about the long-run costs of acquiescing.[4]

The United States has historically used a range of economic, political, and military carrots and sticks to pressure governments during counterinsurgency campaigns. In one of the most extreme examples, the United States supported the overthrow of South Vietnamese President Ngo Dinh Diem on November 1, 1963. As outlined in the U.S. Department of Defense's "Pentagon Papers,"

> [b]eginning in August of 1963 we variously authorized, sanctioned and encouraged the coup efforts of the Vietnamese generals and offered full support for a successor government. In Octo-

---

2 Daniel Byman, Peter Chalk, Bruce Hoffman, William Rosenau, and David Brannan, *Trends in Outside Support for Insurgent Movements*, Santa Monica, Calif.: RAND Corporation, MR-1405-OTI, 2001, p. 23.

3 Byman et al., *Trends in Outside Support for Insurgent Movements*, p. 31.

4 Daniel W. Drezner, *The Sanctions Paradox: Economic Statecraft and International Relations*, New York: Cambridge University Press, 1999, pp. 4–5.

> ber we cut aid to Diem in a direct rebuff, giving a green light to the generals.[5]

The purpose was straightforward: to change the South Vietnam government's prosecution of the war because the United States "wanted to win."[6] However, most cases of persuasion during counterinsurgencies are much less extreme and involve more-subtle efforts to use political, economic, and military instruments to influence behavior. In Afghanistan, the United States used persuasion in several instances to remove unpopular provincial or district governors and to more effectively prosecute counterinsurgency operations.[7]

Consequently, the relationship between counterinsurgency and persuasion is symbiotic. Outside powers generally become involved in insurgencies and counterinsurgencies to influence the behavior and capabilities of their partners to achieve a specific outcome. Because the policy and academic communities have not appreciated this point, little policy or academic research has focused on it thus far. This chapter argues that counterinsurgency and persuasion are fundamentally linked.

The chapter is divided into three sections. The first outlines lessons for conducting successful counterinsurgency operations. The second examines key lessons for successful persuasion. The third offers a brief conclusion. This chapter largely sets up the theoretical basis for the next chapter, which will deal more systematically with policy implications for Pakistan.

Improving Counterinsurgency Capabilities

Most insurgencies, including that in Pakistan, involve four broad sets of actors:

---

[5] U.S. Department of Defense, *United States–Vietnam Relations, 1945–1967*, Book III: *The Overthrow of Ngo Dinh Diem, May–Nov. 1963, Summary and Analysis*, Washington, D.C.: U.S. Government Printing Office, 1971, pp. ii, viii.

[6] U.S. Department of Defense, *United States–Vietnam Relations*, pp. ii, viii.

[7] See, for example, Jones, *In the Graveyard of Empires*, pp. 134–136.

- *Insurgents.* This category includes those who aim to overthrow the national government or to secede from it.[8] In Pakistan, insurgents include the range of militant groups discussed in Chapter Two. Among others, these are the TTP; foreign fighters; and the groups led by Mullah Nazir, Hafiz Gul Bahadur, Mangal Bagh, Maulana Fazlullah, Faqir Mohammad, and others.
- *Local government.* Representatives include Pakistani security forces, such as the army and police, and key national ministries, as well as local officials.
- *External actors.* These include states and nonstate entities that can support the government or insurgents, and range from the United States to al Qa'ida and the international jihadi network. All these can play pivotal roles in tipping wars in favor of insurgents or the government, but can rarely "win it" for either side.
- *Local population.* The people are critical for all actors. Popular support is the sine qua non of victory in counterinsurgency warfare.[9]

Figure 4.1 illustrates the nexus of these actors, with the population at the center.

Securing the support—or at least the acquiescence—of the local population has been critical in past counterinsurgencies. "The only territory you want to hold," one study concluded, "is the six inches between

---

[8] On the definition of insurgency, see Central Intelligence Agency, Guide to the Analysis of Insurgency, Washington, D.C., January 2009, p. 2, and Joint Publication 1-02, DoD Dictionary of Military and Associated Terms, as amended through October 31, 2009, p. 266. On p. 565, JP 1-02 defines unconventional warfare as: "A broad spectrum of military and paramilitary operations, normally of long duration, predominantly conducted through, with, or by indigenous or surrogate forces who are organized, trained, equipped, supported, and directed in varying degrees by an external source. It includes, but is not limited to, guerrilla warfare, subversion, sabotage, intelligence activities, and unconventional assisted recovery." Consequently, conventional war refers to warfare conducted by using conventional military weapons—such as tanks and artillery—and battlefield tactics between two or more states in open confrontation.

[9] Roger Trinquier, *Modern Warfare: A French View of Counterinsurgency*, Westport, Conn.: Praeger Security International, 2006, p. 6.

Figure 4.1
Key Actors in Insurgencies

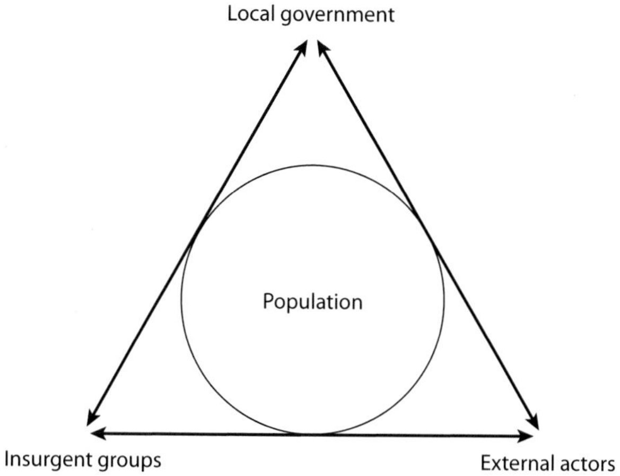

RAND MG982-4.1

the ears of the campesino."[10] British General Sir Frank Kitson argued that the population is a critical element in counterinsurgency operations as "this represents the water in which the fish swims."[11] Kitson borrowed the reference to the water and fish from one of the 20th century's most successful insurgents, Chinese leader Mao Tse-Tung, who wrote that there is an inextricable link in insurgencies "between the people and the troops. The former may be likened to water and the latter to the fish who inhabit it."[12] Insurgencies require a motivated leadership but, more importantly, can only form amid a disillusioned population.

---

[10] Daniel Siegel and Joy Hackel, "El Salvador: Counterinsurgency Revisited," in Michael T. Klare and Peter Kornbluh, eds., *Low Intensity Warfare: Counterinsurgency, Protoinsurgency, and Antiterrorism in the Eighties*, New York: Pantheon Books, 1988, p. 119.

[11] Frank Kitson, *Low Intensity Operations: Subversion, Insurgency and Peacekeeping*, rev. ed., London: Faber and Faber, 1991, p. 49. On counterinsurgency strategies, also see Colonel C. E. Callwell, *Small Wars: Their Principles and Practice*, 3rd ed., Lincoln: University of Nebraska Press, 1996, pp. 34–42; David Galula, *Counterinsurgency Warfare: Theory and Practice*, Westport, Conn.: Praeger Security International, [1964] 2006, pp. 17–42.

[12] Mao Tse-Tung, *On Guerrilla Warfare*, tr. Samuel B. Griffith II, Urbana: University of Illinois Press, 1961, p. 93.

What factors have historically contributed to the success of counterinsurgency operations? Quantitative and qualitative research suggest that multiple factors have been linked to successful counterinsurgency efforts.[13] Several, such as the type of terrain and income distribution, are either outside the control of government forces or virtually impossible to alter in the short term. For example, mountainous terrain and low income per capita appear to increase the likelihood of insurgent success. But governments can do little about these variables: terrain cannot be altered and increasing income per capita can take generations.

To identify the critical variables that have contributed to the success or failure of past insurgencies, RAND constructed a data set aggregating information on insurgencies occurring since World War II.[14] These insurgencies met the following three criteria:

1. They involved fighting between agents of (or claimants to) a state and nonstate groups who sought to take control of a government, take power in a region, or use violence to change government policies
2. At least 1,000 individuals were killed over the course of the conflict, with a yearly average of at least 100
3. At least 100 were killed on both sides (including civilians attacked by rebels).

The analysis indicates that several factors make counterinsurgency more effective. Two in particular have important implications for Pakistan.

---

[13] See, for example, James D. Fearon and David D. Laitin, "Ethnicity, Insurgency, and Civil War," *American Political Science Review*, Vol. 97, No. 1, February 2003, pp. 75–90; Galula, *Counterinsurgency Warfare*; Michael W. Doyle and Nicholas Sambanis, *Making War and Building Peace: The United Nations Since the 1990s*, Princeton, N.J.: Princeton University Press, 2006.

[14] See, for example, David C. Gompert, John Gordon IV, Adam Grissom, David R. Frelinger, Seth G. Jones, Martin C. Libicki, Edward O'Connell, Brooke Stearns Lawson, and Robert E. Hunter, *War by Other Means: Building Complete and Balanced Capabilities for Counterinsurgency*, Santa Monica, Calif.: RAND Corporation, MG-595/2-OSD, 2008, pp. 373–396; Seth G. Jones, *Counterinsurgency in Afghanistan*, Santa Monica, Calif.: RAND Corporation, 2008, pp. 7–24.

Quality of Governance

The first of these factors is improving local governance. Some quantitative analyses indicate that weak central governments render insurgency more feasible and attractive, suggesting that an important remedy is a more competent government.[15] In their study of 151 cases over a 54-year period, political scientists Michael Doyle and Nicholas Sambanis found that governance is critical to prevent and end civil wars and insurgencies. They argued that success requires the "provision of temporary security, the building of new institutions capable of resolving future conflicts peaceably, and an economy capable of offering civilian employment to former soldiers and material progress to future citizens."[16] Another study found that governmental capacity is a negative and significant predictor of civil war, and between 1816 and 1997 "effective bureaucratic and political systems reduced the rate of civil war activity."[17] Weak governance also contributes to lengthier insurgencies and civil wars.[18] As Figure 4.2 shows, RAND data indicate that highly popular governments defeated most of the insurgencies they fought, while unpopular governments lost more than one-half the time.[19]

Governance involves a legitimate authority providing timely services to the population. Governance can include central governments or, as in Pakistan, local government institutions. An insurgency is likely to develop when state control has declined or collapsed—including, as

---

[15] Fearon and Laitin, "Ethnicity, Insurgency, and Civil War," p. 75.

[16] Doyle and Sambanis, *Making War and Building Peace*, p. 5.

[17] Ann Hironaka, *Neverending Wars: The International Community, Weak States, and the Perpetuation of Civil War*, Cambridge, Mass.: Harvard University Press, 2005, p. 45.

[18] Hironaka, *Neverending Wars*, p. 51.

[19] We assessed the popularity of the government by making a qualitative judgment about how popular it was among the local population. We tried to avoid as much as possible the endogeneity problem of coding the government as popular if it won—and unpopular if it lost. Rather, we relied on the judgments of area specialists and historians that covered each insurgency to determine how popular the government was independent of the insurgency, which included examining public opinion polls where available. Unpublished RAND research for the U.S. Department of Defense.

Figure 4.2
Government Popularity and Success

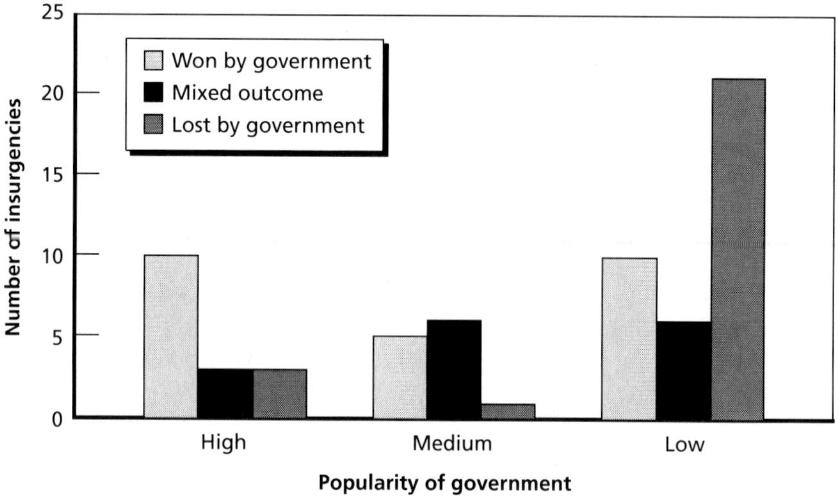

SOURCE: Jones, *Counterinsurgency in Afghanistan*, p. 20.
RAND *MG982-4.2*

in Pakistan, in specific regions of a country.[20] Weak states cannot consolidate authority over all their territory and often do not succeed in maintaining order within the territory they do control.[21]

Indeed, the provision of services can be affected by such factors as the level of corruption, the viability of the justice system, and the influence of warlords and local militias. One basic need of any insurgent group is an attractive cause. As David Galula argues, "[t]he best cause

---

[20] Barry R. Posen, "The Security Dilemma and Ethnic Conflict," in Michael E. Brown, ed., *Ethnic Conflict and International Security*, Princeton, N.J.: Princeton University Press, 1993, pp. 103–124.

[21] William R. Easterly, *The Elusive Quest for Growth: Economists' Adventures and Misadventures in the Tropics*, Cambridge, Mass.: MIT Press, 2001; Robert E. Klitgaard, *Institutional Adjustment and Adjusting to Institutions*, Washington, D.C.: World Bank, 1995; Nicolas van de Walle, *African Economies and the Politics of Permanent Crisis, 1979–1999*, Cambridge, U.K.: Cambridge University Press, 2001; Judith Tendler, *Good Government in the Tropics*, Baltimore, Md.: Johns Hopkins University Press, 1997; Jane Stromseth, David Wippman, and Rosa Brooks, *Can Might Make Rights? Building the Rule of Law After Military Interventions*, New York: Cambridge University Press, 2006, pp. 137–140.

for the insurgent's purpose is one that, by definition, can attract the largest number of supporters and repel the minimum of opponents."[22] Insurgents have taken advantage of all types of problems. Sometimes the cause is social. Class exploitation motivated a number of Marxist-Leninist insurgencies in Latin America, Africa, and Asia during the Cold War. Sometimes it is economic. The Chinese Communists capitalized on the plight of Chinese farmers, who were victims of exactions by authorities and the rapacity of local usurers. Poor governance may indicate disorganization, weakness, or incompetence—creating a window of opportunity for insurgents to win popular support.

In Pakistan, governance challenges may be a significant cause of instability. According to World Bank estimates, governmental effectiveness in Pakistan was in the bottom 25 percent of the world—worse than that of many countries in the region, such as China, Sri Lanka, and India. The same was true in a range of related categories, in which Pakistan ranked low in the rule of law (bottom 19.1 percent in the world) and political stability (bottom 1.4 percent).[23] Figure 4.3 plots the governmental effectiveness of Pakistan and other countries in the region. Even before the upsurge in violence after 2001, governmental effectiveness in Pakistan was low.

Corruption can be a particularly invidious challenge. It can undermine support for the government and increase support for insurgents. Corruption hampers economic growth, disproportionately burdens the poor, undermines the rule of law, and damages government legitimacy. It has a supply side (those who give bribes) and a demand side (public officials who take them).[24] At its core, corruption is the misuse of entrusted power for private gain. It can involve high-level officials with discretionary authority over government policies or lower-level officials who make decisions about enforcing (or not enforcing) regula-

[22] Galula, *Counterinsurgency Warfare*, pp. 19–20.

[23] World Bank, *Governance Matters 2009: Worldwide Governance Indicators, 1996–2008*, Washington, D.C., 2009; Daniel Kaufmann, Aart Kraay, and Massimo Mastruzzi, *Governance Matters VIII: Aggregate and Individual Governance Indicators 1996–2008*, Policy Research Working Paper 4978, Washington, D.C., 2009, p. 6.

[24] Transparency International, *Global Corruption Report 2006*, Berlin, 2006.

Figure 4.3
Government Effectiveness in Pakistan and Neighboring States

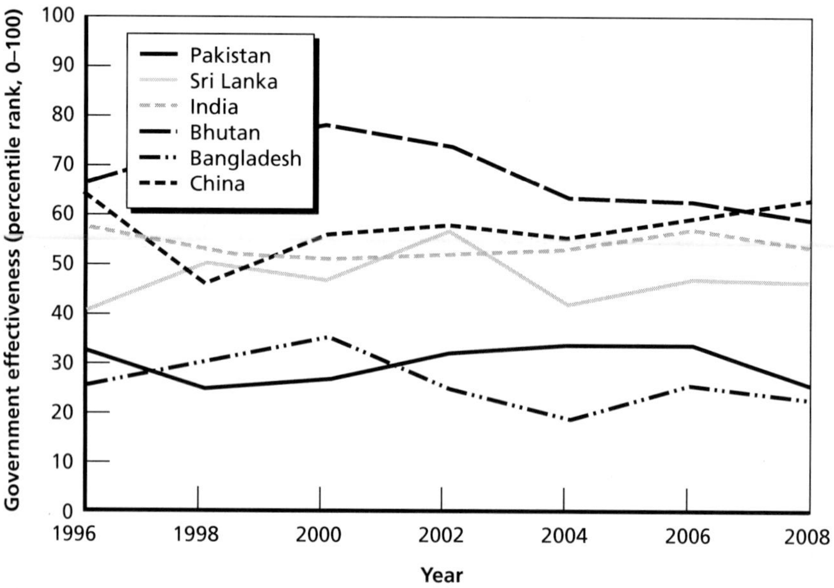

SOURCE: World Bank, *Governance Matters 2009: Worldwide Governance Indicators, 1996–2008*, Washington, D.C., 2009.
RAND *MG982-4.3*

tions. Corruption also slows economic growth. It is often responsible for funneling scarce public resources away from projects that benefit the society and toward projects that benefit specific individuals. However, the most damaging effect of corruption is its consequences for the social fabric of society: Corruption undermines the population's trust in the political system, political institutions, and political leadership.[25] Data from the World Bank and Transparency International indicate that Pakistan was in the bottom 24.6 percent and 23 percent respectively of countries worldwide.[26]

---

[25] Daniel Kaufmann, "Myths and Realities of Governance and Corruption," in World Economic Forum, *Global Competitiveness Report, 2005–2006*, Geneva, 2005, pp. 81–98.

[26] World Bank, *Governance Matters 2009*; Transparency International, *Corruption Perceptions Index 2009*, Berlin, 2009. Transparency International ranked Pakistan 139 out of 180 countries worldwide.

For Pakistan to develop more-effective counterinsurgency strategies it will have to address local grievances. Some of these could be addressed by ensuring better delivery of such services as electricity and water, improving the administration of justice, or implementing more effective anticorruption efforts. As David Kilcullen argues, however, governance in Pakistan does not necessarily mean extending the central government's reach:

> the idea that extending the reach of government into the [FATA] is the solution to all its problems is misguided, since external government (as distinct from self-governance by informal but robust tribal institutions) is both alien and abhorrent to many tribal Pashtuns.[27]

Whether the solution is better central or local governance, or both, the point is still the same: Effective counterinsurgency operations in Pakistan need to address the political, economic, and social grievances that are fueling the insurgency.

The Police

The capabilities of government security forces, especially police, are also key factors in effective counterinsurgency efforts. Both quantitative and qualitative research indicates that insurgents are better able to survive and prosper if the security forces they oppose are relatively weak and lack legitimacy in the eyes of the population.[28] At the tactical and operational levels, such forces have numerous ideal characteristics. Among the most important are a high level of initiative, good intelligence, integration across units and services, quality leadership, motivated soldiers, and the ability to learn and adapt during combat.[29]

---

[27] Kilcullen, *The Accidental Guerrilla*, p. 232.

[28] Fearon and Laitin, "Ethnicity, Insurgency, and Civil War," pp. 75–90; Byman, "Friends Like These: Counterinsurgency and the War on Terrorism," *International Security*, Vol. 31, No. 2, Fall 2006, pp. 79–115; Daniel Byman, *Going to War with the Allies You Have: Allies, Counterinsurgency and the War on Terrorism*, Carlisle, Pa.: Strategic Studies Institute, U.S. Army War College, November 2005.

[29] Daniel Byman, "Friends Like These," pp. 79–115; Byman, *Going to War with the Allies You Have*.

As Figure 4.4 illustrates, there is some correlation between government competence at counterinsurgency and success.[30] Governments with competent security forces won in two-thirds of all completed insurgencies, but governments with medium or low competence defeated less than one-third of the insurgencies.

A condition of emerging anarchy may occur if a government's security forces are feeble and cannot establish, in the German sociologist Max Weber's words, a "monopoly of the legitimate use of physical force within a given territory."[31] The state's security forces may be trained for conventional rather than counterinsurgency war, overpowered by

Figure 4.4
Competency of Security Forces and Success

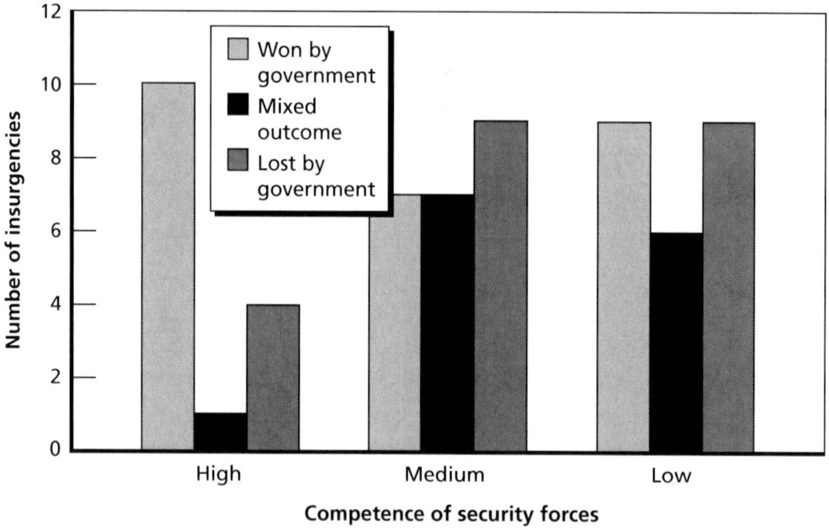

RAND *MG982-4.4*

---

[30] We assessed the capability of government security forces by making a qualitative judgment about how competent their forces were in conducting counterinsurgency warfare. We tried to avoid the endogeneity problem of coding forces as competent if the government won—and incompetent if they lost. Rather, we relied on the judgments of area specialists and historians that covered each insurgency. Unpublished RAND research for the U.S. Department of Defense.

[31] Max Weber, "Politics as a Vocation," in H. H. Gerth and C. Wright Mills, eds., *From Max Weber: Essays in Sociology*, New York: Oxford University Press, 1958, p. 78.

opposition groups, poorly motivated, corrupt, politically divided, and deeply hated by the local population.[32] When a state's security institutions are weak, opposition groups are able to take advantage and engage in competitive state-building.[33] Since the state is too weak to establish law and order within its own territory, groups that can establish order fill the vacuum. The more extreme the decline or absence of authority in a region, the more the population becomes "virgin territory" for those who would create an alternative government.[34] Political entrepreneurs often flourish and finance their private militias through both licit and illicit activity. Simple banditry may become endemic. Criminal activity can also escalate sharply as groups seek to fund their activities.[35]

The police are particularly important. In Pakistan, however, the police suffer from low levels of morale and competence.[36] Public opinion polls have indicated low levels of support for the Pakistani police, especially compared to other Pakistani governance institutions.[37] Like the Frontier Corps and Frontier Constabulary, insurgents have overtaken police stations in Swat and Buner with brute force and set up their own police operations. In spring 2009, when TNSM leader Maulana Fazlullah told police in Swat to leave their jobs or face punishment, 700 of the 1,700 officers deserted their posts.[38] Analysts in Pakistan

---

32 Byman, "Friends Like These," pp. 79–115; Byman, *Going to War with the Allies You Have.*

33 World Bank, *Reforming Public Institutions and Strengthening Governance*, Washington, D.C., 2000; Jessica Einhorn, "The World Bank's Mission Creep," *Foreign Affairs*, Vol. 80, No. 5, 2001, pp. 22–35.

34 Stathis N. Kalyvas, *The Logic of Violence in Civil War*, New York: Cambridge University Press, 2006, p. 216; Timothy P. Wickham-Crowley, *Guerrillas and Revolution in Latin America: A Comparative Study of Insurgents and Regimes Since 1956*, Princeton, N.J.: Princeton University Press, 1992, p. 35.

35 Stromseth, Wippman, and Brooks, *Can Might Make Rights?* pp. 137–140.

36 Abbas, *Police & Law Enforcement Reform in Pakistan.*

37 IRI, "IRI Index: Pakistan Public Opinion Survey, July 15–August 7, 2009," Washington, D.C., 2009.

38 Paul Wiseman and Zafar M. Sheikh, "Pakistani Police Underfunded, Overwhelmed," *USA Today*, May 5, 2009.

interviewed by one of the authors believed that militants had avoided targeting the army out of concern that consistent attacks would provoke a stronger and more-effective response. Thus, targeting the Frontier Constabulary and Frontier Corps strips individuals of their confidence in the armed forces without directly challenging the army.[39] In 2009, however, insurgents increasingly attacked army and ISI targets following the army's operations in Swat. These attacks likely bolstered public opposition to peace deals, increased public support for military action, and galvanized the Pakistan Army to renew its commitment to fighting domestic militants and widening the fight to South Waziristan in fall 2009.

Military and paramilitary forces are, of course, important for counterinsurgency operations, especially if insurgent groups are large, enjoy a robust support base, are equipped like conventional armies, and can hold territory. Pakistan's army and Frontier Corps have struggled. Figure 4.5 highlights World Bank data on the effectiveness of Pakistan's police and other rule-of-law agencies, based on local perceptions. Pakistan has performed worse than most countries in the region.

The Pakistan Army has continued to use large deployments and intense and indiscriminate firepower employing heavy munitions causing extensive collateral damage in its operations in FATA and NWFP. It also uses deeply unpopular cordon-and-search operations, aerial bombardments, and sustained firing of unguided artillery.[40] The army's doctrinal and operational shortcomings are exacerbated by the inhospitable terrain of the tribal areas, the army's weak logistical abilities, shortcomings in Pakistan's technical intelligence, and the unfriendly local population—all of which has motivated the army to counter resistance with excessive force for counterinsurgency operations.[41] The Frontier

---

[39] Author interviews in Pakistan in February and April 2009.

[40] Julian E. Barnes, "Pakistan to Crack Down on Rebels: The Military Plans to Push into Lawless Regions Used by Al Qaeda, a Move the U.S. Has Sought," *Los Angeles Times*, July 29, 2008.

[41] Conversations with U.S. military officials in the Office of Defense Representation Pakistan (ODRP, at the U.S. Embassy in Islamabad in April 2008, with U.S. officials in the Office of the Secretary of Defense in May and July 2008, with U.S. officials at U.S. CENTCOM in August 2008. Also see Tellis, *Pakistan and the War on Terror*.

Figure 4.5
Rule of Law in Pakistan and Neighboring States

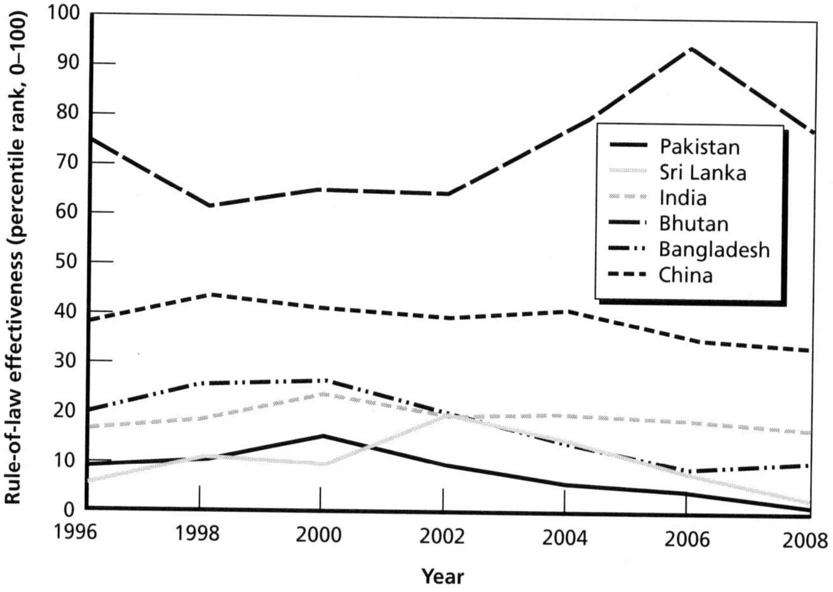

SOURCES: World Bank, *Governance Matters 2009*, and Daniel Kaufmann, Aart Kraay, and Massimo Mastruzzi, *Governance Matters VIII: Aggregate and Individual Governance Indicators, 1996–2008*, Policy Research Working Paper 4978, Washington, D.C.: World Bank, 2009, p. 6.
RAND *MG982-4.5*

Corps has generally not been trained and equipped to be a serious counterinsurgency force, although joint training with U.S. SOF may have improved the corps' competence. Still, it lacks emergency medical evacuation capabilities and other logistical capacity and has a long history of distrusting the army to provide this sort of support.

But police and intelligence units have been particularly critical against insurgent and terrorist groups. One study found that terrorist groups end for two major reasons: Members decide to adopt nonviolent tactics and join the political process (43 percent), or local law enforcement agencies arrest or kill key members of the group (40 percent). Military force has rarely been the primary reason for terrorist groups to end

(7 percent), and few groups have ever achieved victory (10 percent).[42] Among religious groups, the percentage that ends because of police action is even higher: 73 percent of religious groups ended through policing and intelligence operations, while only 11 percent ended through a political settlement, and 16 percent ended through military force.

The police are perhaps the most critical component for ensuring the safety of the people. The police are the primary arm of the government focused on internal security. Unlike the military, they usually have a permanent presence in cities, towns, and villages; a better understanding of the threat environment in these areas; and better intelligence. This makes them a direct target of insurgent forces, who often try to kill or infiltrate them.[43] Nevertheless, an effective police force is critical to establishing law and order.[44] Government military forces may be able to penetrate and garrison an insurgent area and, if well sustained, may reduce guerrilla activity. But once the situation in an area becomes untenable for insurgents, they will simply transfer their activities to another area, and the problem will remain unresolved.[45] A viable indigenous police force with a permanent presence in urban and rural areas is a critical component of counterinsurgency. Without a strong local police force, warlords and political entrepreneurs often flourish and finance their private militias through criminal activity, including trafficking in arms and drugs. Simple banditry—fueled by military desertion, the breakdown of social structures, and demobilization of government forces—may be endemic, and crime will increase.[46]

---

[42] Jones and Libicki, *How Terrorist Groups End*.

[43] Trinquier, *Modern Warfare*, p. 43; Galula, *Counterinsurgency Warfare*, p. 31.

[44] For a series of cases of South Asian counterinsurgency germane to this volume, see Fair and Ganguly, eds., *Treading on Hallowed Ground*.

[45] As David Galula argues: "[C]onventional operations by themselves have at best no more effect than a fly swatter. Some guerrillas are bound to be caught, but new recruits will replace them as fast as they are lost." Galula, *Counterinsurgency Warfare*, p. 72.

[46] Stromseth, Wippman, and Brooks, *Can Might Make Rights?* pp. 137–140.

Police and other security agencies also need to shift focus to protecting the local population. As the U.S. Army and Marine Corps's Counterinsurgency Field Manual noted,

> Progress in building support for the [host nation] government requires protecting the local populace. People who do not believe they are secure from insurgent intimidation, coercion, and reprisals will not risk overtly supporting [counterinsurgency] efforts.[47]

In short, the competence of police and the quality of governance have historically affected the success—or failure—of counterinsurgency efforts. The likelihood of success appears to increase with better police and other security forces, as well as more effective governments that can deliver services to their populations. This suggests focusing more efforts in Pakistan toward better policing and intelligence, rather than concentrating predominantly on the army.

Influencing Political Will

In addition to improving counterinsurgency capabilities, it is also necessary to influence political will. Pakistan's security agencies have targeted some militant groups but not others. Individuals within ISI and other Pakistani agencies have directly assisted Mullah Mohammad Omar's Taliban and the Haqqani network, which pose a threat to U.S. interests in neighboring Afghanistan. But Pakistani security agencies have also targeted a range of militants in South Waziristan, Bajaur, Swat, and other locations.

Pakistan's continuing assistance to some militant groups illustrates a persuasion failure for the United States and other countries. Persuasion, as used here, describes efforts to change the behavior of a state by manipulating its costs and benefits through political, eco-

[47] U.S. Army and U.S. Marine Corps, *Counterinsurgency Field Manual*, Chicago: University of Chicago Press, 2007, p. 179.

nomic, and other instruments.[48] Persuasion generally involves getting another to change its behavior and involves two sets of actors: a sender state, which attempts to persuade another to change its behavior, and a target state, which the sender tries to influence.[49] The sender has a range of political, economic, and military instruments to choose from, which can usefully be divided into two categories.

The first are sticks. States can use economic instruments to persuade a target, such as imposing trade sanctions, boycotting goods, suspending aid, freezing financial assets, and manipulating tariff rates.[50] A sender can also use political instruments to persuade another state, such as recalling ambassadors, refusing to recognize its existence (as many Arab countries have done with Israel), or "shaming" it by revealing potentially embarrassing information about such issues as human rights abuses. In extreme cases, states can use—or threaten to use—military force to influence the behavior of a target. In some instances, this may even include conducting military strikes on another state's territory without its permission, as the United States did in Cambodia during the Vietnam War. The threat of force is sometimes sufficient for persuasion to be successful. As Nobel laureate Thomas Schelling wrote in his book *Arms and Influence*, "It is the threat of damage, or of more damage to come, that can make someone yield or comply."[51]

A second category includes carrots. A sender can provide economic inducements, such as money, debt forgiveness, most favored

---

[48] The *Oxford English Dictionary* defines *to persuade* as "to urge successfully to do something" and "to attract, induce, or entice to something or in a particular direction." See *Oxford English Dictionary*, New York: Oxford University Press, 2009. This is sometimes referred to as *coercion* or *compellence*. See, for example, Thomas C. Schelling, *Arms and Influence*, New Haven, Conn.: Yale University Press, 1966, pp. 100, 103, 172; Thomas C. Schelling, *The Strategy of Conflict*, Cambridge, Mass.: Harvard University Press, 1960, pp. 195–199; Gordon A. Craig and Alexander L. George, *Force and Statecraft: Diplomatic Problems of Our Time*, 3rd ed., New York: Oxford University Press, 1995, p. 196.

[49] Daniel Byman and Matthew Waxman, *The Dynamics of Coercion: American Foreign Policy and the Limits of Military Might*, New York: Cambridge University Press, 2002, pp. 3–4; Paul Huth and Bruce Russett, "Testing Deterrence Theory: Rigor Makes a Difference," *World Politics*, Vol. 42., No. 4, July 1990, p. 475.

[50] Drezner, *The Sanctions Paradox*, p. 3.

[51] Schelling, *Arms and Influence*, pp. 3, 82.

nation trading status, or assistance in acquiring loans from international institutions, such as the World Bank or International Monetary Fund. Another carrot includes political benefits. This can take many forms, such as restoring diplomatic relations and offering entry into an international organization. The European Union, for example, has membership requirements, referred to as the "Copenhagen criteria," which are useful coercive tools toward potential members.[52] Finally, a state can provide military and other security assistance—and can promise more in the future—if the target state changes its behavior. Military aid can involve a vast array of goods, such as arms, weapon systems, technology, and training. It can also include intelligence information that may be of interest to the target state.

Table 4.1 summarizes the range of instruments available to sender states across three categories: military, economic, and political. The table is meant to be illustrative rather than exhaustive but has direct relevance to dealing with Pakistan.

Both carrots and sticks are important. As discussed later in this chapter, however, effectively persuading Pakistan requires a combination of both carrots and sticks that is tailored to the target state's strengths and weaknesses.

Cost-Benefit Calculations

Persuasion is more an art than a science.[53] The challenge of persuasion is convincing the target state that acceding to the sender's demands will be less painful and more beneficial than resisting them. Success and failure depend on the target state's cost-benefit calculation, as well as on the sender's cost-benefit calculation. The target state weighs the values it sets on both its existing position and its new position were it to accede to demands. The sender, on the other hand, must evaluate possible concessions in case negotiations become necessary.[54]

---

[52] European Council, "Conclusions of the Presidency," Copenhagen, June 21–22, 1993.

[53] See, for example, Schelling, Arms and Influence; and Robert A. Pape, *Bombing to Win: Air Power and Coercion in War*, Ithaca: Cornell University Press, 1996.

[54] Schelling, *Arms and Influence*, p. 4.

Table 4.1
Menu of Carrots and Sticks

	Example of Carrots	Example of Sticks
Economic	Financial aid Debt forgiveness Most-favored nation trading status Assistance in getting loans from international financial institutions	Trade sanctions Boycott on goods Suspension of aid Freezing of financial assets Manipulation of tariff rates
Political	Entry into an international institution (e.g., the World Trade Organization) Restoring diplomatic relations	Cutting off diplomatic ties Refusing to recognize a state's existence "Shaming" by revealing embarrassing information
Military	Arms Weapon systems Dual-use technology Intelligence Training	Limited strikes Invasion Threat of attack Aid to a target's adversary

Persuasion succeeds to the extent that the sender can credibly threaten to impose costs on the target that are greater than the value the target assigns to resisting. This involves finding and manipulating the target's pressure points. Persuasion fails when the target assesses that the costs of resisting are lower than they are for acceding to the sender's demands.[55]

Manipulating a target's cost-benefit calculations requires understanding several conditions. One is that costs and benefits are important at two levels: the international level and the domestic level. Political scientist Robert Putnam referred to this as a two-level game.[56] One level involves bargaining between the target and the sender, and the other involves bargaining between the target and its domestic population (and often the sender and its own population). At the domestic level, targets may have to worry about pressure from political parties,

55 Gary Schaub, Jr., "Compellence: Resuscitating the Concept," in Lawrence Freedman, ed., *Strategic Coercion: Concepts and Cases*, New York: Oxford University Press, 1998, p. 44.

56 Robert D. Putnam, "Diplomacy and Domestic Politics: The Logic of Two-Level Games," *International Organization*, Vol. 42, No. 3, Summer 1988, pp. 427–460.

special interest groups, and public opinion within its broader population. In response to U.S. efforts to persuade Pakistan to target militant groups operating on its soil, Pakistani government officials have been forced to consider (a) the effects on their relationship with the United States and other countries, such as India, and (b) the impact among Pakistani constituencies at home. Weighing costs and benefits is important at both levels.

Indeed, successful persuasion needs to involve an understanding of international and domestic factors that influence the target's behavior and its cost-benefit calculation. The sender needs to find ways to manipulate these interests through a combination of carrots and sticks. As political scientist Andrew Moravcsik argued,

> statesmen are typically trying to do two things at once . . . they seek to manipulate domestic and international politics simultaneously. Diplomatic strategies and tactics are constrained both by what other states will accept and by what domestic constituencies will ratify.[57]

Pakistan's domestic political situation has important implications for any persuasion strategy. Pakistani citizens have tended to oppose cooperation with the United States. This does not necessarily indicate that Pakistanis oppose operations against militants on their soil, since polls indicate a growing concern about Taliban and al Qa'ida activity in Pakistan. Instead, it suggests that they oppose operations that appear to be part of a U.S.—not Pakistani—government agenda. Roughly three-quarters of Pakistanis oppose U.S. military incursions into the tribal areas, and over three-quarters opposed U.S. drone strikes in Pakistan (though not necessarily Pakistani drone strikes). In addition, Pakistani

---

[57] Andrew Moravcsik, "Introduction: Integrating International and Domestic Theories of International Bargaining," in Peter B. Evans, Harold K. Jacobson, and Robert D. Putnam, *Double-Edged Diplomacy: International Bargaining and Domestic Politics*, Berkeley: University of California Press, 1993, p. 15.

views of the United States tend to be more negative than those in many other countries, including Saudi Arabia and China.[58]

Beginning in late 2006, IRI periodically asked its nationally representative sample of respondents whether they thought that "Pakistan should cooperate with the United States on its war against terror?" Similar to the findings of the USIP/PIPA poll showing that Pakistanis opposed U.S. military action on Pakistani territory (mentioned in Chapter Three), IRI found that Pakistanis also largely rejected their country's cooperation with the United States. As Figure 4.6 illustrates, opposition fell from a high of 89 percent in January 2008 to 63 percent by October 2008, then rose to 80 percent by July 2009. While Pakistanis generally believed that a wide array of militants threatened their own nation's security, they remained opposed to significant cooperation with the United States.[59] Consequently, any persuasion strategy needs to understand Pakistan's domestic situation, including how Pakistanis view the U.S.-Pakistani relationship.

In addition, persuasion may be easier with allies than with adversaries because the costs of acceding are lower. This is particularly important for the U.S. relationship with Pakistan. Despite disagreements, Pakistan remains an important ally of the United States, for example, in such areas as counterterrorism cooperation between U.S. intelligence and military agencies and the Counterterrorism Wing of the ISI. Much of the literature has focused on efforts to change the behavior of an adversary, such as the Soviet Union during the Cold War (to remove its medium-range ballistic missiles from Cuba) or Iran today (to give up its nuclear weapon program). But states can also seek to persuade allies. As Daniel Drezner found, a state is more likely to try to change the behavior of another state when the target is an ally, not an adversary. The logic is straightforward. The target's conflict expectations determine the magnitude of concessions. Facing an adversary, a

[58] The data in this paragraph are from IRI, "IRI Index: Pakistan Public Opinion Survey, July 15–August 7, 2009," Washington, D.C., 2009.

[59] Data taken from the March 7–30, 2009 poll of Pakistan. See IRI, "IRI Releases Survey of Pakistan Public Opinion, March 7–30, 2009," May 11, 2009. Also see IRI, "IRI Index: Pakistan Public Opinion Survey July 15–August 7, 2009," October 2009.

Figure 4.6
Pakistani Views of the United States

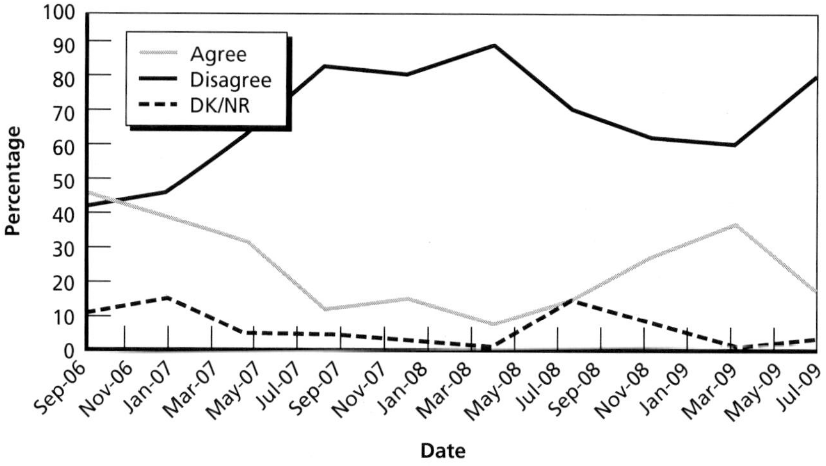

SOURCE: IRI, survey data for July 15–August 7, 2009.
RAND *MG982-4.6*

target may be worried about the long-run implications of acquiescing. Because it expects frequent conflict, the target will be concerned about concessions in the present undercutting its bargaining positions in the future. But allies will anticipate fewer disputes and care less about relative gains and reputation.[60]

Finally, several other variables may affect the outcome of persuasion: the value of the objective under dispute to each of the parties involved, the relative capabilities of the states involved, the power that they are willing to bring to bear on the dispute, and the extent to which they can credibly convey this information to one another. In some cases, for example, an overwhelming imbalance of military capabilities, in which the sender is the stronger state, may help compel the target. As one study concludes, "it may be that an overwhelming imbalance of military capabilities is sufficient to overawe the target state into compliance with the compeller's demands."[61] But an asym-

---

60 Drezner, *The Sanctions Paradox*, pp. 4-5.

61 Schaub "Compellence: Resuscitating the Concept," p. 51.

metry in military capabilities is neither a sufficient nor a necessary condition for effective persuasion, and there are numerous examples of more powerful sender states failing to persuade much weaker targets.[62]

Key Steps

In manipulating the target's costs and benefits, the history of persuasion suggests that the following steps are often critical for success: laying out clear demands, establishing a deadline for compliance, using an array of carrots and sticks, and monitoring compliance. These steps have important implications for Pakistan.

Clear Demands. Successful persuasion generally requires the sender to make a clear, unambiguous demand through written or oral communication. Clarity is important because it helps policymakers in the target state choose from among several possible responses and can help persuade the target of the sender's resilience.[63] It can also be helpful in indicating what is not required of the target and in bounding the sender's demands. As one study concludes,

> clarity of objectives and demands . . . can be of major importance also to the [target's] side. It may desire precise settlement terms to safeguard itself against the possibility that the coercing power has in mind a broader, more sweeping interpretation of the formula for ending the crisis or will be tempted to renew pressure and push for even greater concessions.[64]

Yet discretion is sometimes important. A public threat may undermine the ability of a target to concede if it loses too much support and prestige from its domestic population. "Public communication," one study

---

[62] Byman and Waxman, *The Dynamics of Coercion*, p. 1.

[63] Alexander L. George and William E. Simons, "Findings and Conclusion," in Alexander L. George and Williams E. Simons, eds., *The Limits of Coercive Diplomacy*, 2nd ed., Boulder, Colo.: Westview Press, 1994, pp. 267–294.

[64] Alexander L. George, *Forceful Persuasion: Coercive Diplomacy as an Alternative to War*, Washington, D.C.: U.S. Institute of Peace, 1991, p. 80; Paul Gordon Lauren, "Coercive Diplomacy and Ultimata: Theory and Practice in History," in George and Simons, eds., *The Limits of Coercive Diplomacy*.

concludes, "also has the less desirable effect of making it more difficult for the adversary to comply without a high cost in its power reputation."[65]

Ambiguous demands have often been counterproductive. In the late 1930s, the United States became increasingly concerned about Japanese expansion into China, which the Japanese referred to as creating a "great East Asia coprosperity sphere." In 1939, U.S. policymakers bluntly threatened Japan, placing an embargo on some Japanese military goods, canceling credits, and abrogating the Japanese-American commercial treaty of 1911. But U.S. policymakers never made clear what they wanted the Japanese to do. To maintain leverage, Cordell Hull, the U.S. Secretary of State, was reluctant to stop all trade with Japan. As Gordon Craig and Alexander George argue, the United States sent "conflicting signals, containing elements of both a hard and a moderate line, for some time, reflecting a lack of consensus among policymakers in Washington." The confusion undermined U.S. efforts and "the American failure to clarify and, particularly, to limit policy objectives from the beginning enormously strengthened Japanese motivation not to comply."[66] In dealing with Nicaragua, the Reagan administration's ambiguous demands to the Sandinista regime undermined successful persuasion. "There was much intra-administration disagreement over what U.S. objectives regarding Nicaragua should be—indeed, often over what they were—at any given point in time," concluded one study.[67]

With Pakistan, the United States and its allies—from China to NATO and the European Union—need to establish clear demands that Pakistan end its support to militant groups. Examples include groups conducting attacks in Afghanistan, such as the Haqqani network and

---

[65] Russell Leng, "Influence Strategies and Interstate Conflict," in J. David Singer, ed., *The Correlates of War II: Testing Some Realpolitik Models*, New York: Free Press, 1980, pp. 137–138; and Peter Viggo Jakobsen, "The Strategy of Coercive Diplomacy: Refining Existing Theory to Post–Cold War Realities," in Freedman, ed., *Strategic Coercion*, p. 66.

[66] Craig and George, *Force and Statecraft*, pp. 200–201.

[67] Bruce W. Jentleson, "The Reagan Administration Versus Nicaragua: The Limits of 'Type C' Coercive Diplomacy," in George and Simons, eds., *The Limits of Coercive Diplomacy*, p. 180.

Taliban, and groups targeting India, such as Lashkar-e-Taiba. While discretion is sometimes important, Pakistan's failure to terminate existing links with militant groups should be met with increasing public demands, including through the United Nations. The Pakistan Army has accused the United States of repeatedly changing its demands—then telling Pakistan to do "more." Doing more should not be the U.S. mantra. But there should be clear definitions of what the end game should be, especially cutting ties to militant groups.

Deadline for Compliance. Another factor is establishing a deadline for compliance; the target needs to be convinced that it must alter its behavior by a certain point. "There has to be a deadline," notes Schelling, "otherwise tomorrow never comes." If the target state

> advances like Zeno's tortoise that takes infinitely long to reach the border by traversing, with infinite patience, the infinitely small remaining distances that separate him from collision, it creates no inducement to vacate the border.[68]

When the action carries no clear deadline, there are no consequences for stalling. To be effective, persuasion must be tied to a specific action within a given time frame. As Craig and George argue, "the coercing power must create in the opponent's mind a sense of urgency for compliance with its demand."[69]

---

[68] Schelling, *Arms and Influence*, p. 72. In the paradox of Achilles and the tortoise, Achilles is in a footrace with the tortoise. Achilles allows the tortoise a head start of 100 feet. If we suppose that each racer starts running at some constant speed (one very fast and one very slow), Achilles will have run 100 feet after some finite time, bringing him to the tortoise's starting point. During this time, the tortoise has run a much shorter distance, for example, 10 feet. It will then take Achilles some further time to run that distance, in which time the tortoise will have advanced farther. Then still more time will elapse as Achilles reaches this third point, and the tortoise continues to move ahead. Thus, whenever Achilles reaches somewhere the tortoise has been, he still has farther to go. Therefore, because there are an infinite number of points Achilles must reach where the tortoise has already been, he can never overtake the tortoise.

[69] Craig and George, *Force and Statecraft*, p. 197.

There are several ways to transmit a sense of urgency, most notably through oral or written communication.[70] In setting time limits, states do not need to resort to hours but can use days, weeks, or even months to convey a sense of urgency. Many, however, have chosen short deadlines to maximize pressure—including issuing ultimatums. An ultimatum can be used to deliberately speed up a bargaining process, convey a sense that time is running out because a clock is ticking, and push a target to quickly comply with the demands.[71] With Pakistan, a deadline for ending support to militant groups may be important, although the United States and other countries would need to think carefully about how to do it. Of particular importance may be linking carrots and sticks to a deadline, including U.S. aid.

Carrots and Sticks. Both carrots and sticks are important for manipulating the target's cost-benefit calculations. Relying solely on sticks may convince the target that compliance will result only in more sender demands in the future and may make the target more resolute. Relying solely on carrots creates little pain if the target fails to cooperate.[72]

Carrots are required in most cases because compliance is often extremely costly for the target.[73] When the Soviet Union collapsed in 1991, an independent Ukraine was "born nuclear" with more than 4,000 nuclear weapons on or under its soil. In November 1994, the Rada in Kiev voted overwhelmingly to join the Non-Proliferation Treaty as a nonnuclear state, and all weapons were removed from

---

70 Alexander L. George, "Theory and Practice," in George and Simons, eds., *The Limits of Coercive Diplomacy*, p. 17.

71 Alexander L. George and William E. Simons, "Findings and Conclusion," in George and Simons, eds., *The Limits of Coercive Diplomacy*, p. 282.

72 Glenn H. Snyder and Paul Diesing, *Conflict Among Nations: Bargaining, Decision Making, and System Structure In International Crises*, Princeton, N.J., Princeton University Press, 1977; Paul K. Huth, *Extended Deterrence and the Prevention of War*, New Haven, Conn.: Yale University Press, 1988; Steven Greffenius and Jungil Gill, "Pure Coercion vs. Carrot-and-Stick Offers in Crisis Bargaining," *Journal of Peace Research*, Vol. 29, No. 1, February 1992, pp. 39–52. Game theory work on cooperation also suggests a mix of carrots and sticks. See, for example, Robert Axelrod, *The Evolution of Cooperation*, New York: Basic Books, 1984.

73 Greffenius and Gill, "Pure Coercion," p. 50.

Ukrainian territory by June 1996. Ukraine had many reasons not to take this action. Given the history of Russian expansionism and tensions over Crimea, it seemed logical that Ukraine would keep nuclear weapons as a deterrent against a future revanchist Russia.[74] Economic sticks—and carrots—were critical to Ukraine's decision. The United States and NATO allies encouraged Kiev to give up the arsenal by persuading it that not following the Non-Proliferation Treaty norm would have negative economic consequences.[75] The United States also provided economic inducements, such as Nunn-Lugar payments to help transport and destroy the weapons.[76]

In addition, the historical evidence suggests that sticks alone are usually insufficient to persuade the target state.[77] Target states can often endure substantial amounts of punishment rather than succumb to the demands of senders. Instead of coercing states into changing their behavior, sanctions often have the opposite result: They create a "rally around the flag" effect among populations, as the U.S. sanctions on Fidel Castro's Cuba demonstrate.[78] Leaders may also be able to shift

---

74 John J. Mearsheimer, "The Case for a Ukrainian Nuclear Deterrent," *Foreign Affairs*, Vol. 72, No. 3, Summer 1993, pp. 50–66; Barry R. Posen, "The Security Dilemma and Ethnic Conflict," *Survival*, Vol. 35, No. 1, Spring 1993.

75 Sherman W. Garnett, "Ukraine's Decision to Join the NPT," *Arms Control Today*, Vol. 25, No. 1, January/February 1995, pp. 10–12.

76 Scott D. Sagan, "Why Do States Build Nuclear Weapons? Three Models in Search of a Bomb," *International Security*, Vol. 21, No. 3, Winter 1996–1997, pp. 54–86.

77 On the utility of economic sticks, for example, see, Robert A. Pape, "Why Economic Sanctions Do Not Work," *International Security*, Vol. 22, No. 2, Autumn 1997, p. 93. Also see Robert A. Pape, "Why Economic Sanctions Still Do Not Work," *International Security*, Vol. 23, No. 1, Summer 1998, pp. 66–77; T. Clifton Morgan and Valerie L. Schwebach, "Fools Suffer Gladly: The Use of Economic Sanctions in International Crises," *International Studies Quarterly*, Vol. 41, No. 1, March 1997, pp. 27–50; Johan Galtung, "On the Effects of International Economic Sanctions: With Examples from the Case of Rhodesia," *World Politics*, Vol. 19, No. 3, April 1967, pp. 378–416; Klaus Knorr, "Is International Coercion Waning or Rising?" *International Security*, Vol. 1, No. 4, Spring 1977, p. 103.

78 Susan Kaufman Purcell, "Cuba," in Haass, *Economic Sanctions and American Diplomacy*, pp. 35–56.

the sanctioning costs away from key supporters.[79] Indeed, while economic persuasion may be effective in persuading states to make limited changes in economic policy, it has not tended to be effective in coercing changes of behavior in the security field. In 1968, for example, the United States suspended economic aid to Peru to discourage it from buying military aircraft from France. But the volume of American aid to Peru was small, and Peruvians decided they could do without it.

There is no clear rule of thumb on which combination of carrots and sticks is most likely to be effective; it depends on the target's pressure points and other conditions unique to the sender and target states. With Pakistan, there are both negative and positive lessons for utilizing carrots and sticks. One of the most effective U.S. persuasion efforts came following the September 11, 2001, terrorist attacks. The United States agreed to waive sanctions and provide military and nonmilitary aid, promised to forgive $2 billion of Pakistan's debt, and doled out millions of dollars in "prize money" for helping capture al Qa'ida members.[80] But it also issued a veiled threat of military force if Pakistan did not cooperate. Following blunt messages from Secretary of State Colin Powell and his deputy, Richard Armitage, Musharraf acknowledged: "I war-gamed the United States as an adversary." He concluded that Pakistan's military was significantly weaker than the U.S. military and, consequently, "our military forces would be destroyed."[81] In the end, Musharraf agreed to many of America's requests, although he refused to allow blanket U.S. overflight and landing rights and access to some of Pakistan's naval ports and air bases. The United States agreed to some of Musharraf's requests. U.S. aircraft would not fly over Pakistan's nuclear facilities; the United States would generally not launch combat operations from Pakistani soil; and the United States would provide economic assistance to Pakistan.

---

[79] David Cortright and George A. Lopez, *The Sanctions Decade: Assessing UN Strategies in the 1990s*, Boulder, Colo.: Lynne Rienner, 2000, pp. 37–61; Eric D. K. Melby, "Iraq," in Haass, *Economic Sanctions and American Diplomacy*, pp. 107–128.

[80] See, for example, Cohen and Chollet, "When $10 Billion Is Not Enough," pp. 7–19.

[81] Musharraf, *In the Line of Fire*, pp. 201–202.

There are also plenty of negative examples, such as the U.S. failure to persuade Pakistan to give up its nuclear weapon program. More recently, the U.S. government provided significant aid to persuade Pakistan to target militant groups, including offering coalition support funds, other military aid (such as providing helicopters and air assault training), and counternarcotics assistance. This assistance came through the U.S. Department of Defense, Department of State, CIA, Department of Justice, and other government agencies to support counterterrorism, internal security, and development programs.[82] The coalition support funds were particularly contentious. The United States made payments of roughly $1 billion a year to Pakistan for what it called "reimbursements" to the country's military for conducting counterterrorism efforts along the border with Afghanistan. The monthly payments were intended to reimburse Pakistan's military for the cost of the operations. Some U.S. policymakers complained that, despite the additional funding, Pakistan slashed patrols in areas where al Qa'ida and Taliban fighters were most active.[83] In addition, some Frontier Corps personnel became resentful that a significant portion of the money went to the army and was used for bolstering operations against India.[84] The bottom line, however, is that the predominant focus on carrots failed to affect Pakistan's assistance to militant groups.

Enforcement Mechanism. The final element is an enforcement mechanism to ensure that the target—as well as the sender—complies with the terms of the settlement. As Scott Sagan argues, it "requires that the compelling state appear committed not only to executing its threats if necessary but also to keeping its promises if a political settle-

---

[82] On U.S. aid to Pakistan, see Fair and Chalk, *Fortifying Pakistan*, 2006.

[83] David E. Sanger and David Rohde, "U.S. Pays Pakistan to Fight Terror, but Patrols Ebb," *New York Times*, May 20, 2007, p. 1. There were a number of additional *New York Times* investigative pieces on the coalition support funds. See, for example, David Rohde, Carlotta Gall, Eric Schmitt, and David E. Sanger, "U.S. Officials See Waste in Pakistan Aid," *New York Times*, December 24, 2007, p. A1.

[84] Author interview with Frontier Corps officials, May 2009.

ment is reached."[85] The target will invariably adopt delaying tactics to avoid—or at least postpone—compliance.[86] The target may also test whether the sender is bluffing, hoping to avoid punishment for noncompliance.[87] In Angola, the United Nations experienced substantial enforcement problems in trying to coerce the National Union for the Total Independence of Angola (UNITA) to stop the trade of "conflict diamonds."[88] In the late 1990s a series of embarrassing press reports detailed repeated violations of sanctions in Antwerp, Belgium, where an estimated 80 percent of the world's rough diamonds and more than 50 percent of polished diamonds passed through.[89] As the United Nations' "Fowler Report" stated: "The Panel found that the extremely lax controls and regulations governing the Antwerp market facilitate and perhaps even encourage illegal trading activity."[90]

To make enforcement credible, sender states need to create the impression that they are willing and able to enforce punishment, and that their threats are sufficiently potent to overcome the reluctance of targets to comply.[91] Implementation of the threat must be credible. This often depends on the costs associated with implementation, which might simply reflect the amount of resources and effort involved, as

---

85 Scott D. Sagan, "From Deterrence to Coercion to War: The Road to Pearl Harbor," in George and Simons, eds., *The Limits of Coercive Diplomacy*, p. 85.

86 Byman and Waxman, *The Dynamics of Coercion*, p. 43.

87 Jakobsen, "The Strategy of Coercive Diplomacy," p. 72.

88 For the European Union sanctions, see Council Regulation (EC) No. 1705/98, OJ L 215, 1.8.98; Common Position, 97/759/CFSP, OJ L 309, 12.11.1997; Common Position, 98/425/CFSP, OJ L 190, 4.7.1998.

89 Blaine Harden, "U.N. Sees Violation of a Diamond Ban by Angola Rebels," *New York Times*, March 11, 2000, p. A1. Also see Human Rights Watch, *Angola Unravels: The Rise and Fall of the Lusaka Peace Process*, New York, 1999; United Nations, *Final Report of the Monitoring Mechanism on Angola Sanctions*, New York, S/2000/1225, December 2000; Global Witness, *Conflict Diamonds: Possibilities for the Identification, Certification and Control of Diamonds*, London, May 2000.

90 United Nations, *Final Report of the UN Panel of Experts on Violations of Security Council Sanctions Against Unita: The "Fowler Report,"* New York, S/2000/203, March 2000.

91 Paul Gordon Lauren, "Coercive Diplomacy and Ultimata: Theory and Practice in History," in George and Simons, eds., *The Limits of Coercive Diplomacy*, p. 27.

well as the ability of the target to respond with its own forms of punishment.[92] The sender needs to create in the target's mind a fear of unacceptable escalation if the demand is not accepted.[93] The threat of punishment for noncompliance may be signaled through economic, political, or—in extreme cases—military instruments.[94]

Perhaps the most significant challenge in enforcing persuasion tactics is getting reliable intelligence to verify target behavior. Information may be fragmentary and inadequate.[95] In the economic realm, most actions are reasonably transparent, and information on compliance is often a matter of public record.[96] In the security realm, however, there are limits to transparency and information sharing. States may have an incentive to misrepresent such information, and intentions can change.[97] Despite years of trying to persuade India and Pakistan to eliminate their nuclear weapon programs, U.S. intelligence agencies failed to detect the Indian government's decision to conduct underground tests of three nuclear devices on May 11, 1998. The Indian government followed up with two more tests a few days later; within two weeks, Pakistan responded with its own tests. "We didn't have a clue," acknowledged CIA director George Tenet.[98] Senders have typically

---

[92] Lawrence Freedman, "Strategic Coercion," in Freedman, ed., *Strategic Coercion*, p. 25.

[93] Craig and George, *Force and Statecraft*, p. 197.

[94] Alexander L. George, "Theory and Practice," in George and Simons, eds., *The Limits of Coercive Diplomacy*, p. 17.

[95] See, for example, John J. Mearsheimer, *The Tragedy of Great Power Politics*, New York: W.W. Norton, 2001; Kenneth Waltz, *Theory of International Politics*, Columbus, Ohio: McGraw-Hill, 1979. Also see Robert Jervis, *Perception and Misperception in International Politics*, Princeton, N.J.: Princeton University Press, 1976.

[96] Charles Lipson, "International Cooperation in Economic and Security Affairs," *World Politics*, Vol. 37, No. 1, October 1984, pp. 17–18.

[97] James D. Fearon, "Domestic Political Audiences and the Escalation of International Disputes," *American Political Science Review*, Vol. 88, No. 3, September 1994, pp. 577–592; James D. Fearon, "Rationalist Explanations for War," *International Organization*, Vol. 49, No. 3, Summer 1995, pp. 379–414.

[98] Tenet, *At the Center of the Storm*, p. 44. Also see, for example, Gregory F. Treverton, *Reshaping National Intelligence for an Age of Information*, New York: Cambridge University Press, 2003, pp. 1–5.

verified compliance through dialogues with the target's policymakers, as well as by collecting human, signals, and other forms of intelligence on its own.

With Pakistan, a credible enforcement mechanism would entail frank intelligence-sharing and discussions with Pakistan about Pakistani support to militant groups. When the United States uncovers reliable intelligence on support to militant groups from elements of ISI and other organizations, it must be presented to Pakistan and tied to sticks.

Conclusions

While counterinsurgency and persuasion are different concepts, this chapter argues that they are deeply interlinked. Outside powers involved in a counterinsurgency regularly try to influence the behavior of the local government. For an outside power like the United States, successful counterinsurgency requires effectively persuading its partner through political, economic, and other means to prosecute the war and address its causes. Every counterinsurgency and persuasion case is different and has its own nuances. This is certainly true of Pakistan. Nonetheless, several factors have been critical to success and are important in helping design more-effective operations in Pakistan.

First, successful counterinsurgency operations are usually a function of competent security forces, especially police and intelligence organizations, which have a permanent presence in villages and can help hold territory that has been cleared of insurgents. In addition, governance needs to be improved in areas the insurgency has affected to address the specific political, social, or economic grievances of the local population.

Second, several applicable principles can increase the probability of successful persuasion, which should help guide efforts in Pakistan. One is to issue clear demands, lay out a deadline if possible, apply a combination of carrots and sticks, and implement an enforcement mechanism in case the target fails to comply. Persuasion requires finding a bargain: arranging for the target to be better off doing what the sender wants, and worse off not doing what it wants, when the target takes the punishment into account.[99] In addition, U.S. and broader multilateral efforts to persuade Pakistan must understand several macro-level conditions that are likely to affect success and failure. Persuasion is a two-level game: States negotiate with each other but also need to be concerned about their own domestic constituencies. This means recognizing that Pakistan has to make cost-benefit calculations at the international and domestic levels. "A certain level of political support at home," one study concludes, is needed for any serious use of persuasion.[100]

In Pakistan, the United States needs to better link effective persuasion and counterinsurgency measures. Improving counterinsurgency operations will allow Pakistan to counter militants and protect its own population more effectively, and a more effective persuasion strategy will allow U.S. policymakers to help shape Pakistan's policies and better influence how its aid to Pakistan is being used. The next chapter turns to more concrete policy implications for countering militants in Pakistan.

---

[99] Schelling, *Arms and Influence*, p. 70.

[100] Alexander L. George and William E. Simons, "Findings and Conclusion," in George and Simons, eds., *The Limits of Coercive Diplomacy*, p. 284.

CHAPTER FIVE

A Population-Centric Strategy

The United States has at least two major interests in Pakistan. One is defeating al Qa'ida and other militant groups that threaten the U.S. homeland and its interests overseas. The second is preventing militant groups from acquiring weapons of mass destruction, especially nuclear weapons. Pakistan has similar interests, especially protecting its homeland from militant and state-sponsored threats.

Establishing a more-effective strategy will require Pakistan to shift its cost-benefit calculations and end support to militant groups as a tool of foreign policy. Pakistan views some groups as assets and others as adversaries, a policy that has backfired and undermined Pakistan's own security. Pakistani policymakers have sometimes bristled at U.S. conditions for foreign assistance. As one Pakistani politician remarked about the 2009 Kerry-Lugar-Berman bill, "each and every page of the bill is reflective of the insulting attitude towards Pakistan."[1] Other critiques have bordered on the absurd: "It is an American attempt to capture Pakistan's nuclear assets."[2] Yet Pakistani policymakers need to realize the political reality: When the U.S. government provides aid from U.S. taxpayers, it must ensure that this aid serves American—as well as Pakistani—interests.

This chapter begins by examining Pakistan's political will to counter militant groups. There are at least three categories of groups:

---

1 "Kerry-Lugar Aid Bill Sparks Debate in Parliament," *Dawn* (Karachi), October 7, 2009.

2 Ahmed Hassan, "Kerry-Lugar Bill Widely Opposed, JI Declares," *Dawn* (Karachi), October 24, 2009.

those that Pakistan may be willing to counter because they are enemies of the state; those that are assets of the state; and those toward which Pakistan's will is mixed. The chapter then outlines a counterinsurgency and persuasion strategy.

Discerning Pakistan's Will

At least three types of militant groups receive state support. First are those groups that Pakistan cultivated as state assets and that remain state proxies, such as Lashkar-e-Taiba and Mullah Mohammad Omar's Taliban. In some cases, such as the 2010 capture of the Taliban's second in command, Mullah Abdul Ghani Baradar, Pakistan has been willing to target selected members.

A second group comprises militant groups, such as Jaish-e-Mohammad and Harkat-ul-Jihad-e-Islami, that have a history of state patronage and have long served the state in Afghanistan and India. However, unlike Lashkar-e-Taiba or the Afghan Taliban, these groups developed important fissures that emerged after 2001 in response to Pakistan's participation in the U.S.-led war on terrorism. Elements of Jaish-e-Mohammad, Harkat-ul-Jihad-e-Islami, and other Deobandi militant groups were involved in attacks against President Musharraf, the army, ISI, and Pakistan's civilian leadership. Some individuals from these Deobandi militant groups have also allied with the TTP. Even though elements of these groups have targeted the state, Pakistan has not opted to eliminate them. Rather, the strategy appears to be targeting only the individuals who threaten the state and deterring other group members from conducting attacks in Pakistan. These groups generally remain secure, perhaps because the state presumes that they may be useful at some point for pursuing Pakistan's interests.

A third set of militants includes the TTP and elements of TNSM. In some cases, Pakistani government officials have provided support to militants in these organizations and negotiated peace deals, as discussed in Chapter Three. In other cases, such as in 2009 in South Waziristan and Swat, it has targeted them when they pose a threat to the Pakistan state. Many TTP commanders have consolidated power because they are charismatic leaders, have effectively exploited local grievances, and have coerced the local population through intimidation or targeted assassination. Their rise to power has often been enabled by the absence of state authority or active state complicity. They expand their power through violence—or the threat of violence—while providing basic services, such as rudimentary dispute resolution, in areas where the state is weak. Pakistan seems to have varying strategies for dealing with TTP commanders, depending on their assessment of the costs and benefits of conducting operations against them. While the state has battled various militant groups, it has also shown an inordinate willingness to broker peace deals on terms favorable to militants. This suggests that if the peace deals were effective, the government would have been content to establish a *modus vivendi* with the commanders and their networks. Moreover, Pakistanis, who are at best ambivalent about military action and supportive of peace deals, have tended to favor this strategy.[3]

Other recent events have supported this interpretation. Following the November 2008 Lashkar-e-Taiba attacks in Mumbai, Pakistan braced for an Indian military response. Baitullah Mehsud and his TTP announced a ceasefire against the Pakistan Army to allow it to prepare for an Indian attack. In response, a high-level army official told several Pakistani journalists that Baitullah Mehsud and Maulana Fazlullah were "patriotic" Pakistanis.[4] Such a proclamation was surprising because Baitullah Mehsud had masterminded dozens of attacks against Pakistani paramilitary, military, police, and intelligence targets. Indeed, many Pakistanis believed that the government had been seeking to strike a deal with Baitullah Mehsud if he agreed to stop attacking the state and shift his focus to NATO and Afghan forces in Afghanistan. Similarly, the state has been willing to negotiate with the TNSM's leader, Sufi Mohammad, to secure peace.

3 See various national polls on Pakistani support of peace deals since 2007 conducted by IRI, available on the organization's website.

4 Hamid Mir, "Army Official Calls Baitullah Mehsud, Fazullah 'Patriots,'" *The News*, December 8, 2008.

Elements of a Persuasion Strategy

Pakistan has demonstrated wide variation in will and capacity to counter these militant groups. The United States, working with its allies, must develop a strategy that influences Pakistan's cost-benefit calculations of working with these groups. Such an approach has at least four elements:

- Press Pakistan to phase out all support for militant groups and abandon militancy as a tool of foreign policy.
- Enhance Pakistan's ability to counter militants and prosecute a population-centric counterinsurgency strategy. Even where there is a will to act, Pakistan is ill-prepared for this fight.
- Limit U.S. reliance on Pakistan when possible, including shipment of goods into Afghanistan. This would put Washington in a better bargaining position.
- Establish a better balance between carrots and sticks for a more-comprehensive persuasion strategy.

To accomplish these objectives, the United States needs to respect Pakistan's sovereignty and recognize that there is still considerable anti-Americanism among some Pakistanis.

Issuing a Clear Demand

It is critical that the United States issue a clear demand that Pakistan end its support to militant groups and develop an enforcement mechanism. U.S. President Barack Obama started this process in late 2009 in a letter to Pakistan President Asif Ali Zardari, which was hand delivered by U.S. national security adviser James Jones. The letter bluntly warned Pakistan that it had to cease using insurgent groups to pursue its foreign policy goals.[5] Since 2001—and even earlier—U.S. policy had been inconsistent in its position toward Pakistan's support to militant groups and focused primarily on targeting al Qa'ida.

---

[5] See, for example, Karin Brulliard and Karen DeYoung, "U.S.-Pakistan Cooperation Has Led to Capture of Afghan Taliban Insurgents," *Washington Post*, February 19, 2010, p. A1.

In the 1990s, the United States threatened to put Pakistan on its list of states that support terrorism. The United States did label Harkat-ul-Ansar as a terrorist group in 1997 because of its association with Osama bin Laden. The group renamed itself Harkat-ul-Mujahideen in 1998. After 2001, the United States placed numerous other groups, such as Jaish-e-Mohammad and Lashkar-e-Taiba, on the Department of State's list of foreign terrorist organizations. The Pakistani state also banned these groups, but they reformed under new names, so the banning had little operational effect. Most groups were also banned under their new names in principle, but Lashkar-e-Taiba's successor organization, Jamaat ul Dawa, was not banned.

After 2001, the United States was deeply ambivalent about encouraging Pakistan to end its support to militant groups. In December 2001, Jaish-e-Mohammad attacked the Indian Parliament, significantly increasing India-Pakistan tensions. This forced Pakistan to move forces from its western border with Afghanistan to its eastern border with India, compromising much-needed Pakistani support to Operation Enduring Freedom. Escalation continued after Lashkar-e-Taiba's Kaluchak massacre of the wives and children of Indian army personnel.[6] This prompted U.S. officials, such as Deputy Secretary of State Richard Armitage, to demarche Pakistan to clamp down on militant groups. But Pakistan did not stop the movement of militants into India.[7]

The United States was most interested in securing Pakistani cooperation against al Qa'ida operatives within Pakistan. Initially, U.S. officials paid little attention to the Afghan Taliban in Pakistan, which was shortsighted. Given the significant amount of aid the United States continued to provide Pakistan, Islamabad likely concluded that it could continue supporting some militant groups as long as it was assisting the United States against al Qa'ida and other foreign fighters. This approach was successful, up to a point.

---

6 The Kaluchak massacre occurred in May 2002 near the town of Kaluchak in Jammu and Kashmir. A group of militants attacked a tourist bus from the Indian state of Himachal Pradesh and killed 31 people.

7 Fair and Chalk, *Fortifying Pakistan*, 2006.

Washington must continue encouraging Islamabad to abandon militancy as a tool of foreign policy. This will not happen immediately. Consequently, U.S. policymakers need to work with Islamabad on a time line with measurable benchmarks for success, as well as on establishing an enforcement mechanism through intelligence collection.

Indeed, military aid should be conditioned on success in meeting these objectives. Washington will need to build an international coalition of states that share this view, including China, which has retained a close relationship with Islamabad. China shares many of America's concerns, partly because several militant organizations operating in China, including Uighur separatist groups, have developed bases of operation in Pakistan. Indeed, China may be willing to work within the larger context of Asian security. Saudi Arabia and the United Arab Emirates may also be helpful—especially Saudi Arabia, which has a significant support base within Pakistan.[8]

Ironically, the United States has not placed Pakistan on its list of state sponsors of terrorism—unlike Cuba, Iran, Sudan, and Syria—because Pakistan is an ally, which indicates that the list is political as much as it is substantive. The United States imposes a range of sanctions against countries on the list: restrictions on U.S. foreign assistance, a ban on defense exports and sales, certain controls over exports of dual-use items, and miscellaneous financial and other restrictions. In addition, the U.S. Department of State has identified several groups that have ties to Pakistan's security agencies on its list of "U.S. Government Designated Foreign Terrorist Organizations," including Jaish-e-Mohammad and Lashkar-e-Taiba.[9] The underlying point is straightforward: Unless Pakistan ends its support to militant groups, the United States should not continue to make exceptions on its list of state sponsors of terrorism.

---

[8] IRI, "Pakistan Public Opinion Survey, July 15–August 7, 2009," Washington, D.C., 2009.

[9] To make the list, which is determined by the U.S. Secretary of State, three laws are critical: section 6(j) of the Export Administration Act, section 40 of the Arms Export Control Act, and section 620A of the Foreign Assistance Act. See, for example, U.S. Department of State, *Country Reports on Terrorism 2008*.

Enhancing Pakistan's Counterinsurgency Capabilities

There are several types of assistance that the United States and its partners should provide to Pakistan. One is improving the civilian government's ability to educate its *own* public about militancy. U.S. policymakers sometimes hope that their diplomatic efforts can improve Pakistanis' view of America. This is a mistake. Of far greater importance is the Pakistani government's ability to influence its population about the domestic threat.

Pakistanis have generally believed that militants operating from Pakistani soil are a threat to the state. Where they have tended to be most ambivalent is in the use of *military force* to eliminate insurgents, and the public has been overwhelmingly disposed toward forging peace deals. It remains to be seen whether this shift in public attitude is enduring or transient. Yet the Pakistani civilian government appears to lack any strategy to build consensus for Pakistan's own war on terrorism. Public opinion surveys are an excellent tool for illuminating Pakistanis' positions. Without developing public support for its own war on terrorism, Pakistan's political will to remain engaged in armed struggle remains doubtful. Moreover, without public pressure on the army to eliminate militants, the army may demure from taking action when or if the operations become unpopular with or without the army.

When the Pakistan Army has mustered the will to challenge militant groups, its success has been mixed. Pakistan's security forces have had some success in clearing areas of militants. However, these operations have displaced some four million Pakistanis yet failed to kill or capture many of significant consequence. Most high-value targets that *have* been eliminated, such as Baitullah Mehsud in 2009, were victims of U.S. drone strikes. In addition, MQ-1 Predator and MQ-9 Reaper strikes in Pakistan have killed a number of key al Qa'ida operatives and other militants, as illustrated in Figure 5.1. Beginning in 2008, better U.S. and Pakistani intelligence collection and cooperation against al Qa'ida targets contributed to a deadly campaign from the air.[10] Drones targeted militants in Pakistan's tribal areas, especially North and

---

[10] Author interviews with Pakistan and NATO government officials, Pakistan and Afghanistan, May and October 2009.

Figure 5.1
Example of Predator and Reaper Strikes

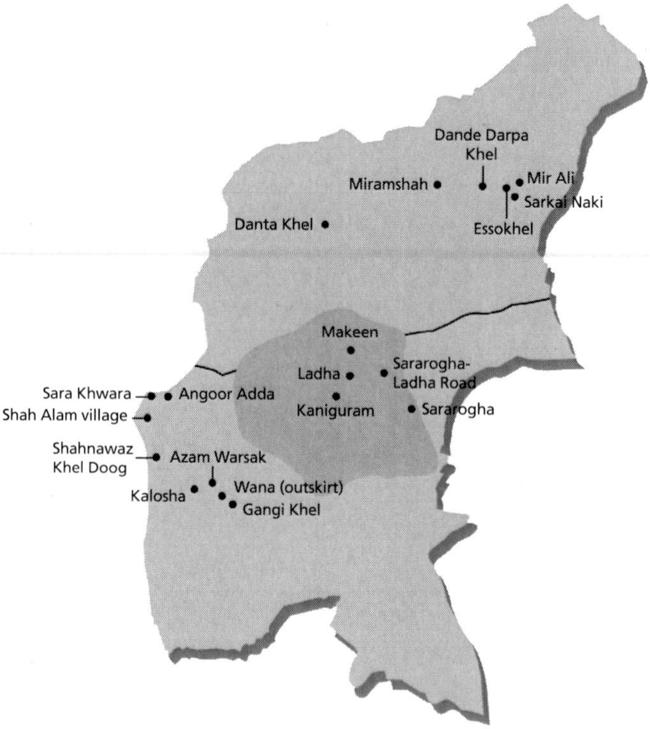

SOURCE: Adapted from Nadia Jajja, "The Path to Deliverance," *The Herald* (Karachi), December 2009, p. 20a.
RAND *MG982-5.1*

South Waziristan. U.S. intelligence indicated that al Qa'ida operatives became increasingly concerned about their operational security, and some considered transiting to other areas, such as Somalia, Yemen, and even the Swat District in Pakistan's NWFP to relieve the pressure.[11] An example of al Qa'ida operatives killed by drone strikes included:

- Abu Layth al-Libi, al Qa'ida emir for Afghanistan (Libyan)
- Abu Khabab al-Masri, al Qa'ida chemical and biological expert (Egyptian)

[11] Eric Schmitt and David E. Sanger, "Some in Qaeda Leave Pakistan for Somalia and Yemen," *New York Times*, June 11, 2009.

- Khalid Habib al-Masri, al Qa'ida commander in Afghanistan (Egyptian)
- Abu Jihad al-Masri, external operations planner (Egyptian)
- Zubayr al-Masri, external operations planner (Egyptian)
- Shaykh Swedan, external operations planner (Kenyan)
- Usama al-Kini, external operations planner (Kenyan).

The United States should continue to deepen cooperation with Pakistan on the use of unmanned aerial vehicles, including MQ-1 Predators, MQ-9 Reapers, and future models. They are extremely useful for intelligence; surveillance; reconnaissance; and, occasionally, targeting militants. Pakistani leaders have repeatedly asked the United States to transfer drone technology to Pakistan to allow it to hit high-value targets in tribal areas, although India has expressed concern that Pakistan could use such drones in Kashmir. In a meeting in Islamabad, for instance, President Asif Ali Zardari asked U.S. Senators John McCain and Joseph Lieberman to "persuade U.S. policymakers to give drone technology to Pakistan so that militants could be targeted by Pakistani security forces themselves rather than foreign troops which raise the question of sovereignty."[12] Drone technology would be helpful, as numerous countries—including Turkey, Israel, the United Kingdom, Mexico, and Italy—have demonstrated. Pakistan's ability to perform the other aspects of classic counterinsurgency—holding territory and building development and other projects—has been inadequate. Therefore, the United States and its partners should focus attention and resources on improving these capabilities once an area is cleared. This has several elements. Holding territory requires sufficient numbers of competent police forces, yet Pakistan's police forces are poorly paid, poorly equipped, and too few in number. There is an urgent need to increase the number and capabilities of Pakistani police, as the Kerry-Lugar-Berman "Enhanced Partnership with Pakistan Act of 2009" tried to do in promoting "police reform, equipping,

---

[12] Syed Irfan Raza, "Zardari Renews Demand for U.S. Drone Technology," *Dawn* (Karachi), January 7, 2010. Also see "Zardari Calls for Transfer of Drone Technology to Pakistan," *Daily Times* (Lahore), February 12, 2010.

and training."[13] Police training is traditionally the responsibility of the U.S. Department of State's Bureau of International Narcotics and Law Enforcement Affairs. But the bureau has a troubled track record, as shown when the Department of Defense took over the responsibilities to train and mentor police in Afghanistan and Iraq.[14] In addition, Pakistan's domestic intelligence agencies, including the police Special Branch, are underdeveloped and overshadowed by Pakistan's ISI. Pakistan requires civilian intelligence capabilities and a more-robust Federal Investigative Agency (FIA). Currently, the FIA is too small to be effective. Planning structures to facilitate military, police, and intelligence cooperation are needed urgently.[15]

Without the ability to build (or rebuild), developing a holding capability will have marginal returns. The government of Pakistan has had too little civil-military coordination, and the bureaucracy has had difficulty organizing relief operations for the millions of refugees, much less rebuilding destroyed villages and devastated infrastructure. U.S. and international assistance to help Pakistan develop civil-military coordination is much needed both for the current situation and for future contingencies. This does not necessarily mean providing funding, although financial support may be helpful. What Pakistan requires is a planning capability to handle these contingencies on its own.

More generally, Pakistan needs consistent encouragement and assistance in improving governance, including the provision of services. Realistically, this is unlikely to happen without serious condi-

---

[13] "Enhanced Partnership with Pakistan Act of 2009," S.962, Report 111-33, U.S. 11th Cong, 1st Sess.

[14] On efforts to rebuild the police in Afghanistan and Iraq see, for example, Jones, *In the Graveyard of Empires*, pp. 163–182; Seth G. Jones, Jeremy M. Wilson, Andrew Rathmell, and K. Jack Riley, *Establishing Law and Order After Conflict*, Santa Monica, Calif.: RAND Corporation, MG-374-RC, 2005; and Andrew Rathmell, Olga Oliker, Terrence K. Kelly, David Brannan, and Keith Crane, *Developing Iraq's Security Sector: The Coalition Provisional Authority's Experience*, Santa Monica, Calif.: RAND Corporation, MG-365-OSD, 2005.

[15] Author interviews with high-level U.S. Department of State officials throughout the summer of 2009. See also Fair and Chalk, *Fortifying Pakistan*; Abbas, *Police & Law Enforcement Reform in Pakistan*.

tioning of aid and changing the way that aid is used in Pakistan. The international community has spent hundreds of millions of dollars on judicial reform and other assistance programs, yet Pakistan remains, in the words of one World Bank analyst, a "graveyard of development programs."[16] Most of these programs have suffered because they have been supply driven and have required too few demand-driven commitments from the Pakistanis. Currently, U.S. assistance focuses too little on conditioning aid on verifiable progress. The logic of this appears to hinge on U.S. fears that it will lose "influence." There seems to be little consideration that large sums of unaccountable aid degrades, rather than improves, governance by creating opportunities for graft and corruption by ministries and officials—and even by aid contractors. The United States clearly needs to rethink how it provides assistance. For example, the United States is running programs that focus on improving governance and development within FATA. Unfortunately, the problems in FATA are symptomatic of a failure to provide governance throughout Pakistan.

FATA's exceptional legal structure is a problem. Under the FCR, there are no regular police in FATA. Justice is draconian and accompanied by corruption, and it lacks any appeal process. The FCR is also a barrier to the free movement of people between FATA and the rest of Pakistan and has enabled residents to demur from accepting the rights and responsibilities of fully being a Pakistani citizen. Pakistan should be encouraged to consider reforming FATA's legal structure; indeed, *any* aid to FATA should be conditioned on efforts to develop a plan for integration. This is inherently a Pakistani process. Nonetheless, Pakistan will need extensive resources.

In addition, the Pakistan Army needs to realize the value of developing a counterinsurgency doctrine and capability. Currently, some in the Pakistan Army view this as a zero sum game: Any move toward counterinsurgency is a move away from its conventional focus on India. Some of the potential political benefits described above could help ameliorate these concerns. Nonetheless, Pakistan's army is likely to remain ineffective as long as it retains its preferred low-intensity

---

[16] Author conversation with World Bank analyst in June 2009.

conflict approach. Pakistan's elite Special Services Group has been effective, but it is a small organization. Thus, the United States should focus its military education and training programs on counterinsurgency and related skills, such as civil-military coordination. Without such measured insistence, Pakistan will continue to conclude that it can use its conventional fears of India to obtain strategic assistance in exchange for tactical or even operational contributions to the war on terrorism. The United States should also focus its foreign military sales and military financing on platforms and equipment needed for counterinsurgency. The U.S. Congress passed legislation intended to do this, especially the Kerry-Lugar-Berman act, but implementation has been problematic.[17]

The Pakistan Army should also strongly consider folding the Frontier Corps into the army and regularizing it (and therefore professionalizing it) as Pakistan did with another paramilitary organization, the Northern Light Infantry in 1999. This would give tribal leaders a greater stake in the organization by offering them more opportunities to become officers. At the same time, regularizing the Frontier Corps as an army unit will also help to integrate FATA residents into Pakistan's social fabric. Currently, they are integrated economically but less so socially and culturally.

Create Space for Persuasion

Pakistan provides an important and affordable land bridge to move lethal and nonlethal supplies to troops in Afghanistan through key LOCs. Although there have been some attacks on the routes through Torkham and Chaman, these LOCs remain open. This demonstrates that Pakistan's forces are capable of restricting militant capabilities when it is in Pakistan's interests to do so. Insurgents could potentially shut down supply lines, given that fuel and lethal supplies effectively move through restricted bottlenecks at border points and other locations along the roads to Kandahar (via Chaman) and Bagram (via Torkham). In October 2009, Pakistan Frontier Corps forces halted

---

[17] "Enhanced Partnership with Pakistan Act of 2009," S.962, Report 111-33, U.S. 11th Cong., 1st Sess.

the movement of nearly 800 trucks along Highway 4 from Quetta, Pakistan, to Spin Boldak, Afghanistan, because of the possibility of U.S. air strikes in Baluchistan. In previous weeks, there had been some unconfirmed media reports that President Obama supported strikes in Baluchistan.[18]

The United States currently relies on two major areas to supply its forces in Afghanistan. The first is through Pakistan, where more than three-quarters of all dry cargo and roughly 42 percent of fuel come into Afghanistan. Nearly 100 percent of NATO fuel comes from Pakistani refineries. The second front is through LOCs in Central Asia (Figure 5.2). Uzbekistan, for example, is critical. Roughly 60 percent of aviation fuel for U.S. operations, 99 percent of fuel for Afghanistan's air corps, and tons of bottled water for U.S. troops transit through Uzbekistan each month, mostly via rail. NATO forces rely on oil that is refined in Azerbaijan, Russia, Kazakhstan, and Turkmenistan, then moves across the Caspian Sea and Central Asia via rail. In addition, some NATO forces use the airspace of Georgia, Azerbaijan, Russia, Kyrgyzstan, Uzbekistan, Turkmenistan, and Tajikistan for cargo and troop movement into Afghanistan.[19]

The United States should continue seeking alternative—if less than ideal—routes for resupply to diminish its reliance on Pakistan. For example, using Iranian supply routes, which some Europeans have already developed, could be a vital pressure point for the Pakistan Army. The United States could also encourage some European countries to negotiate deals with Iran for a supply route, even if the United States could not yet because of tensions over Iran's nuclear program. In addition, the United States could continue to increase LOCs through Central Asia. Examples include using Manas Air Base in Kyrgyzstan and Termez, Uzbekistan. Manas Air Base is home to the U.S. 376th Air Expeditionary Wing and serves as a premier air mobility hub for U.S. and NATO military operations in Afghanistan. The wing's

---

[18] See, for example, Faisal Aziz, "Fear Grows of U.S. Strikes in Pakistan's Baluchistan," *Reuters*, October 12, 2009.

[19] Author interviews with officials from U.S. Transportation Command, September 2009.

Figure 5.2
Northern LOCs into Afghanistan

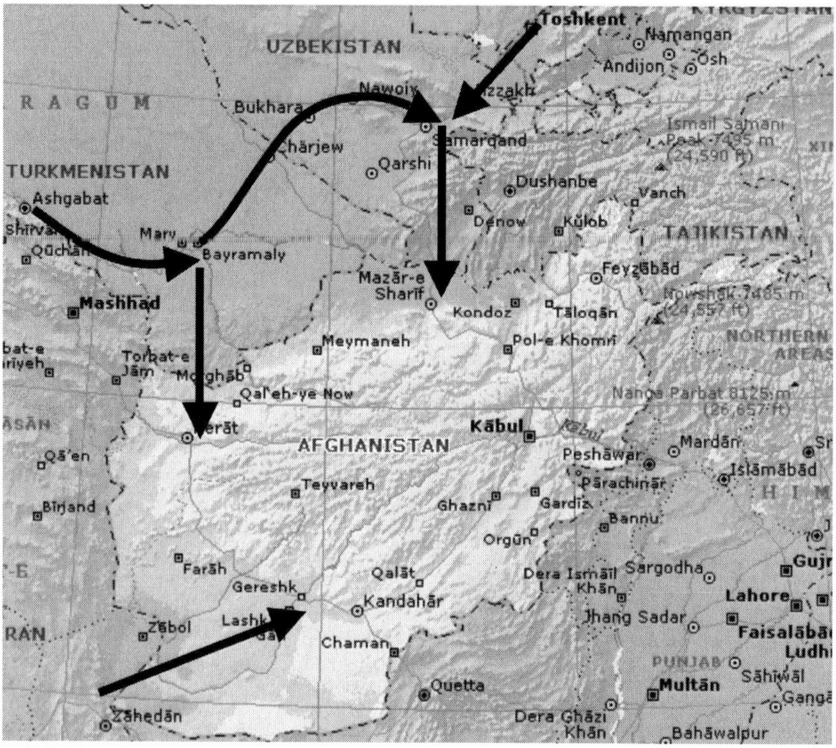

RAND *MG982-5.2*

around-the-clock missions include aerial refueling, combat airlift and airdrop, medical evacuation, and strategic airlift operations.

Seeking alternative routes has two immediate consequences. First, it demonstrates to Pakistan that it needs the United States as much—if not more—than the United States needs Pakistan. Without these logistical routes, key Pakistani stakeholders will lose significant revenues. Second, such a move demonstrates that Washington has the political will to diminish its requirements for Pakistan. Should the United States engage in discussions with Iran or other countries to move more goods into Afghanistan, Pakistan will understand the significance of U.S. intent. Other NATO partners, such as Italy (based in Herat on the Iranian border), have already done so. The United States needs to coordinate its strategy with other partners to minimize Pakistan's ability to cultivate alternative sources of assistance.

Better Sticks, More Appealing Carrots

The United States has generally funneled its "carrots" toward Pakistan's military out of a belief that the Pakistan Army is the most important partner in the war on terrorism.[20] Unfortunately, this has likely bolstered the army's belief that it can continue receiving aid based on its projected relevance to U.S. needs. Yet the army and ISI are the sources of many of the region's problems, even though they provide invaluable cooperation at the same time. Moreover, providing Pakistan with the ability to build up its strategic capabilities while largely ignoring its counterinsurgency needs may have adverse effects and may further encourage Pakistani adventurism under its nuclear umbrella. Table 5.1 illustrates the range of carrots and sticks that should be considered.

While the United States should continue training programs for counterinsurgency and ensure that the vast majority of goods and services that Pakistan obtains are appropriate for counterinsurgency purposes, such systems as F-16s should be withheld until discernible progress is made on U.S. goals. Spare parts for these systems, as well as U.S.-supplied lifetime maintenance, can also be held in abeyance. Pakistan may consider the United States to be an "unreliable partner." This has long been Pakistan's approach to obtaining maximum benefit from the United States while marginally satisfying Washington. The United States should be resolute in ensuring that Pakistan's own choices and actions—not U.S. caprice—will deprive it of the systems that it seeks to fight India. In contrast, the United States should not restrict access to training and platforms needed to develop counterinsurgency capabilities, including police and intelligence agencies.

The United States could also consider economic sanctions against specific individuals and organizations that support terrorism. Equally, visa bans on individuals supporting terrorism may be effective, if legally difficult to enact. Pakistani military and intelligence officials regularly visit the United States and European capitals and enjoy the privilege

---

[20] Fair and Chalk, *Fortifying Pakistan*.

Table 5.1
Example of Carrots and Sticks for Pakistan

	Example of Carrots	Example of Sticks
Economic	Economic and trade concessions, especially for textiles Assistance in acquiring loans from the International Monetary Fund	Economic sanctions against individuals and organizations that support terrorism Visa bans on individuals supporting terrorism
Political	Aid to reform FATA's legal structure and FCR	Some aid should be conditioned on efforts to revise FCR—and broader efforts to develop a plan for reintegration of FATA
Security	Assistance to police Assistance to civilian intelligence agencies, including FIA Military education and training programs on counterinsurgency and related skills Assess possibility of a criteria-based civilian nuclear deal Increased cooperation on UAVs	Assess viability of strategic LOCs for Afghanistan through Iran and Central Asia Make some aid contingent on capture of senior Taliban and Haqqani individuals—as well as ending assistance to militant groups "Shaming" by revealing information on state support to militants

of sending their children abroad for schooling. This will require congressional action. Specific group and individual sanctions can raise the costs on specific government officials while avoiding blunt, punitive penalties that affect entire institutions.

This approach differs substantially from previous periods, in which the United States used widespread sanctions against Pakistan. The 1998 nuclear tests resulted in the Glenn-Symington Amendment sanctions.[21] In 1999, General Musharraf overthrew the democratically

[21] The Symington Amendment prohibits most forms of U.S. assistance to countries that are found to be trafficking in nuclear enrichment equipment or technology outside of international safeguards. The Glenn Amendment prohibits U.S. foreign assistance to nonnuclear weapon states. The nuclear Non-Proliferation Treaty defines the legal status of a "nuclear weapon state." For more information about these sanctions, see Robert Hathaway, "Confrontation and Retreat: The U.S. Congress and the South Asian Nuclear Tests," *Arms Control Today*, January/February 2000; Barbara LePoer et al., *India-Pakistan Nuclear Tests and U.S. Response*, CRS Report 98-570, updated November 24, 1998; and Jeanne Grimmett, *Nuclear Sanctions: Section 102(b) of the Arms Export Control Act and Its Application to India and Pakistan*, Washington, D.C., Congressional Research Service, Report 98-486, October 5, 2001.

elected Nawaz Sharif, after which the United States applied sanctions under Section 508.[22] In addition, specific entities in Pakistan had been sanctioned under the Missile Technology Control Regime for proscribed acquisition of missile technology from China. On March 24, 2003, the United States imposed a new set of sanctions on Pakistan's Khan Research Laboratories for a "specific missile-related transfer" from North Korea's Changgwang Sinyong Corporation.[23] Washington also threatened to label Pakistan a state that supports terrorism on several occasions throughout the 1990s.

As a consequence of these sanctions and the ways in which they were applied, security cooperation between the United States and Pakistan deteriorated. Although the Glenn-Symington Amendment did not technically require termination of the International Military Education and Training program for Pakistan, the program was largely unavailable to Pakistan after 1990.[24] The suspension of this and other training opportunities and exchanges resulted in a much-diminished mutual understanding among low- and mid-level military officers of both countries. Pakistan mid- and low-level officers were no longer "Westward looking" as a result of the cessation of such programs, and the U.S. military lost the opportunity to appreciate and understand the ethos, capabilities, orientation, and competence of the Pakistani military.

Ultimately, U.S. sanctions failed to prevent Pakistan from proliferating and relying on militancy as a tool of foreign policy. In the end,

---

[22] Under Section 508 of the 1999 Foreign Operations Appropriations Act, no U.S. assistance may be given to any country "whose duly elected head of government is deposed by military coup or decree." See U. Dianne E. Rennack, *India and Pakistan: Current U.S. Economic Sanctions Specialist in Foreign Policy Legislation*, Washington, D.C.: Congressional Research Service, October 12, 2001.

[23] See Fair, *The Counterterror Coalitions*; C. Christine Fair, *The Cuisines of the Axis of Evil and Other Irritating States*, Guilford, Conn.: Globe Pequot Press, 2008; See U.S. Department of State, "North Korea–Pakistan: Missile-Related Sanctions and Executive Order 12938 Penalties," April 1, 2003. See also "U.S. Explains Sanctions," BBC News, April 3, 2003.

[24] The International Military Education and Training program is a funding component of U.S. security assistance that provides training on a grant basis to students from allied and friendly nations. Fair, *The Counterterror Coalitions*.

the United States may have suffered the most from the way it sought to punish Pakistan for its misdeeds. The United States lost critical contact with the military and visibility into areas of U.S. national interest, such as the evolving state of Pakistan's nuclear program. Fortunately, the senior leadership of both militaries likely had maintained fairly robust ties dating back to the Soviet invasion of Afghanistan when security cooperation was strong. Moreover, both militaries participated in UN-sponsored and U.S.-led peacekeeping operations. These peacekeeping operations afforded Pakistan opportunities to obtain some military-to-military contact with the United States at a time when more usual avenues of interaction were blocked by layers of sanctions. In addition, Pakistan was able to procure limited spare parts to support these operations. For example, on August 13, 2001, President Bush granted a one-time waiver of sanctions that permitted the sale of spare parts for Pakistan's Cobra helicopters, armored personnel carriers, and ammunition to support Pakistan's peacekeeping activities in Sierra Leone.[25]

The period of sanctions in the 1990s should serve as a lesson. Despite repeated warnings that India would test a nuclear device, the United States did not develop and preposition a package of Pakistani inducements to launch the "day after" or the "day of" a potential Indian test. According to one Department of Defense official involved in persuading Pakistan to resist testing, the United States went to Pakistan largely empty handed.[26]

While the United States must develop a judicious ensemble of sticks, Washington must also offer a selection of meaningful carrots. Pakistan has come to view U.S. assistance as an entitlement.[27] Therefore, offering more aid (as in the Kerry-Lugar-Berman legislation) is unlikely to persuade Pakistan to stop using militants as a tool of foreign policy. Indeed, restricting or diminishing aid will have the effect of a sanction, given the way in which Pakistan has become accustomed to aid and has developed a narrative that Pakistan *deserves* financial

[25] See discussion in Fair, "Time for Sober Realism."

[26] See C. Christine Fair, "Learning to Think the Unthinkable: Lessons from India's Nuclear Test," *India Review*, Vol. 4, No. 1, January 2005; Fair, *The Counterterror Coalitions*.

[27] See discussion in Fair, "Time for Sober Realism."

allocations as a just reward for cooperating with the United States. Much of the aid and reimbursements disbursed to Pakistan since 2001 was grossly misused, siphoned off to support Pakistan's economy and to build up forces to defeat India. Washington was also culpable. The United States had an inadequate footprint to track the flow of funds and seek accountability for U.S. resources dispensed to Pakistan.[28]

The United States should consider more politically valuable initiatives, given the willingness and equities of other regional parties. While an effective U.S. role in reaching an Indo-Pakistani accommodation on Kashmir is unlikely, partly because of Indian opposition, there are at least two initiatives that could benefit Pakistan.

First is a criteria-based civilian nuclear deal for Pakistan.[29] Pakistan complained about the exceptionalism of the Indo-U.S. nuclear deal, in which India agreed to separate its civil and military nuclear facilities and place its civil nuclear facilities under International Atomic Energy Agency safeguards. In exchange, the United States agreed to work toward full civil nuclear cooperation with India. Pakistani officials argued that its sacrifices in cooperating with the United States should merit comparable consideration. Pakistan legitimately fears that the agreement may allow India to improve and expand its nuclear weapon arsenal.[30] Pakistan sought to undermine the Indo-U.S. deal, arguing that it would spark an arms race on the subcontinent.[31]

Since the Indo-U.S. nuclear agreement has cleared the U.S. Congress, the Nuclear Suppliers Group, and the International Atomic Energy Agency, Pakistan has become increasingly insistent that it merits a comparable deal. During a meeting at the International Insti-

---

[28] Kathy Gannon, "Billions in US Aid Never Reached Pakistan Army," *Washington Post*, October 4, 2009.

[29] See, for example, C. Christine Fair, "Pakistan Needs Its Own Nuclear Deal," *Wall Street Journal*, February 10, 2010.

[30] Leonard Weiss, "U.S.-India Nuclear Cooperation," *The Nonproliferation Review*, Vol. 14, No. 3, November 2007, pp. 429–457.

[31] Bruce Loudon, "Pakistan: Nuke Deal to Spark Arms Race," *The Australian*, website, July 25, 2008; Paul K. Kerr and Mar Beth Nikitin, *Pakistan's Nuclear Weapons: Proliferation and Security Issues*, Washington, D.C.: Congressional Research Service, May 15, 2009.

tute of Strategic Studies, Foreign Minister Shah Mahmood Qureshi expressed his country's desire for a similar agreement. He emphasized that the Indo-U.S. nuclear agreement must not be discriminatory.[32] Pakistan had argued for such a deal during President George W. Bush's March 2006 visit to India and Pakistan. President Bush bluntly rejected such appeals, arguing that India and Pakistan "had different needs and different histories," in a reference to the A. Q. Khan affair.[33] A. Q. Khan is regarded as the founder of Pakistan's nuclear program and was accused of providing nuclear weapon technology to Iran, North Korea, Libya, and other states.[34] In February 2009, the Islamabad High Court declared A. Q. Khan a "free citizen" of Pakistan, lifting the restrictions imposed on him since 2004, when he publicly confessed to running an illicit nuclear network.

Some prominent Pakistani analysts have suggested that a criteria-based approach with Pakistan could be possible.[35] The explicit criteria could be tied to access to A. Q. Khan, greater visibility into Pakistan's program, submission to safeguards, a strategic decision to abandon militancy as a tool of foreign and domestic policy, and empirically verifiable metrics in eliminating militant groups operating in and from Pakistan. The deal could have elements that are much more restrictive than the Indian deal. For example, it could be based on an exclusive relationship with the United States, rather than seeking broad accommodation with the Nuclear Supplier's group and other regimes that

[32] "Pakistan Wants India-Like Nuclear Deal with US Qureshi," *Business Recorder*, website, July 25, 2008.

[33] Bush Rejects Nuke Deal with Pakistan," *The Times of India,* March 4, 2006.

[34] On the A. Q. Khan affair, see, for example, Kenley Butler, Sammy Salama, and Leonard S. Spector, "Special Report: The Khan Network," *Bulletin of the Atomic Scientists*, Vol. 62, No. 6, November/December 2006, pp. 25–34, 62–63; Nawaz, *Crossed Swords*, pp. 551–556. Also see Pakistan and United States accusations on A. Q. Khan's proliferation in Musharraf, *In the Line of Fire*, pp. 286–296; Tenet, *At the Center of the Storm*, pp. 262–263, 281–287.

[35] Stephen P. Cohen is one of the proponents of this view. He has articulated this possible policy option in a number of forums, including during his review of this manuscript. Members of a recent Asia Society task force also put forward some way of trying to bring Pakistan into the "global nonproliferation regime" by beginning a dialogue to explore means of recognizing Pakistan as a de jure nuclear power. See Asia Society, *Back from the Brink? A Strategy for Stabilizing Afghanistan-Pakistan*, Asia Society Task Force Report, April 2009.

limit the proliferation of nuclear technology and access to materials for nuclear programs.

Such a deal would confer acceptance of Islamabad's nuclear weapon program and reward it for the improvements in nuclear security it has made since 2002. In the long shadow of A. Q. Khan and continued uncertainty about the status of his networks, it is easy to forget that Pakistan has established a Strategic Plans Division that has done much to improve the safety of the country's nuclear assets. In exchange for fundamental recognition of its nuclear status and civilian assistance, Pakistan would have to meet two criteria: It would have to provide the kind of access and cooperation on nuclear suppliers' networks identified in the Kerry-Lugar-Berman legislation. Pakistan would also have to demonstrate sustained and verifiable commitment in combating all terrorist groups on its soil. Such a civilian nuclear deal could achieve the goals that Kerry-Lugar-Berman could not because it would offer Pakistan benefits that it actually values and that only the United States can meaningfully confer.

A nuclear deal will not be an easy sale either in Washington or in Islamabad, much less in Delhi. Details of the Indo-U.S. deal are still being negotiated more than five years after the idea was initially floated. A deal with Islamabad will be even more protracted than the deal with New Delhi because of A. Q. Khan's activities and the clout of domestic lobbies in Washington. It is possible that even this deal may not provide Pakistan adequate incentives to eliminate terror groups or provide access to such individuals as A. Q. Khan.

Second, a serious economic carrot should be considered. Pakistan has long sought access to economic and trade concessions, especially for textiles.[36] Some U.S. economic initiatives are unlikely to be useful. For example, setting up Reconstruction Economic Zones in FATA, Kashmir, and the earthquake-affected areas is unlikely to have an appreciable effect on local economic activity even if it would have some public-relations value. Moreover, it is likely that goods would be

[36] See Office of the Press Secretary, "Joint Statement on United States–Pakistan Strategic Partnership," website, July 28, 2008; Office of the Press Secretary, "Joint Statement on United States–Pakistan Strategic Partnership," website, March 4, 2006.

manufactured outside the target zones and routed through the zones to receive the economic dispensation. If the United States seeks to achieve a greater economic effect, Washington and Islamabad should consider signing a free trade agreement, which would affect more people. As with other inducements, this too would be subject to the usual requirements about a phased and verifiable cessation of support for militant groups and greater access to—and visibility—into Pakistan's nuclear weapons.

Conclusion

A key objective of U.S. policy must be to alter Pakistan's strategic calculus and end its support to militant groups. Pakistan is unlikely to abandon militancy as a tool of foreign policy without a serious effort to alter its cost-benefit calculus. This requires the United States to clarify what its goals are, develop an international consensus on most (if not all) of these goals, and issue a clear demand to Pakistan regarding these objectives. At the same time, the United States and its partners must understand that Pakistan's ability to act effectively, even against those it views as a threat, is limited. Efforts to increase Pakistan's counterinsurgency capabilities may help bolster Pakistan's *will* to contain these threats as its capabilities expand. Given the U.S. perception that it needs Pakistan more than Pakistan needs the United States, the United States will have to create space for persuasion and forge more creative carrots and sticks.

There is a long history of cooperation between the United States and Pakistan, although policymakers in both countries have often forgotten—or ignored—that history. The relationship has tended to be stronger when both had a mutual interest in responding to security threats. As the Greek historian Thucydides noted, mutual "interest is the surest of bonds whether between states or individuals."[37] Cooperation between Pakistan and the United States has waxed and waned

[37] Thucydides, *The History of the Peloponnesian War*, tr. Rex Warner, New York: Penguin Books, 1977, p. 53.

depending on the existence of mutual interests. During the Cold War, they developed a close relationship to balance against the Soviet Union. Pakistani Prime Minister Liaquat Ali Khan somewhat jokingly quipped that Pakistan would have "no further need to maintain an army," and certainly not a large one, if the United States could "guarantee Pakistan's frontiers."[38] Today, the threats to Pakistan and the United States are serious and real, and they require substantive cooperation. Disagreements will continue, as they do between all countries. The true mettle of policymakers is whether they can effectively deal with today's threats despite their disagreements. A great deal is now at stake.

[38] Ayesha Jalal, *The State of Martial Law*, New York: Cambridge University Press, 1990, p. 111. Also see Haqqani, *Pakistan: Between Mosque and Military*, p. 32.

About the Authors

Seth G. Jones is a senior political scientist at the RAND Corporation and author, most recently, of *In the Graveyard of Empires: America's War in Afghanistan* (W.W. Norton, 2009). In 2009, he served as a plans officer and adviser to the Commanding General, U.S. Special Operations Forces, in Afghanistan. In addition, he has been an adjunct professor in the Security Studies Program at Georgetown University, as well as the Center for Homeland Defense at the U.S. Naval Postgraduate School. He is the author of *The Rise of European Security Cooperation* (Cambridge University Press, 2007). He has also published a range of journal articles on Afghanistan, Pakistan, and other national security subjects in *International Security*, *Foreign Affairs*, *The National Interest*, *Security Studies*, *Chicago Journal of International Law*, *International Affairs*, and *Survival*, as well as such newspapers as *The New York Times*, *Wall Street Journal*, and *Washington Post*. His most recent RAND publications include *Counterinsurgency in Afghanistan* (2008) and *How Terrorist Groups End: Lessons for Countering Al Qa'ida* (2008). He received his M.A. and Ph.D. from the University of Chicago.

C. Christine Fair is an assistant professor in the Center for Peace and Security Studies in Georgetown University's Edmund A. Walsh School of Foreign Service. Previously, she has served as a senior political scientist with the RAND Corporation, a political officer to the United Nations Assistance Mission to Afghanistan in Kabul, and as a senior research associate in United States Institute of Peace's Center for Conflict Analysis and Prevention. She is also a senior fellow with the Counter Terrorism Center at West Point. Her research focuses on political and military affairs in South Asia. She has authored, coauthored, and coedited several books including *Treading Softly on Sacred Ground: Counterinsurgency Operations on Sacred Space* (Oxford University Press, 2008), *The Madrassah Challenge: Militancy and Religious Education in Pakistan* (United States Institute of Peace, 2008), and *Fortifying Pakistan: The Role of U.S. Internal Security Assistance* (United States Institute of Peace, 2006). She is a member of the International Institute of Strategic Studies and the Council on Foreign Relations, serves on the editorial board of *Studies in Conflict and Terrorism*. She publishes widely on political and military affairs spanning Iran, Afghanistan, Pakistan, India, Sri Lanka, and Bangladesh. Her most recent RAND publications include *Pakistan: Can the United States Secure an Insecure State?* (2010). She completed an M.A. from the Harris School of Public Policy and an M.A. in South Asian Languages and Civilizations in 1997 at the University of Chicago. In 2004, she received a Ph.D. in South Asian Languages and Civilizations at the University of Chicago.

Bibliography

Abbas, Hassan, "Transforming Pakistan's Frontier Corps," *Terrorism Monitor*, Vol. 5, No. 6, March 30, 2007.

———, "Increasing Talibanization in Pakistan's Seven Tribal Agencies," *Terrorism Monitor*, Vol. 5, No. 18, September 27, 2007, pp. 1–5.

———, "Is the NWFP Slipping out of Pakistan's Control?" *Terrorism Monitor*, Vol. 5, No. 22, November 26, 2007.

———, A Profile of Tehrik-i-Taliban Pakistan," *CTC Sentinel,* Vol. 1, No. 2, January 2008, pp. 1–4.

———, *Police & Law Enforcement Reform in Pakistan: Crucial for Counterinsurgency and Counterterrorism Success*, Clinton, Mich.: Institute for Social Policy and Understanding, April 2009.

Abbas, Zaffar, "Operation Eyewash," *The Herald* (Karachi), August 2005.

———, "Taliban Ousted, but Spinkai Is Now a Ghost Town," *Dawn* (Karachi), May 19, 2008.

Abid, Abdur Rehman, "Buner Falls into the Hands of Swat Taliban," *Dawn* (Karachi), April 22, 2009.

———, "Taliban Ambush FC Convoy, Foil Buner Deployment," *Dawn* (Karachi), April 23, 2009.

"Accord in Bajaur to Curb Terrorists," *Dawn* (Karachi), May 31, 2005.

Afridi, Qaiser Khan, *UNHCR Helps South Waziristan's Displaced in Neighbouring Districts*, Geneva: Office of the United Nations High Commissioner for Refugees, December 2009.

Ahmed, Iftikhar, "Islam, Democracy and Citizenship Education: An Examination of the Social Studies Curriculum in Pakistan," *Current Issues in Comparative Education*, Vol. 7, No. 1, December 15, 2004.

"Al-Jazeera TV Interviews Pakistan Taliban Chief," BBC, May 29, 2008.

"Al-Qaeda 'Rebuilding' in Pakistan," BBC News, January 12, 2007. As of April 23, 2010:
http://news.bbc.co.uk/2/hi/south_asia/6254375.stm

Ali, Mohammad, "Peace Deal in Bajaur Soon, Says Aurakzai," *Dawn* (Karachi), February 24, 2007.

Ali, Zulfiqar, "Peshwar: Over 4,000 Houses Destroyed in Waziristan Operation: Report," *Dawn* (Karachi), November 8, 2008.

Almeida, Cyril, "Kayani Spells out Threat Posed by Indian Doctrine," *Dawn* (Karachi), February 4, 2010.

Amin, Akhtar, "Government Moves Additional Army Continents to Swat," *Daily Times* (Lahore), October 19, 2007.

Amir, Intikhab, "Waziristan: No Man's Land?" *The Herald* (Karachi), April 2006.

———, "Whose Writ Is It Anyway?" *The Herald* (Karachi), Vol. 37, No. 4, April 2006.

Ansari, Massoud, "Security: A Series of Unfortunate Events," *The Herald* (Karachi), November 2009.

Arquilla, John, and David Ronfeldt, eds., *In Athena's Camp: Preparing for Conflict in the Information Age*, Santa Monica, Calif.: RAND Corporation, MR-880-OSD/RC, 1997. As of March 25, 2010:
http://www.rand.org/pubs/monograph_reports/MR880/

———, *Networks and Netwars: The Future of Terror, Crime and Militancy,* Santa Monica, Calif.: RAND Corporation, MR-1382-OSD, 2001. As of March 25, 2010:
http://www.rand.org/pubs/monograph_reports/MR1382/

Art, Robert J., "To What Ends Military Power," *International Security*, Vol. 4, No. 4, Spring 1980.

Asia Society, *Back from the Brink? A Strategy for Stabilizing Afghanistan-Pakistan.* Asia Society Task Force Report, April 2009.

Axelrod, Rob, *The Evolution of Cooperation*, New York: Basic Books, 1984.

Aziz, Faisal, "Fear Grows of U.S. Strikes in Pakistan's Baluchistan," Reuters, October 12, 2009

Aziz, K. K., *Murder of History: A Critique of History Textbooks Used in Pakistan*, Lahore: Vanguard Books, 1998.

"The Bajaur Massacre," *Dawn* (Karachi), November 1, 2006.

Bakhtiar, Idrees, "Between the Lines," *The Herald* (Karachi), July 2007.

Barnes, Julian, E., "Pakistan to Crack Down on Rebels: The Military Plans to Push into Lawless Regions Used by Al Qaeda, a Move the U.S. Has Sought," *Los Angeles Times*, July 29, 2008.

Barno, Lieutenant General David W., Testimony Before the Committee on Foreign Affairs, U.S. House of Representatives, February 15, 2007, p. 21.

Beaumont, Peter, and Mark Townsend, "Pakistan Troops 'Aid Taliban': New Classified U.S. Documents Reveal That Mass Infiltration of Frontier Corps by Afghan Insurgents Is Helping Latest Offensive," *The Observer* (London), June 22, 2008.

Berntsen, Gary, and Ralph Pezzullo, *Jawbreaker: The Attack on bin Laden and Al-Qaeda: A Personal Account by the CIA's Key Field Commander*, New York: Crown Publishers, 2005.

Border Roads Organization, *Vision, Mission, Role*, Delhi, 2010.

Brockes, Emma, "British Man Named as Bomber Who Killed 10," *The Guardian*, December 28, 2000.

Brulliard, Karin, and Karen DeYoung, "U.S.-Pakistan Cooperation Has Led to Capture of Afghan Taliban Insurgents," *Washington Post*, February 19, 2010, p. A1.

Brzezinski, Zbigniew, *Power and Principle: Memoirs of the National Security Adviser, 1977–1981*, New York: Farrar, Straus, and Giroux, 1983.

Bundy, McGeorge, *Danger and Survival: Choices About the Bomb in the First Fifty Years*, New York: Random House, 1988.

"Bush Rejects Nuke Deal with Pakistan," *The Times of India,* March 4, 2006.

Butler, Kenley, Sammy Salama, and Leonard S. Spector, "Special Report: The Khan Network," *Bulletin of the Atomic Scientists*, Vol. 62, No. 6, November / December 2006, pp. 25–34, 62–63.

Byman, Daniel, *Going to War with the Allies You Have: Allies, Counterinsurgency and the War on Terrorism*, Carlisle, Pa.: Strategic Studies Institute, U.S. Army War College, November 2005.

———, "Friends Like These: Counterinsurgency and the War on Terrorism," *International Security*, Vol. 31, No. 2, Fall 2006, pp. 79–115.

Byman, Daniel, Peter Chalk, Bruce Hoffman, William Rosenau, and David Brannan, *Trends in Outside Support for Insurgent Movements*, Santa Monica, Calif.: RAND Corporation, MR-1405-OTI, 2001. As of March 25, 2010: http://www.rand.org/pubs/monograph_reports/MR1405/

Byman, Daniel, and Matthew Waxman, *The Dynamics of Coercion: American Foreign Policy and the Limits of Military Might*, New York: Cambridge University Press, 2002.

Callwell, C. W., *Small Wars: Their Principles and Practice*, 3rd ed., Lincoln: University of Nebraska Press, 1996.

Central Intelligence Agency, *Guide to the Analysis of Insurgency*, Washington, D.C., January 2009.

Cheema, Pervaiz Iqbal, *The Armed Forces of Pakistan*, New York: New York University Press, 2002.

Coates, Sam, and Jeremy Page, "Pakistan 'Linked to 75% of All UK Terror Plots,' Warns Gordon Brown," *The Times* (London), December 15, 2008.

Coghlan, Tom, Zahid Hussain, and Jeremy Page, "Secrecy and Denial as Pakistan Lets CIA Use Airbase to Strike Militants," *The Times* (London), February 2009.

Cohen, Craig, and Derek Chollet, "When $10 Billion Is Not Enough: Rethinking U.S. Strategy Toward Pakistan," *Washington Quarterly*, Vol. 30, No. 2, Spring 2007.

Cohen, Stephen P., *The Pakistan Army*, Berkeley, Calif.: University of California Press, 1984.

———, *The Idea of Pakistan*, Washington, D.C.: Brookings Institution Press, 2004.

Collier, David, "The Comparative Method: Two Decades of Change," in Dankwart A. Rustow and Kenneth Paul Erickson, eds. *Comparative Political Dynamics: Global Research Perspectives*, New York: HarperCollins Publishers, 1991, pp. 7–31.

Constable, Pamela, and Kamran Khan, "Suicide Bombing Kills 41 Troops at Pakistani Army Base: Attack Called Reprisal for Strike on School," *Washington Post*, November 9, 2006.

Cortright, David, and George A. Lopez, *The Sanctions Decade: Assessing UN Strategies in the 1990s*, Boulder, Colo.: Lynne Rienner Publishers, 2000.

Craig, Gordon A., and Alexander L. George, *Force and Statecraft: Diplomatic Problems of Our Time*, 3rd ed., New York: Oxford University Press, 1995.

Daalder, Ivo H. and Michael E. O'Hanlon, *Winning Ugly: NATO's War to Save Kosovo,* Washington, D.C.: Brookings Institution Press, 2000.

Doyle, Michael W., and Nicholas Sambanis, *Making War and Building Peace: The United Nations Since the 1990s*, Princeton, N.J.: Princeton University Press, 2006.

Dreazen, Yochi J., "Al Qaeda's Global Base Is Pakistan, Says Petraeus," *Wall Street Journal*, May 11, 2009.

Drezner, Daniel W., *The Sanctions Paradox: Economic Statecraft and International Relations*, New York: Cambridge University Press, 1999.

Easterly, William R., *The Elusive Quest for Growth: Economists' Adventures and Misadventures in the Tropics*, Cambridge, Mass.: MIT Press, 2002.

Einhorn, Jessica, "The World Bank's Mission Creep," *Foreign Affairs*, Vol. 80, No. 5, 2001.

El-Edroos, S. A., "A Plea for a People's Army," *Pakistan Army Journal*, Vol. 4, June 1962, pp. 19–25.

———, "Afro Asian Revolutionary Warfare and Our Military Thought," *Pakistan Army Journal*, Vol. 4, December 1962, pp. 35–41.

European Council, "Conclusions of the Presidency," Cophenhagen, June 21–22, 1993.

European Union, Council Regulation (EC) No. 1705/98, OJ L 215, 1.8.98; Common Position, 97/759/CFSP, OJ L 309, 12.11.1997; Common Position, 98/425/CFSP, OJ L 190, 4.7.1998

Evans, Alexander, "The Kashmir Insurgency: As Bad as It Gets," *Small Wars and Insurgencies*, Vol. 11, No. 1, Spring 2000, pp. 69–81.

[Excised] to DIA Washington, D.C., Cable, "Pakistan Interservice Intelligence/ Pakistan (PK) Directorate Supplying the Taliban Forces," October 22, 1996. Released by the National Security Archive.

Fair, C. Christine, *The Counterterror Coalitions: Cooperation with India and Pakistan*, MG-141-AF, Santa Monica, Calif.: RAND Corporation, MG-141-AF, 2004. As of March 25, 2010:
http://www.rand.org/pubs/monographs/MG141/

———, "Militant Recruitment in Pakistan: Implications for Al-Qaeda and Other Organizations, *Studies in Conflict and Terrorism*, Vol. 27, No. 6, November 2004, pp. 489–504.

———, "Learning to Think the Unthinkable: Lessons from India's Nuclear Test," *India Review*, Vol. 4, No. 1, January 2005.

———, "Pakistan Loses Swat to Local Taliban," *Terrorism Focus*, Vol. 4, No. 37, November 14, 2007.

———, *The Cuisines of the Axis of Evil and Other Irritating States: A Dinner Party Approach to International Relations*, Guilford, Conn.: Globe Pequot Press, 2008.

———, "Who Are Pakistan's Militants and Their Families?" *Terrorism and Political Violence*, 2008, Vol. 20, No. 1, January 2008, pp. 49–65.

———, "Should Pakistan Get a Nuke Deal?" *Foreign Policy*, March 23, 2010. As of May 26, 2010:
http://www.foreignpolicy.com/articles/2010/03/23/should_pakistan_get_a_nuke_deal

———, "Pakistan's Relations with Central Asia: Is Past Prologue?" *Journal of Strategic Studies*, Vol. 31, No. 2, April 2008, pp. 201–227.

———, "Antecedents and Implications of the November 2008 Lashkar-e-Taiba (LeT) Attack upon Several Targets in the Indian Mega-City of Mumbai," testimony presented before the House Homeland Security Committee, Subcommittee on Transportation Security and Infrastructure Protection on March 11, 2009.

———, "Pakistan's Own War on Terror: What the Pakistani Public Thinks," *Journal of International Affairs*, Vol. 63, No. 1, 2009, pp. 39–56.

———, "Time for Sober Realism: Renegotiating U.S. Relations with Pakistan," *Washington Quarterly*, Vol. 32, No. 2, April 2009.

———, "From Strategy to Implementation: The Future of the U.S.-Pakistan Relationship," Testimony presented before the House Foreign Affairs Committee on May 5, 2009.

———, "Militants in the Kargil Conflict: Myths, Realities, and Impacts," in Peter Lavoy, ed., *Asymmetric Warfare in South Asia: The Causes and Consequences of Kargil*, Cambridge, U.K.: Cambridge University Press, December 2009.

———, "Pakistan Needs Its Own Nuclear Deal," *Wall Street Journal*, February 10, 2010.

———, "Leader-Led Jihad in Pakistan: The Case of Lashkar-e-Taiba," in Bruce Hoffman and Fernando Reinares, eds., *Leader-Led Jihad*, New York: Columbia University Press, forthcoming.

———, "Pakistani Attitudes Towards Militancy and State Responses to Counter Militancy," written while the author was a Luce Fellow at the University of Washington in 2009. This paper is forthcoming in an edited volume by James Wellman.

Fair, Christine C., and Peter Chalk, *Fortifying Pakistan: The Role of U.S. Internal Security Assistance*, Washington, D.C.: United States Institute of Peace, 2006.

Fair, Christine C., and Sumit Ganguly, eds., *Treading on Hallowed Ground: Counterinsurgency Operations in Sacred Spaces*, New York: Oxford University Press, 2008.

Fair, Christine C., and Seth G. Jones, "Pakistan's War Within," *Survival*, Vol. 51, No. 6, December 2009–January 2010, pp. 161–188.

Fair, Christine C., Clay Ramsay, and Steve Kull, "Pakistani Public Opinion on Democracy, Islamist Militancy, and Relations with the U.S.," Washington, D.C.: USIP/PIPA, January 7, 2008.

Farooq, Ghulam, "Taliban Step into Shangla as Buner Showdown Looms," *Daily Times* (Lahore), April 24, 2009.

Fearon, James D., "Domestic Political Audiences and the Escalation of International Disputes," *American Political Science Review*, Vol. 88, No. 3, September 1994, pp. 577–592.

———, "Rationalist Explanations for War," *International Organization*, Vol. 49, No. 3, Summer 1995, pp. 379–414.

Fearon, James D., and David D. Laitin, "Ethnicity, Insurgency, and Civil War," in *American Political Science Review*, Vol. 97, No. 1, February 2003, pp. 75–90.

Federation of American Scientists, "Pakiston [sic]: Total Military Force," 2008. As of May 6, 2010:
http://www.fas.org/programs/ssp/man/militarysumfolder/pakistan.html

"Fifteen Militants Killed in Waziristan Operation: ISPR," *Dawn* (Karachi), December 28, 2009.

"Five More Militants Killed in South Waziristan: ISPR," *Dawn* (Karachi), December 10, 2009.

Freedman, Lawrence, ed., *Strategic Coercion: Concepts and Cases*, New York: Oxford University Press, 1998.

———, "Strategic Coercion," in Lawrence Freedman, ed., *Strategic Coercion: Concepts and Cases*, New York: Oxford University Press, 1998.

Frontier Police, "Incentive for Martyred Families," Pakistan, 2006.

Galula, David, *Counterinsurgency Warfare: Theory and Practice*, Westport, Conn.: Praeger Security International, [1964] 2006.

Galtung, Johan, "On the Effects of International Economic Sanctions: With Examples from the Case of Rhodesia," *World Politics*, Vol. 19, No. 3, April 1967, pp. 378–416.

Ganguly, Sumit, *The Crisis in Kashmir: Portents of War, Hopes of Peace*, Cambridge, Mass.: Cambridge University Press, 1999.

———, "A Mosque, A Shrine and Two Sieges," in C. Christine Fair and Sumit Ganguly, Eds., *Treading on Hallowed Ground: Counterinsurgency in Sacred Spaces*, New York: Oxford University Press, 2008.

Gannon, Kathy, "Billions in U.S. Aid Never Reached Pakistan Army," *Washington Post*, October 4, 2009.

Garnett, Sherman W., "Ukraine's Decision to Join the NPT," *Arms Control Today*, Vol. 25, No. 1, January/February 1995, pp. 7–12.

George, Alexander L., "Case Studies and Theory Development: The Method of Structured, Focused Comparison," in Paul Gordon Lauren, ed., *Diplomacy: New Approaches in History, Theory, and Policy*, New York: Free Press, 1979, pp. 43–68.

———, *Forceful Persuasion: Coercive Diplomacy as an Alternative to War*, Washington, D.C: United States Institute of Peace, 1992.

———, "Theory and Practice," in Alexander L. George and William E. Simons, eds., *The Limits of Coercive Diplomacy*, 2nd ed., Boulder, Colo.: Westview Press, 1994.

George, Alexander L., and Timothy J. McKeown, "Case Studies and Theories of Organizational Decision Making," in Robert F. Coulam and Richard A. Smith, eds., *Advances in Information Processing in Organizations: A Research Annual*, Vol. 2, Greenwich, Conn.: JAI Press, 1985, pp. 43–68.

George, Alexander L., and William E. Simons, *The Limits of Coercive Diplomacy*, 2nd ed., Boulder, Colo.: Westview Press, 1994.

———, "Finding and Conclusions," in George and Simons, *The Limits of Coercive Diplomacy*.

Giustozzi, Antonio, *Empires of Mud: Wars and Warlords in Afghanistan*, New York: Columbia University Press, 2009.

Global Witness, *Conflict Diamonds: Possibilities for the Identification, Certification and Control of Diamonds*, London, June 2000.

Gompert, David C., John Gordon IV, Adam Grissom, David R. Frelinger, Seth G. Jones, Martin C. Libicki, Edward O'Connell, Brooke Stearns Lawson, and Robert E. Hunter, *War by Other Means: Building Complete and Balanced Capabilities for Counterinsurgency*, Santa Monica, Calif.: RAND Corporation, MG-595/2-OSD, 2008. As of March 25, 2010:
http://www.rand.org/pubs/monographs/MG595.2/

Gopal, Anand, "Pakistani Taliban in Swat Refuse to Give Up Arms: The Militants Had Struck a Deal to Relinquish Their Weapons in Return for Islamic Law in the Region," *Christian Science Monitor*, April 16, 2009.

Graham, Stephen, "Ghost Village Haunts Pakistani Plans to Make Peace with Tribal Militants," Associated Press, May 19, 2008.

Gray, Andrew, "U.S. Senator Doubts Pakistan, Blasts 'Pitiful' NATO," Reuters, April 1, 2009.

Greffenius, Steven, and Jungil Gill, "Pure Coercion vs. Carrot-and-Stick Offers in Crisis Bargaining," *Journal of Peace Research*, Vol. 29, No. 1, February 1992, pp. 39–52.

Grimmett, Jeanne J., *Nuclear Sanctions: Section 102(b) of the Arms Export Control Act and Its Application to India and Pakistan*, Washington, D.C., Congressional Research Service, Report 98-486, October 5, 2001.

Haqqani, Husain, *Pakistan: Between Mosque and Military*, Washington, D.C.: Carnegie Endowment for International Peace, 2005.

Harden, Blaine, "U.N. Sees Violation of a Diamond Ban by Angola Rebels," *New York Times*, March 11, 2000, p. A1.

Hasan, Syed Shoaib, "Profile: Baitullah Mehsud," BBC News, December 28, 2007.

Hassan, Ahmed, "Kerry-Lugar Bill Widely Opposed, JI Declares," *Dawn* (Karachi), October 24, 2009.

Hastert, Paul L., "Operation Anaconda: Perception Meets Reality in the Hills of Afghanistan," *Studies in Conflict and Terrorism*, Vol. 28, No. 1, January–February 2005, pp. 11–20.

Hathaway, Robert, "Confrontation and Retreat: The U.S. Congress and the South Asian Nuclear Tests," *Arms Control Today*, January/February 2000.

Herrmann, Richard, "Coercive Diplomacy and the Crisis over Kuwait, 1990–1991," in Alexander L. George et al., *The Limits of Coercive Diplomacy*, 2nd ed., Boulder, Colo.: Westview Press, 1994.

Hironaka, Ann, *Neverending Wars: The International Community, Weak States, and the Perpetuation of Civil War*, Cambridge, Mass.: Harvard University Press, 2005.

"Hit and Run," *The Herald* (Karachi), February 2006.

Hoyt, Timothy, "Politics, Proximity and Paranoia: The Evolution of Kashmir as a Nuclear Flashpoint," *The India Review*, Vol. 2, No. 3, July 2003, pp. 117–144.

———, "Kargil: The Nuclear Dimension," in Peter R. Lavoy, ed., *Asymmetric Warfare in South Asia: The Causes and Consequences of the Kargil Conflict*, Cambridge: Cambridge University Press, 2009.

Human Rights Watch, *Angola Unravels: The Rise and Fall of the Lusaka Peace Process*, New York, 1999.

———, "'Everyone Lives in Fear': Patterns of Impunity in Jammu and Kashmir," *Human Rights Reports*, Vol. 18, No. 11, September 11, 2006. As of March 25, 2009:
http://www.hrw.org/en/reports/2006/09/11/everyone-lives-fear

Hussain, Rizwan, *Pakistan and the Emergence of Islamic Democracy in Afghanistan*, Burlington, Vt.: Ashgate, 2005.

Hussain, Zahid, "Al-Qaeda's New Face," *Newsline* (Karachi), August 2004.

———, "The Battle for the Soul of Pakistan," *Newsline* (Karachi), July 2007.

———, "From Much Sought After to 'Most Wanted,'" *Dawn* (Karachi), May 21, 2009.

———, "Laddah, Sararogha Cleared; Street Fighting in Making," *Dawn* (Karachi), November 18, 2009.

Hussein, Gen. Safdar, comments made during the peace accords in Shakai, "Return of the Taliban," *Frontline*, October 2006. As of April 1, 2010: http://www.pbs.org/wgbh/pages/frontline/taliban/etc/script.html

Huth, Paul K., *Extended Deterrence and the Prevention of War*, New Haven, Conn.: Yale University Press, 1988.

Huth, Paul, and Bruce Russett, "Testing Deterrence Theory: Rigor Makes a Difference," *World Politics*, Vol. 42, No. 4, July 1990.

International Committee of the Red Cross, *Pakistan: ICRC and Pakistan Red Crescent Substantially Expanding Operations,* news release, Islamabad, June 2009.

International Crisis Group, *The State of Sectarianism in Pakistan*, Crisis Group Asia Report, No. 95, Brussels, Islamabad: International Crisis Group, 2005.

———, *Pakistan's Tribal Areas: Appeasing the Militants*, Islamabad/Brussels, December 2006.

———, *Reforming Pakistan's Police*, Crisis Group Asia Report, No. 157, Brussels, Islamabad, July 14, 2008.

International Institute for Strategic Studies, *The Military Balance 2009*, London: Routledge, 2009.

International Republican Institute, "IRI Releases Survey of Pakistan Public Opinion," press release linking to survey data for October 15–30, 2008, December 18, 2008. As of April 22, 2010: http://www.iri.org/news-events-press-center/news/iri-releases-survey-pakistan-public-opinion-4

———, "IRI Releases Survey of Pakistan Public Opinion," press release linking to survey data for March 7–30, 2009, May 11, 2009. As of April 22, 2010: http://www.iri.org/news-events-press-center/news/iri-releases-survey-pakistan-public-opinion-7

———, "IRI Releases Survey of Pakistan Public Opinion," press release linking to survey data for July 15–August 7, 2009, October 1, 2009. As of April 22, 2010: http://www.iri.org/news-events-press-center/news/iri-releases-survey-pakistan-public-opinion

IRI—*See* International Republican Institute.

Jajja, Nadia, "The Path to Deliverance," *The Herald* (Karachi), December 2009, p. 20.

Jakobsen, Peter Viggo, "The Strategy of Coercive Diplomacy: Refining Existing Theory to Post–Cold War Realities," in Lawrence Freedman, *Strategic Coercion: Concepts and Cases,* New York: Oxford University Press, 1998.

Jalal, Ayesha, *The State of Martial Law*, New York: Cambridge University Press, 1990.

———, *Partisans of Allah*, Lahore: Sang-e-Meel, 2008.

Jentleson, Bruce W., "The Reagan Administration Versus Nicaragua: The Limits of 'Type C' Coercive Diplomacy," in Alexander L. George and William E. Simons, *The Limits of Coercive Diplomacy,* 2nd ed., Boulder, Colo.: Westview Press, 1994.

Jervis, Robert, *Perception and Misperception in International Politics*, Princeton, N.J.: Princeton University Press, 1976.

———, *The Meaning of the Nuclear Revolution*, Ithaca, N.Y.: Cornell University Press, 1989.

Joeck, Neil, *Maintaining Nuclear Stability*, New York: Oxford University Press for the International Institute for Strategic Studies, Adelphi Paper, 0567-932X, 1997.

Joint Publication 1-02, DoD Dictionary of Military and Assocated Terms, online ed., as amended through October 31, 2009. As of March 25, 2010: http://www.dtic.mil/doctrine/dod_dictionary/

Jones, Seth G., "Pakistan's Dangerous Game," *Survival*, Vol. 49 No. 1, Spring 2007.

———, *Counterinsurgency in Afghanistan*, Santa Monica, Calif.: RAND Corporation, MG-595-OSD, 2008. As of March 25, 2010: http://www.rand.org/pubs/monographs/MG595/

———, *In the Graveyard of Empires: America's War in Afghanistan*, New York: W.W. Norton, 2009.

Jones, Seth G., and Martin C. Libicki, *How Terrorist Groups End: Lessons for Countering al Qa'ida*, Santa Monica, Calif.: RAND Corporation, MG-741-1-RC, 2008. As of March 25, 2010: http://www.rand.org/pubs/monographs/MG741-1/

Jones, Seth G., Jeremy M. Wilson, Andrew Rathmell, and K. Jack Riley, *Establishing Law and Order After Conflict*, Santa Monica, Calif.: RAND Corporation, MG-374-RC, 2005. As of March 25, 2010: http://www.rand.org/pubs/monographs/MG374/

Kalyvas, Stathis N., *The Logic of Violence in Civil War*, New York: Cambridge University Press, 2006.

Kargil Review Committee, *From Surprise to Reckoning: The Kargil Review Committee Report*, New Delhi: Sage Publications, December 15, 1999.

Kanwal, Gurmeet, "Losing Ground: Pak Army Strategy in FATA and the NWFP," New Dehli: Institute of Peace and Conflict Studies, Issue Brief No. 84, October 2008.

Kapur, Paul S., *Dangerous Deterrent: Nuclear Weapons Proliferation and Conflict in South Asia*, Stanford: Stanford University Press, 2007.

"Kashmiris Don't Want to Join Pak: Survey," *The Times of India*, September 27, 2002.

Katz, Ian, "Gates Says Militant Sanctuaries Pose Biggest Afghanistan Threat," *Bloomberg News*, March 1, 2009.

Kaufmann, Daniel, "Myths and Realities of Governance and Corruption," in *World Economic Forum, Global Competitiveness Report, 2005–2006*, Geneva, 2005.

Kaufmann, Daniel, Aart Kraay, and Massimo Mastruzzi, *Governance Matters VIII: Aggregate and Individual Governance Indicators, 1996–2008*, Policy Research Working Paper 4978, Washington, D.C.: World Bank, 2009.

Kayani, General Ashfaq Parvez, Chief of the Army Staff, letter to Mehsud Tribes, October 2009.

Kennedy, Robert F., *Thirteen Days: A Memoir of the Cuban Missile Crisis*, New York: W.W. Norton, 1969.

Kerr, Paul K., and Mar Beth Nikitin, *Pakistan's Nuclear Weapons: Proliferation and Security Issues*, Washington, D.C: Congressional Research Service, May 15, 2009.

"Kerry-Lugar Aid Bill Sparks Debate in Parliament," *Dawn* (Karachi), October 7, 2009.

Khan, Amir Mohammad, "Spiralling into Chaos," *Newsline* (Karachi), March 2004.

Khan, Anwarullah, "ISI Official, Three Others Killed in Bajaur Ambush," *Dawn* (Karachi), March 28, 2007.

Khan, Ghafar Ali, "The Lost Frontier," *The Herald* (Karachi), July 2007.

Khan, Iftikhar A., "Security Forces Advance on Strategic Kamber Bridge," *Dawn* (Karachi), May 21, 2009.

———, "Army Takes 'Complete Control' over Mingora," *Dawn* (Karachi), May 30, 2009.

———, "Kayani Writes to Mehsuds, Seeks Tribe's Support," *Dawn* (Karachi), October 20, 2009.

Khan, M. Ilyas, "Descent into Anarchy," *The Herald* (Karachi), March 2004.

———, "Mixed Signals," *The Herald* (Karachi), March 2004.

———, "Who Are These People?" *The Herald* (Karachi), April 2004.

Khan, Ismail, "Five Militants Pardoned for Peaceful Life: Alien Asked to Surrender by 30th," *The Dawn* (Karachi), April 25, 2004.

———, "Why the Waziristan Deal Is a Hard Sell," *Dawn* (Karachi), October 14, 2006.

———, "Talibanisation Imperils Security, NSC Warned: Immediate Action Urged," *Dawn* (Karachi), June 22, 2007.

———, "Battle to Be Won or Lost in Bajaur," *Dawn* (Karachi), September 21, 2008.

Khan, Ismail, and Alamgir Bhittani, "42 Uzbeks Among 58 Dead: Fierce Clashes in S. Waziristan," *Dawn* (Karachi), March 21, 2007.

Khan, Ismail, and Dilawar Khan Wazir, "Night Raid Kills Nek, Four Other Militants," *Dawn* (Karachi), July 19, 2004.

Khattak, Daud, and Delwar Jan, "Operation Against Taliban on Government Mind," *The News*, April 24, 2009.

Khattak, Iqbal, "I Did Not Surrender to the Military, Says Nek Mohammad," *Friday Timess* (Lahore), April 30–May 6, 2004.

———, "Deserted Towns Shows Human Cost of Operation Zalzala," *Daily Times* (Lahore), May 20, 2008.

———, "Army in Waziristan Better Equipped, More Relaxed," *Daily Times*, May 21, 2008.

———, "Pakistan: Mehsud Says Local Taliban to Begin Media War; Slams Reporter's Murder," *Daily Timess* (Lahore), May 27, 2008.

Khan, Khashnud Ali, "Why and How Did the Operation Commence in Mohmand Agency and Bajaur Agency?" *Jinnah*, September 30, 2008.

Khan, Mukhtar A., "A Profile of Militant Groups in Bajaur Tribal Agency," *Terrorism Monitor*, Vol. 7, No. 6, March 19, 2009.

Kilcullen, David, *The Accidental Guerilla: Fighting Small Wars in the Midst of a Big One*, New York: Oxford University Press, 2009.

Kitson, Frank, *Low Intensity Operations: Subversion, Insurgency and Peacekeeping*, rev. ed., London: Faber and Faber, 1991.

Klitgaard, Robert E., *Institutional Adjustment and Adjusting to Institutions*, Washington, D.C.: World Bank, 1995.

Knorr, Klaus, "Is International Coercion Waning or Rising?" *International Security*, Vol. 1, No. 4, Spring 1977.

Kramer, Mark, "Counterinsurgency in Chechnya," *International Security*, Vol. 29, No. 3, Winter 2004/05.

Krepon, Michael and Chris Cagné, "Introduction," in Michael Krepon and Chris Gagné, eds., *The Stability-Instability Paradox: Nuclear Weapons and Brinkmanship in South Asia*, Washington, D.C.: Stimson Center, June 2001.

Kronstadt, K. Alan, *Pakistan—U.S. Anti-Terrorism Cooperation*, Washington, D.C: Congressional Research Service, March 2003.

———, *U.S.-Pakistan Relations*, Washington, D.C: Congressional Research Service, 2008.

Kux, Dennis, *The United States and Pakistan, 1947–2000: Disenchanted Allies*, Baltimore: Johns Hopkins University Press, 2001.

Lauren, Paul Gordon, "Coercive Diplomacy and Ultimata: Theory and Practice in History," in Alexander L. George and William E. Simons, *The Limits of Coercive Diplomacy*, 2nd ed., Boulder, Colo.: Westview Press, 1994.

Leng, Russel, "Influence Strategic and Interstate Conflict," in J. David Singer, ed., *The Correlates of War II: Testing Some Realpolitik Models*, New York: Free Press, 1980.

LePoer, Barbara, et al., *India-Pakistan Nuclear Tests and U.S. Response,* CRS Report 98-570, November 24, 1999.

Lesser, Ian O., Bruce Hoffman, John Arquilla, David Ronfeldt, Michele Zanini, and Brian Michael Jenkins, *Countering the New Terrorism*, Santa Monica, Calif.: RAND Corporation, MR-989-AF, 1999. As of March 25, 2010: http://www.rand.org/pubs/monograph_reports/MR989/

Levin, Carl, "Opening Statement of Senator Carl Levin, Senate Armed Services Committee Hearing on Afghanistan and Pakistan," February 26, 2009.

Lipson, Charles, "International Cooperation in Economic and Security Affairs," *World Politics*, Vol. 37, No. 1, October 1984, pp. 1–23.

Lloyd, Anthony, "Captured Battle Plan Shows Strength and Training of Taleban Forces," *The Times*, November 11, 2008.

Loudon, Bruce, "Pakistan: Nuke Deal to Spark Arms Race," *The Australian*, July 25, 2008.

Loyn, David, *Butcher and Bolt: Two Hundred Years of Foreign Engagement in Afghanistan*, London: Hutchinson, 2008.

Mahsud, Saliab, "Caught in the Crossfire," *The Herald* (Karachi), April 2004.

"Many Killed in 'U.S. Drone Attack,'" BBC News, April 1, 2009.

Maples, LTG Michael D., *Current and Projected National Security Threats to the United States, Statement for the Record, Senate Select Committee on Intelligence Committee*, Washington, D.C: Defense Intelligence Agency, January 2007.

———, *Annual Threat Assessment: Statement Before the Committee on Armed Services United States Senate*, Washington, D.C: Defense Intelligence Agency, February 2008.

McMullen, Ron, Afghanistan Desk, U.S. Department of State, "Developments in Afghanistan," cable, December 5, 1994. Released by the National Security Archive.

Mearsheimer, John J., "The Case for a Ukrainian Nuclear Deterrent," *Foreign Affairs*, Vol. 72, No. 3, Summer 1993, pp. 50–66.

———, *The Tragedy of Great Power Politics,* New York: W.W. Norton, 2001.

Mehsud, Sailab, "Army Embarks on Rah-i-Nijat Finally," *Dawn* (Karachi), October 18, 2009.

Melby, Eric D. K., "Iraq," in Richard N. Haass, *Economics Sanctions and American Diplomacy,* New York: Council on Foreign Relations Press, 1998.

"Militants Overrun Pakistan Fort," BBC News, January 17, 2008.

Mir, Amir, "Story Behind Manawan Fidayee Attack," *The News*, April 1, 2009.

Mir, Hamid, "Army Official Calls Baitullah Mehsud, Fazullah 'Patriots,'" *The News*, December 8, 2008.

Moravesik, Andrew, "Introduction: Integrating International and Domestic Theories of International Bargaining," in Peter B. Evans, Harold B. Jacobson, and Robert B. Putnam, *Double-Edged Diplomacy: International Bargaining and Domestic Politics*, Berkeley, Calif.: University of California Press, 1993.

Morgan, T. Clifton, and Valerie L. Schwebach, "Fools Suffer Glady: The Use of Economic Sanctions in International Crises," *International Studies Quarterly*, Vol. 41, No. 1, March 1997, pp. 27–50.

Mulford, David C., U.S. Ambassador to India, *Afghanistan Has Made a Remarkable Transition*, New Delhi: U.S. Department of State, February 2006.

Musharraf, Pervez, *In the Line of Fire*, New York: Free Press, 2006.

———, interview conducted for "Return of the Taliban," *Frontline*, June 8, 2006. As of March 31, 2010:
http://www.pbs.org/wgbh/pages/frontline/taliban/interviews/musharraf.html

Nasr, S. V. R., "Islam, the State and the Rise of Sectarian Militancy in Pakistan," in Cristopher Jafferlot, *Pakistan: Nationalism Without a Nation?* London: Zed Books, 2002.

Nasr, Vali R., "International Politics, Domestic Imperatives, and Identity Mobilization: Sectarianism in Pakistan, 1979–1998," *Comparative Politics*, Vol. 32, No. 2, January 2000, pp. 170–191.

Nawaz, Shuja, *Crossed Swords: Pakistan, Its Army, and the Wars Within*, New York: Oxford University Press, 2008.

———, "The First Kashmir War Revisited," *India Review*, Vol. 7, No. 2, 2008.

———, *FATA—A Most Dangerous Place: Meeting the Challenge of Militancy and Terror in the Federally Administered Tribal Areas of Pakistan*, Washington, D.C.: Center for Strategic and International Studies, January 2009.

Naylor, Sean, *Not a Good Day to Die: The Untold Story of Operation Anaconda*, New York: Berkley Books, 2005.

Nayyar, A. H., and Ahmed Salim, *The Subtle Subversion: The State of Curricula and Textbooks in Pakistan—Urdu, English, Social Studies and Civics*, Islamabad: Sustainable Development Policy Institute, 2003.

Office of the Press Secretary, "Joint Statement on United States–Pakistan Strategic Partnership," March 4, 2006.

Office of the Press Secretary, "Joint Statement on United States–Pakistan Strategic Partnership," July 28, 2008.

Office of the United Nations High Commissioner for Refugees, *Newly Displaced Pakistani Civilians Report Grim Conditions in Swat Valley*, Islamabad, June 2009.

Oxford English Dictionary, New York: Oxford University Press, 2009.

"Pak Army Needs No Foreign Training: COAS," *The Nation*, May 16, 2009.

Pakistan Army, General Headquarters, Military Operations Directorate, *Record on Pakistan's War on Terror*, December 28, 2006.

Pakistan Institute for Peace Studies, *Pakistan Security Report 2008*, Islamabad, 2009.

———, *Pakistan Security Report 2009*, Islamabad, 2010.

Pakistan Ministry of Interior, *The Talibanisation Problem*, Islamabad: Ministry of Interior, 2007.

"Pakistan Taliban to Increase Suicide Attacks," *Xinhua General News Service*, November 14, 2009.

"Pakistani Troops 'Flee Border Post,'" Al Jazeera, January 17, 2008.

"Pakistan Wants India-Like Nuclear Deal with US Qureshi," *Business Recorder*, website, July 25, 2008.

Pape, Robert A., *Bombing to Win: Air Power and Coercion in War*, Ithaca: Cornell University Press, 1996.

———, *Why Economic Sanctions Do Not Work*, Cambridge, Mass.: MIT Press, 1997.

———, "Why Economic Sanctions Do Not Work," *International Security*, Vol. 22, No. 2, Autumn 1997, pp. 90–136.

———, "Why Economic Sanctions Still Do Not Work," *International Security*, Vol. 23, No. 1, Summer 1998, pp. 66–77.

Pardesi, Manjeet Singh, "Battle for the Soul of Pakistan at Islamabad's Red Mosque," in C. Christine Fair and Sumit Ganguly, eds., *Treading on Hallowed Ground: Counterinsurgency Operations in Sacred Spaces*, New York: Oxford University Press, 2008, pp. 88–116.

Partlow, Joshua, and Haq Nawaz Khan, "Tribe Members Held Accountable: Pakistani Order Says Mehsuds Can Be Targeted Over Taliban Leader's Crimes," *Washington Post*, July 21, 2009.

Patchell, Peter, "Pakistan's Secret War in Baluchistan," *The Guardian*, December 21, 2007.

Posen, Barry R., "The Security Dilemma and Ethnic Conflict," in Michael E. Brown, ed. *Ethnic Conflict and International Security*, Princeton, N.J: Princeton University Press, 1993.

———, "The Security Dilemma and Ethnic Conflict," *Survival*, Vol. 35, No. 1, Spring 1993.

Purcell, Susan Kaufman, "Cuba," in Richard N. Haass, ed., *Economics Sanctions and American Diplomacy*, New York: Council on Foreign Relations Press, 1998

Putnam, Robert D., "Diplomacy and Domestic Politics: The Logic of Two-Level Games," *International Organization*, Vol. 42, No. 3, Summer 1988.

Rabasa, Angel, Robert D. Blackwill, Peter Chalk, Kim Cragin, C. Christine Fair, Brian A. Jackson, Brian Michael Jenkins, Seth G. Jones, Nathaniel Shestak, and Ashley J. Tellis, "The Lessons of Mumbai," Santa Monica, Calif.: RAND Corporation, OP-249-RC, 2009. As of March 25, 2010: http://www.rand.org/pubs/occasional_papers/OP249/

Ragin, Charles C., "Comparative Sociology and the Comparative Method," *International Journal of Comparative Sociology*, Vol. 22, Nos. 1–2, March–June 1981.

Rajghatta, Chidanand, and Kamal Siddiqui, "Pak Cries Foul over US Revenge Strike," *Indian Express*, August 22, 1998.

Rashid, Ahmed, *Descent into Chaos*, New York: Viking Penguin, 2008.

———, "Pakistan's Worrisome Pullback," *Washington Post*, June 6, 2008.

Rathmell, Andrew, Olga Oliker, Terrence K. Kelly, David Brannan, and Keith Crane, *Developing Iraq's Security Sector: The Coalition Provisional Authority's Experience*, Santa Monica, Calif.: RAND Corporation, MG-365-OSD, 2005. As of March 25, 2009: http://www.rand.org/pubs/monographs/MG365/

Raza, Syed Irfan, "Zardari Renews Demand for U.S. Drone Technology," *Dawn* (Karachi), January 7, 2010

Rennack, U. Dianne E., "India and Pakistan: Current U.S. Economic Sanctions Specialist in Foreign Policy Legislation," Washington, D.C.: Congressional Research Service, October 12, 2001.

Riedel, Bruce, "American Diplomacy and the 1999 Kargil Summit at Blair House," policy paper, Philadelphia: University of Pennsylvania, Center for the Advanced Study of India, 2002.

Rizvi, Hassan Askari, *The Military and Politics in Pakistan: 1947–1997*, Lahore, Pakistan: Sang-e-Meel, 2000.

———, *Military, State and Society in Pakistan*, London: Palgrave, 2000.

"Reporters See Wrecked Buddhas," *BBC News*, March 26, 2001.

Rohde, David, Carlotta Gall, Eric Schmidt, and David E. Sanger, "U.S. Office See Waste in Pakistan Aid," *New York Times,* December 24, 2007, p. A1.

Rubin, Barnett R. *The Fragmentation of Afghanistan*, New Haven, Conn.: Yale University Press, 2002.

———, "Saving Afghanistan," *Foreign Affairs*, January/February 2007.

Ruttig, Thomas, "Loya Paktia's Insurgency: The Haqqani Network as an Autonomous Entity," in Antonio Giustozzi, ed., *Decoding the New Taliban: Insights from the Afghan Field*, New York: Columbia University Press, 2009, pp. 57–101

Sagan, Scott D., "From Deterrence to Coercion to War: The Road to Pearl Harbor," in Alexander L. George and William E. Simons, *The Limits of Coercive Diplomacy,* 2nd ed., Boulder, Colo.: Westview Press, 1994.

———, "Why Do States Build Nuclear Weapons? Three Models in Search of a Bomb," *International Security*, Vol. 21, No. 3, Winter 1996–1997.

Sagan, Scott D., and Kenneth Waltz, *The Spread of Nuclear Weapons: A Debate*, New York: W.W. Norton, 1995.

Sanger, David E., and David Rohde, "U.S. Pays Pakistan to Fight Terror, but Patrols Ebb," *New York Times*, May 20, 2007, p. 1.

Schaub, Gary, Jr., "Compellence: Resuscitating the Concept," in Freedman, ed., *Strategic Coercion*, 1998.

Schelling, Thomas C., *The Strategy of Conflict*, Cambridge, Mass.: Harvard University Press, 1960.

———, *Arms and Influence*, New Haven, Conn.: Yale University Press, 1966.

Schmitt, Eric, and David E. Sanger, "Some in Qaeda Leave Pakistan for Somalia and Yemen," *New York Times*, June 11, 2009.

Shafi, Major Mohammad, "The Effectiveness of Guerilla War," *Pakistan Army Journal*, Vol. 5, June 1963.

Shah, Saeed, "Taliban Rivals Unite to Fight U.S. Troops Surge," *The Guardian*, March 3, 2009.

Shapiro, Jacob N., and C. Christine Fair, "Why Support Islamist Militancy? Evidence from Pakistan," *International Security*, Vol. 34, No. 3, Winter 2009/2010.

Siddiqa, Ayesha, "In the Line of Fire," *The Herald* (Karachi), December 2006.

Siegel, Daniel, and Joy Hackel, "El Salvador: Counterinsurgency Revisited," in Michael T. Klare and Peter Kornbluth, eds., *Low Intensity Wafare: Counterinsurgency, Protoinsurgency, and Antiterrorism in the Eighties*, New York: Pantheon Books, 1988.

Skocpol, Theda, and Margaret Somers, "The Uses of Comparative History in Macrosocial Inquiry," *Comparative Studies in Society and History*, Vol. 22, No. 2, 1980.

Snyder, Glenn, "The Balance of Power and the Balance of Terror," in Paul Seaburry, ed., *The Balance of Power*, San Francisco: Chandler, 1964.

Snyder, Glenn H., and Paul Diesing, *Conflict Among Nations: Bargaining, Decision Making, and System Structure in International Crises*, Princeton, N.J., Princeton University Press, 1977.

Sorbo, A. H., "Paradise Lost," *The Herald* (Karachi), June 1988.

"Street Battles Rage in Uzbek Militants' Stronghold," *Dawn* (Karachi), November 2, 2009.

Stromseth, Jane, David Wippman, and Rosa Brooks, *Can Might Make Rights? Building the Rule of Law After Military Interventions*, New York: Cambridge University Press, 2006.

Swami, Praveen, *India, Pakistan and the Secret Jihad: The Covert War in Kashmir, 1947–2005*, London: Routledge, 2007.

"Taliban Chief Ideologist Survives 'Zalzala,'" *Daily Times*, May 26, 2008.

"Taliban Turn Troops Back from Mingora," *The News*, April 26, 2009.

Tarzi, Amin, "Afghanistan: Kabul's India Ties Worry Pakistan," *Radio Free Europe/Radio Liberty*, April 16, 2006.

Tavernise, Sabrina, Richard A. Oppel, Jr., and Eric Schmitt, "United Militants Threaten Pakistan's Populous Heart," *New York Times*, April 13, 2009.

Tellis, Ashley J., *Pakistan and the War on Terror: Conflicted Goals, Compromised Performance*, Washington, D.C.: Carnegie Endowment for International Peace.

Tellis, Ashley J., C. Christine Fair, and Jamison Jo Medby, *Limited Conflicts Under the Nuclear Umbrella: Indian and Pakistani Lessons from the Kargil Crisis*, MG-1450-USCA, Santa Monica, Calif.: RAND Corporation, 2001. As of March 25, 2010:
http://www.rand.org/pubs/monograph_reports/MR1450/

Tendler, Judith, *Good Government in the Tropics*, Baltimore: Johns Hopkins University, 1997.

Tenet, George, with Bill Harlow, *At the Center of the Storm: My Years at the CIA*, New York: HarperCollins, 2007.

"Text of Pakistan's Shari'ah Law 2009," BBC Monitoring South Asia, April 14, 2009.

Thucydides, *The History of the Peloponnesian War*, trans. Rex Warner, New York: Penguin Books, 1977.

Tilly, Charles, "Means and Ends of Comparison in Macrosociology," in Frederick Engelstad, Kalleberg Ragnvald, and Grete Brochman, eds., *Comparative Social Research*, Vol. 16, Greenwich, Conn.: JAI Press, 1997.

Tohid, Owais, "The New Frontier," *Newsline* (Karachi), April 2004.

———, "The Warror Tribes," *Newsline* (Karachi), April 2004.

Transparency International, *Global Corruption Report 2006*, Berlin, 2006.

———, *Corruption Perceptions Index 2009*, Berlin, 2009.

Treverton, Gregory F., *Reshaping National Intelligence for an Age of Information*, New York: Cambridge University Press, 2003.

Trinquier, Roger, *Modern Warfare: A French View of Counterinsurgency*, Westport, Conn.: Praeger Security International, 2006.

Tripodi, Christian, "Peacemaking Through Bribes or Cultural Empathy? The Political Officer and Britain's Strategy Towards the North-West Frontier, 1901–1945," *Journal of Strategic Studies*, Vol. 31, No. 1, February 2008.

Tse-Tung, Mao, *On Guerilla Warfare*, translated by Samuel B. Griffith II, Urbana: University of Illinois Press, 1961.

"TTP Claims Peshawar Suicide Bombing," *The News* (Pakistan), December 27, 2009.

United Nations, *Final Report on UN Panel of Experts on Violations of Security Council Sanctions Against Unita: The "Fowler Report,"* New York, S/2000/203, March 10, 2000.

———, *Final Report of the Monitoring Mechanism on Angola Sanctions*, New York, S/2000/1225, December 21, 2000.

U.S. Air Force, Office of Lessons Learned, *Operation Anaconda: An Air Power Perspective*, Washington, D.C.: Headquarters U.S. Air Force, *February 2005.*

U.S. Army and U.S. Marine Corps, *Counterinsurgency Field Manuel*, Chicago: University of Chicago Press, 2007.

U.S. Congress, "Enhanced Partnership with Pakistan Act of 2009," S962, Report 111-33, 11th Cong., 1st Sess., June 24, 2009.

U.S. Consulate, Peshawar, Cable, "Afghan-Pak Border Relations at Torkham Tense," October 2, 1996. Released by the National Security Archive.

U.S. Department of Defense, *United States–Vietnam Relations, 1945–1967*, Book III: *The Overthrow of Ngo Dinh Diem, May–November 1963, Summary and Analysis*, Washington, D.C: United States Government Printing Office, 1971.

U.S. Department of State, "North Korea–Pakistan: Missile-Related Sanctions and Executive Order 12938 Penalties," April 1, 2003.

———, *Country Reports on Terrorism 2008*, Washington, D.C., April 2009.

U.S. District Court, Eastern District of New York, United States of America Against Najibullah Zazi, 09 CR 663(S-1), February 22, 2010.

U.S. Embassy, Islamabad, "Afghanistan: [Excised] Criticizes GOP's Afghan Policy; Says It Is Letting Policy Drift," cable, June 16, 1998. Released by the National Security Archive.

———, "U.S. Embassy Teams Up With the Ministry of Interior to Bolster Frontier Constabulary Capacity in Frontier Regions: MOU Signed Worth US $2.7 Million," press release, August 3, 2006.

"U.S. Explains Sanctions," BBC News, April 3, 2003.

van de Walle, Nicolas, *African Economies and the Politics of Permanent Crisis, 1979–1999*, Cambridge, U.K.: Cambridge University Press, 2001.

Van Evera, Stephen, *Guide to Methods for Students of Political Science*, Ithaca, NY: Cornell University Press, 1997.

Walsh, Declan, "Demolished by the Pakistan Army: The Frontier Village Punished for Harbouring the Taliban," *The Guardian*, May 20, 2008.

Waltz, Kenneth, *Theory of International Politics,* New York: McGraw-Hill, 1979.

Warrick, Joby, "CIA Places Blame for Bhutto Assassination," *Washington Post*, January 18, 2008.

Weber, Max, "Politics as a Vocation," in H. H. Gerth and C. Wright Mills, eds. *From Max Weber: Essays in Sociology,* New York: Oxford University Press, 1958.

Weiss, Leonard, "U.S.–India Nuclear Coöperation," *The Nonproliferation Review*, Vol. 14, No. 3, November 2007, pp. 429–457.

Wickham-Crowley, Timothy P., *Guerillas and Revolution in Latin America: A Comparative Study of Insurgents and Regimes Since 1956*, Princeton, N.J.: Princeton University Press, 1992.

Wiseman, Paul, and Zafar M. Sheikh, "Pakistani Police Underfunded, Overwhelmed," *USA Today,* May 5, 2009.

Wisler, Dominique, maintainer, "Pakistan," World Database on Policing, website, Geneva, Switzerland: COGINTA, undated. As of March 25, 2010: http://coginta.com/WDP/pakistan.html

Wirsing, Robert G., *India, Pakistan and the Kashmir Dispute: On Regional Conflict and Its Resolution*, New York: St. Martin's Press, 1994.

Woodward, Bob, *Bush at War*, New York: Simon and Schuster, 2002.

World Bank, *Reforming Public Institutions and Strengthening Governance*, Washington, D.C., 2000.

———, *Governance Matters 2009: Worldwide Governance Indicators, 1996–2008*, Washington, D.C., 2009.

Yousaf, Mohammad, and Mark Adkin, *Afghanistan the Bear Trap: The Defeat of a Superpower*, Havertown, Pa.: Casemate, 2001.

Yusufzai, Rahimullah, "Fall of the Last Frontier?" *Newsline* (Karachi), June 2002.

———, "Whose Country Is It Anyway?" *The Herald* (Karachi), February 2006.

———, "Eviction or Safe Passage?" *Newsline* (Karachi), May 2007.

———, "The Emergence of the Pakistani Taliban," *Jane's Information Group*, December 11, 2007.

Zaeef, Abdul Salam, *My Life with the Taliban*, London: Hurst and Company, 2009.

Zahab, Mariam Abou, "The Regional Dimension of Sectarian Conflicts," in Cristopher Jafferlot, ed., *Pakistan: Nationalism Without a Nation?* London: Zed Books, 2002.

———, "Changing Patterns of Social and Political Life Among the Tribal Pashtuns in Pakistan," Draft Paper, 2007.

Zahab, Mariam Abou, and Olivier Roy, *Islamist Networks: The Afghan-Pakistan Connection*, London: C. Hurst, 2004.

Zaman, Muhammad Qasim, "Sectarianism in Pakistan: The Radicalization of Shi'i and Sunni Identities," *Modern Asian Studies*, Vol. 32, 1998, pp. 689–716.

"Zardari Calls for Transfer of Drone Technology to Pakistan," *Daily Times* (Pakistan), February 12, 2010.

Zimmerman, Tim, "Coercive Diplomacy," in George and Simons, eds., *The Limits of Coercive Diplomacy,* 1994.

Index